Counseling Psychology
Perspectives and Functions

Counseling Psychology
Perspectives and Functions

Gerald L. Stone
The University of Iowa

Brooks/Cole Publishing Company
Monterey, California

Brooks/Cole Publishing Company
A Division of Wadsworth, Inc.

Printed in the United States of America

10   9   8   7   6   5   4   3   2   1

Library of Congress Cataloging in Publication Data

Stone, Gerald L.
  Counseling psychology.

  Bibliography; p.
  Includes index.
  1. Counseling.   I. Title.
BF637.C6S777   1985   158'.3   85-16593

ISBN 0-534-05142-1

Sponsoring Editor: *Claire Verduin*
Editorial Assistant: *Pat Carnahan*
Production Editor: *Penelope Sky*
Production Assistant: *Dorothy Bell*
Manuscript Editor: *Diane Hammond*
Permissions Editor: *Carline Haga*
Interior and Cover Design: *Sharon Kinghan*
Art Coordinator: *Judith L. Macdonald*
Interior Illustration: *Tim Keenan*
Typesetting: *Omegatype Typography, Inc., Champaign, Illinois*
Printing and Binding: *R. R. Donnelley & Sons Co., Crawfordsville, Indiana*

To Cheryl, my wife,
and Corby and Carrie, my children,
who provide me with unlimited
challenge and support.

Preface

Counseling Psychology: Perspectives and Functions is intended to be a challenging book, one that requires more from students than does an introductory text. I do not simply reproduce typical counseling theories or enumerate lists of skills; rather, students are persuaded to recognize the need for cognitive work in addressing the issues confronting counseling psychology.

In presenting my ideas I have emphasized the following significant aspects of the field:

1. *Theory in relation to history, philosophy, and psychology.* Contemporary counseling approaches are integrated with historical influences and with ideas from a wide range of helping perspectives.
2. *Theory combined with research and application.* Conceptual analyses of various counseling methods are illustrated consistently with both case examples and research examples.
3. *Description supported by commentary.* Descriptions of counseling approaches are followed by critical commentaries that assess the strengths and weaknesses of each method.

In organizing the material I have highlighted the multifaceted nature of our discipline by integrating theories and practices within a framework based on the generic processes of counseling. In each chapter I present a different perspective on counseling, but in common terms: historical influences, generic counseling processes, and clinical and research examples, ending with a critical commentary. In the final chapter I develop an integrative overview of these perspectives.

A book that achieves a coherent ordering of a complex subject results in part from challenging contributions from many individuals. My colleagues at Michigan State University, the University of Western Ontario, and the University of Iowa deserve special thanks, and I am grateful to the many theorists and researchers whose work has influenced my own integrative efforts. I would also like to thank Reta Litton and Virginia

Travis for their diligent work in preparing the manuscript, and to acknowledge the reviewers: Cheryl Bartholomew of the State University of New York at Oswego; William Cormier of West Virginia University at Morgantown; Tom McGovern of Virginia Commonwealth University; Frank Nugent of Western Washington University; and Geoffrey Yager of the University of Cincinnati. Finally, I salute those students who provided permission, support, and challenge in my thoughtful ("blue sky") periods during my classes and research meetings.

Gerald L. Stone

Contents

10   *Organizing*   166

11   *Perspective on perspectives*   184

References   196

Author index   212

Subject index   217

Counseling Psychology
Perspectives and Functions

Introduction

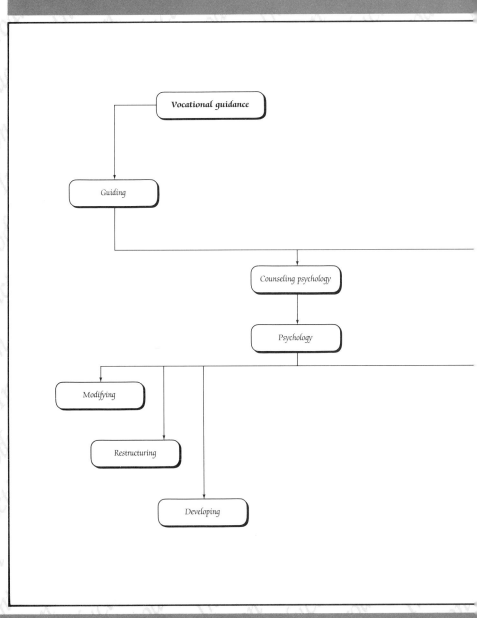

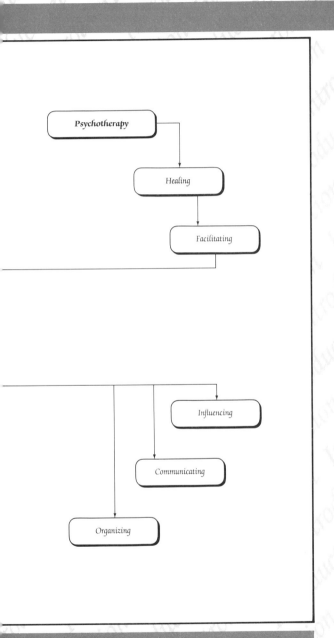

1

One way to learn about applied psychology is to examine the difficulties in integrating science and practice. These difficulties have contributed to controversies over the role and functions of counseling psychologists—in particular, the controversy over the scientist/practitioner approach, in which the counseling psychologist is regarded as both a scientist in the field of psychology and an applied practitioner. Difficulties can arise from such a synthesis because of differences in the methods and ideologies of scientists and practitioners.

When faced with the question of appropriate treatment for an anxiety disorder, the scientist may begin a research project to study the question or search for recommendations based on past research. The practitioner, on the other hand, is confronted by a person in need of assistance and develops the best possible treatment plan based on available information. Scientists and practitioners seriously criticize one another's approaches: the practitioner claims that the scientist is unrealistic and uses dehumanizing and inappropriate research methods, whereas the scientist criticizes the practitioner's lack of scientific integrity in making treatment decisions without an adequate conceptual understanding or data base.

The real differences in ideology revealed in these debates often reflect, to some degree, different approaches to counseling. The purpose of this book is to examine these different approaches in order to identify some of the reasons for the divergence and in so doing come to a better understanding of counseling psychology as a science and a profession.

Orientation

This book systematically reviews different approaches to counseling, called perspectives. The term **perspective** is adopted for conceptual, social, and historical reasons. Conceptually, the term denotes a broad framework for understanding the explanations of counseling theorists and practitioners. It is evident that ideas about counseling do not occur in a vacuum, but are influenced by social conditions (see Levine & Levine, 1970). A perspective is therefore not only conceptual, but also conveys the dependence of knowledge on its social context; that is, *perspective* implies a relationship, a point of view occurring in a context and directed somewhere. Perspectives can also provide a useful historical introduction to the counseling field, and it seems appropriate to begin with such an introduction, with more extensive discussion presented in each of the following chapters.

Historical background

As depicted in the Perspectives Overview at the beginning of this chapter, three perspectives—guiding, healing, and facilitating—are associated with the two major historical traditions of vocational guidance and psychotherapy. Vocational guidance viewed counseling primarily as a rational method of enhancing the match between a worker and a job, relying on accurate information, testing, and problem-solving activities. Psychotherapy, on the other hand, dealt with emotional issues and interpersonal relationships and rejected the notion that counseling was an adjunct to information dissemination and decision making. Rather, counseling as a personal helping relationship was central. These traditions and associated perspectives blended together and helped form counseling psychology (see Stone, 1984). The other perspectives reviewed in this book became associated with counseling as the field increasingly identified itself with psychology. As psychologists, counseling theorists adopted or created new perspectives based on contributions from other areas of psychology, including learning, cognition, development, social, personality, clinical psychology, and others.

In summary, counseling psychology evolved by the blending of vocational guidance and psychotherapy into a program that developed new concepts and methods based on the field of psychology. In the following chapters, notable events are outlined and persons associated with the major traditions and perspectives of counseling psychology are discussed.

Plan of the book

The format of each chapter on perspectives (chapters 2 through 10) is the same: a perspective is presented in terms of a representative counseling approach intersected by a common set of counseling-related activities called **functions**, along with sections on history, examples, and critical commentary. Visual and verbal guides are found at the beginning and end of each chapter.

A few words should be said about the book's organization, including the selection of perspectives, counseling approaches, and counseling functions. As described earlier, the three perspectives of guiding, healing, and facilitating are easily derived from the history of counseling psychology, and the other perspectives represent trends in the psychological literature that appear to be important in counseling psychology. These include (with the psychological term in parentheses) modifying (learning), restructuring (cognition), developing (development), influencing (social), communicating (communications theory), and organizing (community). Thus a total of nine perspectives are presented in a sequence that reflects their relative impact on counseling psychology.

Special consideration was given to selecting an approach both relevant to the counseling situation and representative of the family of approaches related to a particular perspective. For instance, for the healing perspective a time-limited approach to therapy was selected, because it is often more relevant to a counseling situation than is long-term therapy based on classical psychoanalysis.

Functions

In selecting the counseling functions, a problem-solving framework for understanding counseling activities was adopted. On the basis of John Dewey's (1916, 1933/1960) approach to problem solving, four basic counseling functions (with problem-solving stages in parentheses) were defined (see Stone, 1980): establishment (problem orientation), conceptualization (problem identification), intervention (experimentation), and evaluation (evaluation). A professional development function was also included to provide information about training and education.

Establishment

The **establishment** phase consists of the activities associated with developing a problem-solving orientation. The counselor may help clients develop an effective reorientation to their problems by lowering anxiety, increasing motivation, or improving the processing of information.

Two conditions are highlighted in describing the establishment function; one, the relationship between counselor and client, and two, social influence. In discussing the first condition—the working relationship between the counselor and client—three overlapping descriptions will be used: counselor roles, counselor-client transactions, and client behavior. The roles of a counselor can vary greatly. Some concern themselves with personal adjustment, others facilitate communication in a group, while still others become human-resource consultants in large industries. In counselor-client transactions, the basic factor is the degree of structure within the counseling process. The transaction, though often determined by the counselor, sometimes is determined by both, equally, or by the client, should the counselor decide to place the client in control. Finally, various kinds of client behavior are reinforced. Some counselors help the client learn to express feelings; others reinforce the client for using behavioral language or for completing homework assignments.

The second establishment condition is social influence (see McGuire, 1969). Writers have recently been stressing the similarities between counseling-like situations and social influence (for example, Bergin, 1962; Frank, 1961/1973; Goldstein, Heller, & Sechrest, 1966; Strong, 1968, 1978). In discussing social influence as an establishment condition, two components of the influence process will be examined: setting and communications. Counseling occurs in diverse settings, including colleges and universities, clinics, hospitals, private practice, industry, and vocational agencies. In addition, all forms of counseling are based on a rationale that includes communication—an explanation of the problem and of the relevance of the proposed intervention. Some counselors believe that problems emerge as a result of unconscious conflicts, whereas others point to environmental causes.

Conceptualization

Closely related to the rationale process of the establishment phase is the **conceptualization** stage. In this function, assessment is central. Some counselors are interested in assessing the client's personality, others want to develop measures that assess the environment. Another group, of course, believes assessment to be inappropriate. The description of the conceptualization function focuses on the methods various counselors use in helping their clients redefine their concerns through language that leads to understanding and corrective action.

Intervention

The discussion of the **intervention** function provides a description of the methods counselors use in helping clients. For example, one counselor may present and interpret information about the client's interests and various occupations. Given this information, the client, with the aid of the counselor, may interact with a computer, watch and listen to audiovisual materials, and visit a number of businesses in order to observe the work situation and talk with employees. Other counselors emphasize verbal communication, performance tasks, or institutional change. Whatever the action, it is designed to change the problematic situation (now that it has been conceptualized within the established relationship between counselor and client).

Evaluation

Most perspectives are associated with characteristic ways of **evaluation**. That is, some perspectives are identified with a case-study approach, and others with correlational methods and experimental procedures. More recent perspectives encourage an individualized or program evaluation.

Professional development

Finally, the **professional development** function is the teaching and learning of counseling. Some training models emphasize a therapeutic approach, whereas others stress the learning of basic communication skills.

Summary

Counseling functions	*Characteristics*
Establishment	Relationship and social influence conditions
Conceptualization	Goals and assessment activities
Intervention	Treatment strategies and methods of behavior change
Evaluation	Research methods
Professional development	Training approach

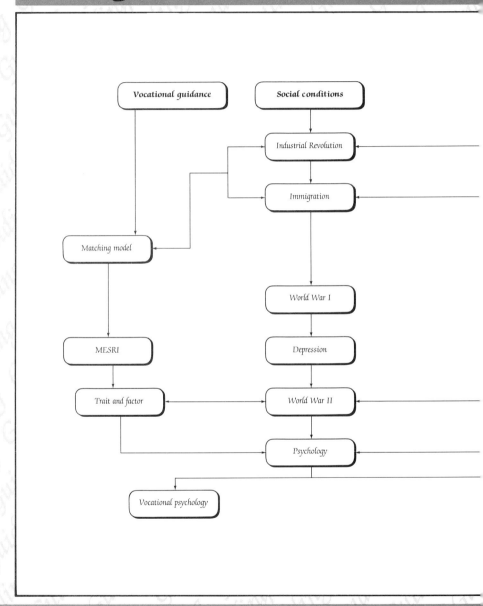

2

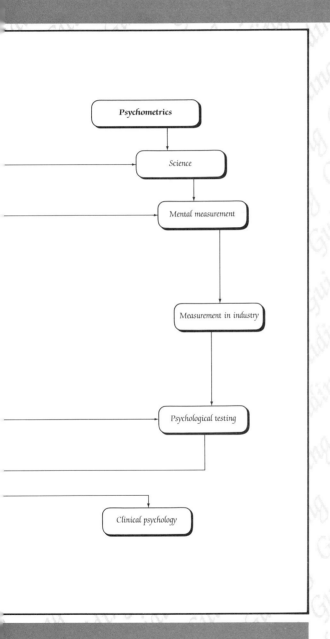

Psychometrics

Science

Mental measurement

Measurement in industry

Psychological testing

Clinical psychology

Guiding can be a loaded term, since it often carries different meanings acquired through its association with the guidance movement in education and vocational psychology. Thus it will be helpful to distinguish *guiding* from other terms. One term that has caused confusion is *coercion*. Guiding need not mean coercion in the sense of ignoring or overriding an individual's point of view. On the other hand, guiding is more than passively reflecting an individual's viewpoint. An analogy may clarify these distinctions.

Assume that we are contemplating a change of career and want a guide. From this guide we expect certain things, among them familiarity with careers, with economic conditions of employment, with job requirements, and with the methods used to help individuals make wise career decisions. On many issues we expect our guide to know more than we do.

About other matters, however, we expect our guide to pay attention to us because our own knowledge is greater. For example, although careers with great potential for promotion and earnings may be available to us, we may desire a more limited career because of our present interests in family and leisurely pursuits. However knowledgeable the expert, there are important areas in which the guide's fund of knowledge is irrelevant unless it is supplemented by specific knowledge of us, our goals, and our idiosyncrasies.

On the other hand, guides should not be coerced by us into denying their expertise. If we expect to obtain a specific job magically, without paying sufficient attention to the skills and experiences needed, it is proper for the guide to remind us of these qualifications instead of simply agreeing with us.

If the association of guidance and education has led to unfortunate connotations, it has also provided a useful context for description. That is, such an association suggests that guiding can be seen as an educational perspective (Brewer, 1932)—the "bringing out," through external resources, of something either from within the person or potentially available to the person. Here the emphasis is not on external coercion of a client or on the coercion that arises from the refusal of counselor and client to make use of appropriate external resources. Educative guides are experts but are never solely external in their guidance. Rather, they proceed by making contact with the client's resources, or internal world. Thus guiding does not preclude the need for instruction and information, but these external resources are part of an active interchange between counselor and client directed toward mutual understanding, problem resolution, and the pursuit of excellence.

Historical background

Antecedents

Throughout human history, many people have recognized the necessity of working together for common protection and comfort and have often realized the benefit of seeking advice and counsel from others. Until the late 19th century, much of the advice giving occurred in a religious context and concerned the preservation of the religious community as well as the welfare of the individual (see McNeill, 1951).

Although earlier antecedents can be identified (see Beck, 1963), most historians of the guidance movement, such as John Brewer (1942), E. G. Williamson (1965), and W. R. Stephens (1970), suggest that guidance is a 20th-century phenomenon. At the end of the 19th century, two movements—one cultural, the other ideological—combined to provide the impetus for broadening and secularizing guidance functions. Between 1890 and 1920 a great number of changes occurred in association with industrialization. As factories grew, increasing numbers of people from rural areas and foreign lands sought employment in the cities. New kinds of work multiplied with the introduction of new machines and technology.

These social changes, including technology, specialization, urbanization, and secularization, generated needs that could not be met by a predominantly agrarian society. The creation of new areas of work produced increasing demands for training. Newly arrived immigrants needed to learn a different language, to understand new customs, and to develop new skills. Rapid industrialization also changed the nature of the family. The home was no longer the center of work, and parents working outside the home were often hard pressed to give their children the guidance they needed to respond to rapid social change.

In response to these needs, a reform ideology began to develop. Its basic sentiment was humanitarian and arose in part from the individualism expressed in religion, the ideas of the Enlightenment, the pioneer spirit of the frontier, and the ideals of democracy. Whatever its sources, this humanitarian concern, stressing the improvability of humankind through the application of reason and scientific procedures, was expressed in diverse forms and in many localities.

Development of guidance

This humanitarian concern or ideology had a profound impact on the development of guidance. Of the multitude of expressions of this concern, two individuals and their works seem to be most relevant.

John Dewey

The first is John Dewey (1916), with his pragmatic philosophy and emphasis on the school as a place to prepare children for participation in society. The basic concepts Dewey espoused seem similar to much of our American heritage. Dewey's pragmatic approach stressed the individual's active experience, paralleling the long Puritan tradition in this country of the importance of work (see Weber, 1958). The pragmatic approach also emphasized the social responsibilities of the school in helping people make realistic choices by means of scientific and objective procedures. For Dewey and many others, the school could become a useful tool for meeting some of the needs of a highly industrialized democracy. That is, the school could increase social and economic efficiency by providing education, training, socialization, and procedures for the allocation and conservation of human talent. In addition, the school would provide a laboratory in which the skills and concepts associated with a democratic society could be practiced. It was these beliefs—the importance of work, of making realistic choices, and of utilitarian education—that provided the fertile ground for the growth of guidance.

Frank Parsons

Another particularly important pioneer in this field was Frank Parsons, the man usually credited with initiating the guidance movement in the United States. Though devoted to social and economic reform (see Rockwell & Rothney, 1961), Parsons brought more than a reformer's zeal to guidance. In his book, *Choosing a Vocation* (1909), he outlined one of the major approaches of a guiding perspective:

> In a wise choice there are three broad factors: (1) a clear understanding of yourself, your aptitudes, abilities, interests, ambitions, resources, limitations, and their causes; (2) a knowledge of the requirements and conditions of success, advantages and the disadvantages, compensation, opportunities, and prospects in different lines of work; (3) true reasoning on the relations of these two groups of facts. (p. 5)

Psychometrics

Parsons's formulation reflects at least two traditions that helped establish the guidance field. One, the **psychometric tradition**, had to do with the spirit of individualism, but was here cast in the terminology of scientific measurement rather than religion or ideology. The psychometric tradition, involving the development of instruments and methods for appraisal, elaborated the first step of Parsons's model and continued to grow in response to social needs.

In industry, for example, the early work of Munsterberg (1899) on the application of experimental psychology to industry was followed by

Frederick Taylor's time and motion studies; Walter Dill Scott's research on the selection of salespeople; the development of a technology for assessing interests by Edward K. Strong, Walter Bingham, Bruce Moore, and others; and, during the depression of the 1930s, the establishment by Donald Paterson, John Darley, and their colleagues at the University of Minnesota of a program (Minnesota Employment Stabilization Research Institute—MESRI) for the scientific study of vocational choice and adjustment.

Intelligence testing, which is almost synonymous with the psychometric tradition, began with the work of Binet and colleagues in France, and sprang from humanitarian and practical concern for the appropriate placement of mentally retarded children. Stimulated by Binet and by J. M. Cattell's and E. L. Thorndike's early mental-testing work, intelligence testing continued to develop and expand with the translation and adaptions of the Binet-Simon Scales by Lewis Terman and associates, the development of group intelligence tests (Army Alpha and Beta) during World War I by Robert Yerkes and associates, and the provision of an individual intelligence test for adults, the Wechsler-Bellevue Scale, by David Wechsler. With the activity during and after World War II (for example, the establishment of the U.S. Veterans Administration), psychological testing, including intelligence and vocational assessment, became a major, if not a primary, activity of many clinical and counseling psychologists.

Vocational guidance

The second tradition in Parsons's model was that of **vocational guidance**. In its early development, vocational guidance emphasized vocational education, primarily occupational information and advice. In Brooklyn, Eli Weaver helped students find summer jobs. In Grand Rapids, Michigan, Jesse Davis helped teachers shape curricula to convey information about the working world and a democratic society. In Middletown, Connecticut, William Wheatley provided occupational information to students through social studies classes and occupational courses. The seminal work of Frank Parsons caught on, of course, in the Boston school system, and by 1911 Harvard University was offering a special training course for vocational counselors.

A reformulation

Since individual appraisal and dissemination of occupational information were stressed in the third aspect of the Parsons model, it is easy to understand why many people perceived counseling ("true reasoning") as a rather directive, testing-oriented, and information-giving undertaking. Historically, because of either a lack of psychological tests or a lack of interest in them, there was more emphasis on occupational information than on individual appraisal. It was not until the late 1920s and the 1930s that psychologists reentered the field and applied scientific and clinical procedures.

Three psychologists—Morris Viteles, Donald Paterson, and E. G. Williamson—deserve mention for their contributions to a psychological reformulation of guidance. Viteles, a student of the early clinical psychologist Lightner Witmer, applied to guidance the new psychological methods and clinical techniques that were used at the University of Pennsylvania in the diagnosis of children's learning disabilities. Paterson, a representative of differential psychology, brought to the University of Minnesota a measurement technology from his graduate studies at Ohio State University and his army experience and applied them to vocational concerns, developing in the process many psychological devices for vocational and educational counseling. Williamson, a student of Paterson at the University of Minnesota, integrated the technology of differential psychology and the techniques of the clinician in his work as Director of the University Testing Bureau at Minnesota. His contributions helped reinstate Parsons's formulation on a scientific basis and redefined vocational guidance as counseling.

Summary

In sum, the guiding perspective has been associated predominately with educational and vocational guidance. Guidance activities have been based on social needs for economic and social efficiency, and guidance concepts reflect many traditional American beliefs: the value of the individual, the importance of work, the usefulness of education, and the value of objectivity and quantification. Historically, the guidance perspective has been associated with such external activities as moral instruction and dissemination of occupational information. It was not until the 1930s that the importance of understanding the individual became salient. Unfortunately, the debates about the value of directive counseling between Williamson and Carl Rogers, the latter an advocate of a nondirective approach, tended to dehumanize guidance. Such debates emphasized guidance workers' use of scientific measurement, ignoring their concern with the importance of human relationships. Criticism of the guidance field increased as the psychotherapy movement and the anti-intellectualism and calls for "relevance" of the 1950s and 1960s gained momentum.

At present, however, although many counseling psychologists still consider the guiding perspective a minor viewpoint, or of historical interest only, a renewed interest in Parsons's formulation is reflected in recent concern with individual differences, occupational mental health, vocational theories and practices relevant to women, adult development, and cognitive counseling. In addition, a slow national economy has increased the saliency of career choice. Given the close association in the past between social needs and the emergence of a guiding perspective, it may be that we will witness its reemergence in the following decades.

Approach

Let us now turn to an examination of a guiding-perspective approach. The description of the approach, known as guidance counseling or trait and factor counseling, is based on a distillation of the works of Williamson (1939a, 1939b, 1950, 1965; Williamson & Biggs, 1979).

Orientation

The guiding perspective applied to counseling can be seen as a direct reflection of the thinking of John Dewey. In *Democracy and Education,* Dewey (1916) recommended that the school serve as a laboratory for democracy in which students would participate in the development of a social process, thereby gradually learning how to apply the scientific method toward the betterment of society. A major emphasis was on teaching the scientific method. In an analogous manner, the problem-solving counselor within the guiding tradition provided a social environment in which clients could apply the scientific method to learn about themselves and society.

It was hoped that through such experiences clients would gain problem-solving skills that would enable them to address future concerns and contribute to the growth of a humane society. Such a perspective, emphasizing the problem-solving aspects of the counseling process, has been applied primarily to clients' educational and vocational concerns.

In these applications, Parsons's model was elaborated in terms of trait and factor theory and actually implemented with scientific methodology at the University of Minnesota. Trait and factor theory assumed that individuals differ in their aptitudes for work and school activities and, moreover, that effective performance of these activities yields the individual maximum satisfaction. In the convergence of these two assumptions, which parallel the first two steps of Parsons's model, true reasoning becomes a matter of **matching persons and environments**, one of the major approaches within the guiding perspective. The matching process used scientific procedures to gather accurate information, generate a hypothesis, conduct an experiment, and evaluate the outcome. These problem-solving steps helped define a major method of guidance-oriented counseling. Williamson outlined a six-step counseling method (the parallel problem-solving steps are in parentheses):

(1) analysis (information gathering), (2) synthesis (information gathering), (3) diagnosis (hypothesis generation), (4) prognosis (hypothesis generation), (5) counseling (experimentation), and (6) follow-up (evaluation).

In sum, the orientation of a guiding-influenced approach is problem solving, a rational process implemented and evaluated in terms of the needs of the individual and society for responsible self-development.

Establishment

In developing a counseling relationship, a problem-solving counselor focuses on enhancing client learning and counselor influence. In terms of client learning, the role of the counselor is to become an educator, but not in the sense of giving the client answers. As in the classroom, good teaching in the consultation office involves much more than providing information. Effective teaching and effective counseling both depend on a personal connection between the teacher and the learner. Most counselors rely on a good counseling relationship, and the problem-solving counselor is no exception. In such a relationship, the client's learning is improved through increased attention to information, confidence, and commitment to counseling tasks. Such a personalized relationship enables the counselor, as educator, to improve a client's self-understanding by teaching decision-making skills, including the gathering of valid information and the implementation of problem-solving strategies. In a sense, the client learns how to become a personal scientist.

The counseling relationship also involves interpersonal influence. Guidance counselors, as scientific experts who are also knowledgeable about occupations and personal decision making, use their influencing power to maintain rapport, reduce unnecessary anxiety, and motivate clients to strive for excellence—to challenge a client's view with alternative possibilities of the "good life" based on the full utilization of the client's abilities.

Another focus for problem-solving counselors is the use of the scientific method. Through role modeling, the client observes how the counselor gathers valid information and tests various alternatives. By participating with the counselor in these activities, the client also gains experience in gathering information and making decisions. From these active learning experiences new skills can be learned and used, offering clients the opportunity to observe themselves actively addressing their problem instead of passively accepting it.

The convergence of these factors—rapport, influence, and problem-solving skills—serves to establish a counseling relationship.

To summarize, the problem-solving counselor takes on an educational role. Many counselor-client transactions take place in school settings and can be characterized as instructional. In many transactions the counselor will ask questions, use concrete language, and focus on rational problem-solving methods. At the same time, the counselor personalizes these transactions by using relationship skills directed toward enhancing client self-understanding. The client is encouraged to adopt a problem-solving approach, to become a scientist: gathering information, experimenting, and evaluating. Such client behavior is encouraged because it is based on the assumption that the application of science and objective knowledge can play a major role in the solution of human problems. This assumption serves as a rationale for the problem-solving counselor. It assumes the rather optimistic view that once scientific skills are learned and objective knowledge about alternatives is available, the client will be able to make good decisions.

Conceptualization

The traditional emphasis in guidance counseling has been on the conceptualization function—that is, assessment activities (in Williamson's terminology, *differential diagnosis*). Although the use of diagnosis by trait and factor counselors suggests to some a medical approach, the guidance use of diagnosis is much more in the problem-solving tradition.

Another common misconception about trait and factor counselors is their assumed reliance on tests as the only data of significance. However, clinical information, much of it nonquantitative, on personal values and decision-making strategies from both self-evaluations and observations of others, is important to guidance counselors in formulating a complete picture of the individual and forms an important part of the basis for planning and evaluation.

Although trait and factor counselors are more than testers, a special feature of this approach is the use of **social comparison** information in the collection of data. Notable examples of tests constructed on the basis of social comparison are the Vocational Interest Blank, developed by E. K. Strong of Stanford, and the Minnesota Multiphasic Personality Inventory (MMPI), developed by Hathaway, McKinley, and Meehl at the University of Minnesota. The principal technique for determining the vocational relevance of a client's test response is the use of contrasted groups. Occupational preference begins to take on meaning when it can be related to the occupational preferences of a known and well-defined group, called the criterion or standard comparison group, having a given occupation, such as architecture or law. In addition, the preferences of architects or lawyers take on meaning only to the extent that they differ from the preferences of the general populace. The MMPI uses external criterion groups in a similar way: client responses take on psychological meaning on the basis of their relation to the responses of various psychiatric diagnostic groups that served as criterion groups in the scale construction of the MMPI.

Social comparison strategies point to the importance of social and cultural factors in client self-understanding. The following case history illustrates a trait and factor approach using social comparison data. In this case, the counselor, after establishing a relationship with the client, employs social comparison data—for example, data from personality and vocational interest inventories—to help the client achieve a broader self-understanding.

The case of Roger.   Roger was an 18-year-old freshman in his second semester at the university when he first came to the university counseling center. Of medium build and stature, Roger, an only child, described his childhood in a typical middle-class suburb as a happy one. His descriptions included memories of parental values, relationship with parents, relationship with peers, vocational fantasies, and early heroes. He recalled that materialism, trust, honesty, and responsibility were valued in his home; he suggested that he had had a pleasant relationship with both parents, but had relied on his father to a greater extent; he remembered some difficulties in making friends as he got older, due to a move during his high school years; he reported that early on he thought about becoming a parachutist, a mountain climber, or an actor; his father, Einstein, and Robin Hood were his early heroes.

Roger's father, a college graduate, had been a mechanical engineer for the last 20 years; his mother had completed high school and had had many part-time jobs, including her present job as a bookkeeper. According to test data, Roger's scores on university entrance examinations and the Scholastic Aptitude Test placed him at the 25th percentile for entering first-year students.

During the initial interview, Roger said it had been difficult to adjust to the university at first, but was getting better, except for his being unable to study and his low grades (Ds) in science and math. He indicated that he had planned to be a medical doctor until he was in high school, when his interest in veterinary medicine had begun to grow. Although he was registered in the preveterinarian medicine program, he was unsure of his vocational preference and wanted help in evaluating his plans for a change of study.

Roger had worked in many part-time positions (for example, paper boy, golf caddy). At the time of the initial interview he was employed as a part-time stockman in a shoe store. When asked to evaluate his job experience, he was mostly concerned about the wages he received.

Roger said he liked to breed tropical fish, collect coins and stamps, and to "fool around" with photography; other interests included candle-making, reading, and working with wood and on engines and motorcycles. He did not participate much in extracurricular activities at the university. In fact, Roger was not enthusiastic about school, thinking he was not smart enough. Attending the university was his parents' idea; they thought it would give him a secure occupational future.

Meanwhile, Roger was anxious to find out more about his interests and needs. He wanted to take the Strong-Campbell Interest Inventory (SCII). I (the counselor) also assigned the Personality Research Form (PRF), because I thought it might help Roger understand the relation between his needs and various occupations. He filled out these two inventories.

In about two weeks Roger returned. Before showing him the results of the inventories, I asked Roger to fill out a PRF profile of traits (achievement, order, and others) and their descriptions, which would help me assess his self-awareness. Then we discussed the SCII. On the basis of his scores on various scales, his interests were primarily in the human relations area (for example, social-service interest scale, social-worker occupational scale, and social-theme scale scores were all high). Roger had little to say in response to these findings except to question why he was having so much trouble in school if he had such interests.

We moved on to the PRF. On the basis of self-descriptions, he considered himself shy and introverted (abasement scale). He also described himself as logical, sensible, and nonviolent (understanding and harm-avoidance scales). He would have liked to be more intelligent, relaxed, and outgoing (achievement, affiliation, and impulsivity scales). The results of the PRF disclosed that Roger was high in achievement, nurturance, and succorance and low in autonomy and endurance. As we discussed his profile, I suggested that such a profile indicated many kinds of needs, including a need to please other people. This suggestion was acceptable to Roger. He said he was having problems breaking away from his parents, especially with regard to his education and the prospect of changing majors.

In the weeks that followed, Roger began to explore his needs and the types of careers that would be compatible with these needs. He contacted the Veterinary School advisor and explored the university's career resources. In addition, he enrolled in a study skills course.

After the exploration period, we spent some time talking about how important it was for Roger to discover his identity as being different from his family's expectation. We retuned to his Interest Inventory and Personality Research Form and developed some career directions and work experiences to evaluate these possibilities. At this point, counseling was discontinued to give Roger some time for further thinking and planning.

The following year Roger returned to the counseling center. He had decided to withdraw from school in order to obtain more experience in the working world. He said he had talked about his plans to his parents, who, although concerned, indicated that they would be supportive. We talked further about Roger's hopes for the future and about the types of experience he was seeking. We agreed to stay in contact over the year. He stopped by one more time and said he was feeling good about his decision. He was working as an aide in a clinic for disturbed children. This case illustrates the use of objective inventories for both a vocational problem and a developmental and emotional problem, that of Roger's dependence on his family.

In sum, a salient feature of the trait and factor approach is the conceptualization phase, in which counselors assist clients in broadening their self-understanding. Special emphasis is placed on the use of social comparison data or normative information. Although such data are not the only significant informational sources, it is assumed that clients need to be influenced by social criteria in order to maximize their potential within society.

Intervention

In guidance counseling, the decision-making interview is a major process. It can be used to collect information, evaluate progress, teach problem-solving skills, treat problems, or facilitate the development of potentiality. Many interventions have already been reviewed, including rapport building, interpersonal influence, and diagnosis. Another major function has to do with the teaching nature of counseling. In the following case, a middle-aged woman, returning to school after a 15-year absence, is concerned about her ability to accomplish her academic goals. Despite receiving straight As in her first semester, she finds herself extremely anxious and riddled by self-doubts. The following edited excerpt, including commentary, picks up the interaction after rapport and informational procedures have been initiated.

	Excerpt	*Commentary*
1. *Client:*	Good morning.	
2. *Counselor:*	Good morning. What has happened this week?	
3. *Client:*	I just don't think I am going to make it. I mean, this is just too hard for me. School is so unreal. I am unprepared. I don't think like a student anymore.	
4. *Counselor:*	It may help us if you could be specific. Give me an example.	The problem-solving counselor helps the client be specific (4, 6). In a very

| *Excerpt* | *Commentary* |

real sense, the counselor is helping the client become more scientific. In both situations, counseling and science, clients and students need to specify the problem. One way of doing this is to translate abstract language into specifics in order to reduce misunderstanding.

5. *Client:* OK. I am taking a math course this semester. I was terrible in math in high school. I seem to spend hours on studying math and I still don't understand it. I just don't see how I can get through it.

6. *Counselor:* I hear that you don't have much confidence in your math ability, but what is your evidence for such a statement?

In the following exchanges (6–13), the counselor is using the counseling interview to teach the client the scientific method. In this case, the counselor is helping the client discover the bases of her self-evaluations. As indicated by the counselor (10, 16), the client seems to use a limited amount of information, resulting from selective perception.

7. *Client:* Evidence? What do you mean?

8. *Counselor:* I mean, like a scientist, what evidence do you use to come to your conclusion? What information?

9. *Client:* Well . . . I don't consider myself a scientist, but I just feel incompetent in math. Although I have always received good grades, I don't think it reflects my ability. I

Excerpt   *Commentary*

spend hours on home-
work and yet feel that I
don't understand it.

10. *Counselor:* It might help us to think
like scientists here. It
seems that you consider
certain things as facts
and others as irrelevant
in evaluating yourself,
especially concerning
math.

11.   *Client:* Uh-huh. I guess so.

12. *Counselor:* Help me with this. What
facts are you using in
making these negative
judgments about math?

13.   *Client:* Oh . . . I don't know. It's
just a feeling. Yes, and
then there are the long
hours of study. . . . Also,
my father was bright in
math and helped me in
high school. He had little
patience with me. I
seemed to be so slow. I
always thought women
couldn't do math.

14. *Counselor:* Is there other information available?

15.   *Client:* What do you mean?

16. *Counselor:* Is this all the information? I mean, from our
earlier meetings don't we
have information about
your grades in math from
last semester, scores on
achievement tests,
teacher comments, and
other sources?

17.   *Client:* Oh, yeah.

Excerpt   *Commentary*

18. *Counselor:* I wonder, why does this
                  information (which is
                  very positive) become
                  lost in talking about your
                  math?

19.   *Client:* I know. But I still don't
                  feel confident.

The above is a typical example of the teaching nature of counseling. In this case, the counselor helped the client discover the so-called facts on which she was basing her self-evaluation. In the ensuing interactions, the counselor could help the client develop methods of increasing self-knowledge and replacing faulty self-appraisal skills. To be sure, the task is not a simple one, nor does it appear that the earlier procedures of trait and factor counseling concerned with the presentation of objective information will be effective. In fact, the counselor may have to consider some additional client work (for example, consciousness raising, assertiveness training, women's support group) before starting the client on an apprenticeship in becoming a personal scientist.

Evaluation

A hallmark of trait and factor counseling was the continued espousal and practice of research. Research was seen as a crucial counseling function. In the words of Williamson (1965), "research is a vital and necessary underpinning of counseling, and every counselor needs to carry on and prosecute some form of research as part of his professional obligation" (p. 121).

Trait and factor research, belonging to the individual-difference tradition of Galton, Cattell, Binet, Terman, and Thurstone, emphasized the importance of naturally occurring variation among individuals and groups. The research approach, introduced into vocational psychology by Hugo Munsterberg, involved the use of psychological methods to identify individual capabilities related to successful performance. This research approach, sometimes referred to as a correlational approach, was reinstated by the vocational guidance movement and broadened by Paterson and his colleagues at Minnesota to include information about aptitudes, interests, and personality from tests and correlational methodologies. The correlational approach emphasized the importance of individual differences, whereas experimentalists treated individual variation as error and concentrated on experimenter-created variation as opposed to natural variation. It may be helpful at this point to illustrate these points with a brief discussion of a study that is representative of a trait and factor approach to research.

In 1961, all high school seniors in Minnesota were asked to report their post–high-school plans. Such information provided a data pool for a 1966 study by Ralph Berdie and Albert Hood of the University of Minnesota on the relationship of a great many variables to post–high-school plans. From an initial group of students, a large random sample (3817) was drawn from those who planned either to attend college or to seek employment after high school. These plans were considered the dependent variable, with 17 independent variables (high-school percentile rank, Minnesota Scholastic Aptitude Test [MSAT], farm-nonfarm status, number of books in the home, sex, father's occupation, father's education level, mother's education level, source of family income, family affluence, and seven other indexes derived from 25 personality-inventory items from the Minnesota Counseling Inventory [MCI]). These data were then subjected to multiple correlational analyses in order to assess the extent to which one can predict which students will plan for college and which ones will not. Although a correlational methodology is a questionable procedure, given the nature of the data (for example, dichotomous variables and possible curvilinear relationships), the evidence suggests that each of the predictor variables helps a little in explaining plans for college attendance, with ability and academic achievement carrying the most weight, followed by family background and personality. The most impressive findings, however, concern the limits faced in making such predictions. With all the information available, only 38% of the variance in plans was accounted for by the numerous predictor variables. In addition, no great importance could be attached to any one predictor variable.

This study reveals many traditional features of trait and factor research: the issue of college attendance and the use of a great variety of variables, underscoring the researchers' emphasis on information. Normative and social-comparison information, much of it based on scientific research, came from the following variables: high-school percentile rank, MSAT, and personality inventory items from the MCI. (The latter is in fact based on the trait and factor methodology of contrasted groups and is an MMPI-type of inventory for adolescents.) Finally, correlational methodologies were used to assess the extent to which predictor variables account for the existing variance in plans for college attendance. Taken together, an educational-vocational context, multiple variables, social-comparison data, and correlational methodologies seem to be the major ingredients of a trait and factor approach to research.

Professional development

There appears to be little information available on the systematic formulation of a trait and factor approach to the professional training of counseling psychologists. Such a situation may reflect the ambiguity and variety of opinions about training on the part of the early pioneers of the Minnesota school—especially those of Donald Paterson, who was more interested in developing traditional Ph.D.s in individual difference psychology, and E. G. Williamson, who became identified with the broader field of student development and student personnel work in higher education. Whatever the reason, little systematic thinking on professional development exists in the trait and factor literature.

Historically, Paterson, Williamson, and others devoted much effort to transforming the training of guidance workers into the training of psychologists. This transformation had several consequences. The first was a shift in focus from *techniques* to *philosophy and research*—Williamson concentrated his earlier interest on the delineation of counseling techniques but later became immersed in the questions of the philosophy and research evidence underlying the techniques. These philosophical interests led to the issues of values and the relationship of methods and goals, in which ideals are integrated with the technology to accomplish them. Indeed, counseling techniques should never become isolated from philosophy and research, which is basic to good technique.

A second consequence was reflected in the *curriculum*. A psychological counselor needed exposure to research design, measurement, psychological theory and research, philosophy of science, and vocational psychology. In later years Williamson (1975) suggested that counselor educators should have been counseled and should counsel before they teach. These suggestions relate to appropriate practical experience within the curriculum. Little has been written about practicum or supervision, and in the early years such experiences were not readily available other than through didactic seminars and part-time positions in the testing bureau. Nevertheless, a few points can be made. There were skills and a technology to master. One had to become familiar with psychological testing, information gathering, and objective case preparation. There were various tests to learn and observational skills to use. In terms of practical experience, perhaps as Vance (1968), a Paterson student, suggests, the student was to carry the empirical tradition to the consulting room. The student's goal was to become an empirical clinician by using his or her own experience as a basis for testing constructs and improving performance.

A third consequence involved the *development of applied programs*, such as counseling psychology within a psychology department with programs in general, theoretical, comparative, and experimental areas. As a result, counseling psychologists at Minnesota were exposed to the discipline of psychology, including statistics, history and systems, theory, and experimental, learning, and differential psychology. They also specialized in personnel psychology, vocational psychology, vocational and educational counseling, industrial psychology, tests and measurements of special value to educational and vocational counseling, and appropriate practical experience. Such specialization led to a distinction from other applied programs, such as clinical psychology, that emphasized abnormal psychology, psychodynamics, and psychiatry.

Another consequence, although not so much a result of the transformation of guidance workers into psychologists as a result of the *educational context* in which the transformation was taking place, concerned the scope of counseling practice. In response to college students' needs and academic goals, counseling practice was conceptualized as a broad enterprise interrelated with several other student services. It was suggested that counseling psychologists become specialists and contributing members of a broad interdisciplinary approach rather than superficial generalists operating alone. Moreover, the postsecondary educational context in which guiding approaches developed probably influenced the content and process of professional preparation. That is, intellectual values, occupational and educational needs, and individual and social responsibilities are probable environmental pressures encountered in such educational contexts. It is not difficult to envision how professional training would focus on such issues and adopt a rational, problem-solving strategy seemingly well suited to such an environment.

Commentary

The guidance approach has at least four areas of renewed emphasis, each representing a positive contribution, that need to be recognized in an age characterized by a mental-health approach and individual psychotherapy. These areas are cognition, research, social responsibility, and vocational development.

In terms of cognition, counselors and therapists have been preoccupied with unconscious processes, feelings, or behaviors. Although the information-centered approach used in decision-making counseling in the past is inadequate, the trait and factor writers continue to remind us of the important role that rational processes can play in counseling (see Stone, 1980).

Just as cognitive processes have been neglected, many counselors ignore research as a fundamental basis for practice. Conceptions of research change, but the trait and factor approach highlights the relationship between counseling practice and science.

The third area, social responsibility, seems to have been overridden by the conflicts of the 1960s and the self-absorption of the 1970s. In an era of selfish development, it is refreshing to read Williamson and Dewey on the interdependent society and individual social responsibility.

Although trait and factor counselors may have been more concerned with social criteria, and present-day counselors with personal development, it seems important to integrate these concerns.

Finally, although many counseling psychologists favor psychotherapy, a few have reminded the profession of our heritage in educational and vocational counseling. Such reminders seem necessary for a profession that is tempted, for financial reasons, to succumb to a mental health zeitgeist and to neglect a socially relevant part of our tradition. Moreover, other applied psychologists, such as industrial and organizational psychologists, seem quite willing and eager to provide a vocational service.

In addition to the positive points, a few criticisms should be mentioned. From a modern information-processing viewpoint, Williamson's assumptions about information processing are outdated. That is, Williamson discusses information primarily in terms of such externals as test results, observations, and grades, while neglecting the personal meaning associated with the "objective" information selected and processed by the client.

Another criticism focuses on the counseling environment in higher education. As stated earlier, an educational context for counseling leads to an emphasis on certain social needs, including personal adjustment, school discipline, intellectual values, and the development of a work force. These social needs are not necessarily bad, but their influence can overshadow the internal reality of the client.

Finally, the need to create and maintain a psychological profession may have led the early leaders of the guiding approaches to emphasize scientific methodology and psychological procedures and to overlook the positive aspects of the traditions of humanism and psychotherapy. Thus the experimental and measurement orientation of a guidance approach is criticized for being impersonal, but such "objectivity" may have more to do with the perceived needs of an emerging psychological profession than the actual counseling experience would reveal.

In sum, many of the apparent failings of the guiding approach are simply functions of history. The guiding approach arose during a time when counselors were not encouraged or permitted to do therapy, which was restricted to psychiatrists. To a certain extent, the guiding approach reflected this sharp dichotomy, in that clients with complex emotional conflicts were referred to psychiatrists.

Thus, although this externally based information approach to counseling has many positive characteristics, it seems to need a major updating of psychological concepts, philosophy, methodology, research strategies, and training procedures. At the same time, the guiding tradition has made major contributions to career-development theory and vocational psychology (see Crites, 1969), both of which are modern descendants of the guiding tradition.

Summary

Counseling function	*Characteristic*
Establishment	Relationship and social influence variables are an adjunct to the educational and scientific aspects of counseling.
Conceptualization	Use of scientific procedures for the gathering of socially valid information is emphasized.
Intervention	Counseling is similar to teaching, with a focus on problem-solving skills.
Evaluation	A correlational approach is preferred.
Professional development	Scientific education in psychology with practical experience is recommended.

Healing

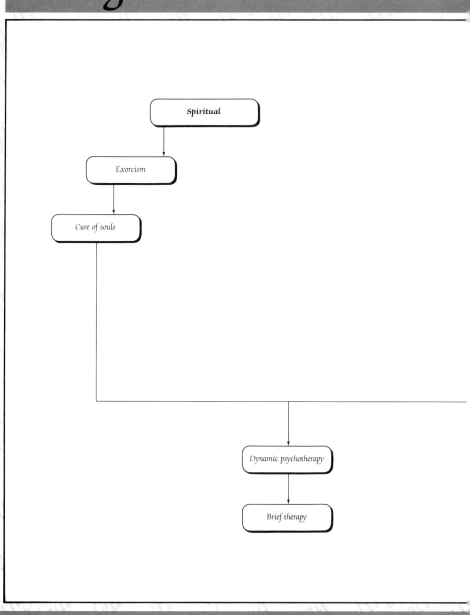

Spiritual

Exorcism

Cure of souls

Dynamic psychotherapy

Brief therapy

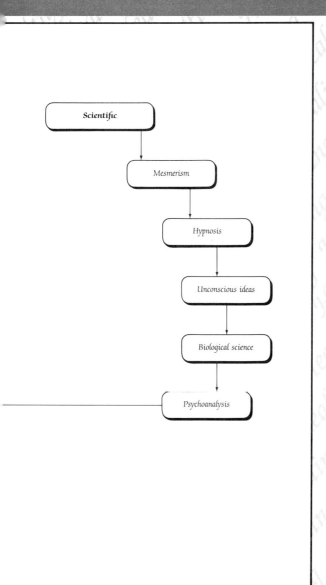

3

The term **healing** can take on many definitions, since it has been closely associated with differing ideas about illness. That is, ideas about human suffering have shaped the meaning of healing. For example, in many primitive societies abnormal behavior was considered to be a function of spiritual or magical possession. Under these conditions, healing became a spiritual/magical ritual to undo spiritual possession through the sacred words and rites of an exorcism, which was conducted by a healer.

Another common disease theory in North America maintained that disease was caused by the presence of a harmful foreign substance in the body, which could be removed by a medicine man. This early disease theory was a precursor of the modern model of disease and treatment that is concerned with infection. With infectious disease, physical symptoms are traceable to foreign bacterial processes within the body, which are treated by appropriate medical and surgical interventions. When extended to the domains of psychiatry and psychology, the infectious-disease model implies that maladaptive behaviors are symptoms resulting from psychopathological processes similar to pathological bacterial processes.

Although there are several other disease models, all imply some degree of loss or impairment, and consequently treatment is often concerned with a restoration of wholeness. To be sure, the wholeness need not mean structured wholeness nor does it have to imply a state that once actually existed. Surgery often restores function but does not necessarily restore the same structural details, such as the insertion of a pacemaker for heartbeat regulation. Thus healing is primarily interpreted to mean restoration of functional wholeness.

Unfortunately, such a definition of healing is not so clear-cut as it appears. When healing is applied to humankind from a psychological point of view, a new order of complexity emerges. What contributes wholeness is both more variable and more culture conditioned, as the point of view moves from biology to psychology. It will not be possible to resolve such an issue, but readers should be warned against assuming that healing goals are dictated solely by nature when psychological healing is used.

Historical background

The modern healing perspective in counseling psychology is rooted in the many historical traditions underlying dynamic psychotherapy, especially the spiritual and scientific traditions.

Spiritual tradition

The spiritual tradition regards many forms of human suffering as caused by spiritual possession. Major forms of treatment were borrowed from primitive societies by the Catholic Church and the Protestant community.

Exorcism is a prototype of a well-structured psychotherapy. Typically, the sufferers would present themselves to an exorcist, expecting help. The exorcist, a culturally recognized healer, would induce the spiritual intruder residing within the suffering person to speak, and after lengthy discussions, struggles, and appeals, a so-called victory was often accomplished with the dismissal of the intruder. Father Johann Joseph Gassner was considered one of the most renowned exorcists of the 18th century. He would dress in ceremonial garments and sit in an appointed place, with the sufferers kneeling before him in the presence of numerous witnesses. Gassner would make requests of the sufferers, focusing on their names, the nature of their illnesses, and the strength of their faith in his powers. After the requests, Gassner would say (in Latin), "If there be anything preternatural about this disease, I order in the name of Jesus that it manifest itself immediately." Subsequently, the sufferers would often show symptoms, such as convulsions. Such evidence was used by Gassner as proof of spiritual possession as opposed to natural ailments. He then ordered the spirit to produce symptoms in other bodily parts of the sufferers, and these demonstrations provided further evidence of Gassner's power. Finally, once the spiritual intruder had been subdued, Gassner expelled it.

The **curing of souls**, a tradition within Protestant communities and related to the older practice of confession, is another important spiritual forerunner of dynamic psychotherapy. The curing of souls was often associated with spiritually gifted ministers, who enabled suffering parishioners to disclose alarming secrets, resulting in a reduction of their personal difficulties.

Both exorcism and the curing of souls show some similarities to modern psychotherapies, in which patients and clients seek help from socially recognized healers (psychiatrists, psychologists, and other health professionals). Such help is usually found in a clinical setting—a hospital, an outpatient clinic, or a private office. These suffering individuals, expecting to be helped, are invited by the practitioner to engage in verbal discussion about their problem. After educating patients about the nature of their problems, therapists help the patients to reveal conflicts through therapeutic transactions and to take corrective actions. Thus expectations for help, sanctioned settings and healers, shared beliefs about suffering, and verbal unmasking of the sufferer's problem are the methods of spiritual healing that evolved into the methods of modern psychotherapy.

Among the many similarities, one deserves special emphasis, namely, the making manifest of the distress. In exorcism, the healer demanded that the demon make manifest the symptoms of the disturbance, while the Protestant ministers elicited the manifestation of a burdening secret.

Such an emphasis would be later consolidated and elaborated into theories of unconscious motivation and therapeutic practices aimed at client disclosure.

Scientific tradition

With the Enlightenment of the 18th century, the scientific era, came an emphasis on the power of the mind and a declining interest in mystical explanations. Within the scientific tradition, one source of dynamic psychology deserves special mention: **hypnotism**. Beginning with mesmerism (Mesmer, 1949) hypnotic procedures were the chief methods of gaining access to the unconscious mind. Although the hypnotic condition was called other things—artificial somnambulism, magnetic sleep, perfect crisis—and different explanations were offered, it was recognized that hypnotism opened an access to psychological processes that were inaccessible during the normal waking state. From the beginning, several factors associated with the hypnotic situation were the object of speculation. These factors can be seen as directly related to later principles of dynamic psychotherapy.

The rapport—the special relationship between healer and patient—a cornerstone of modern psychotherapy, impressed the early mesmerists. According to Mesmer, the therapeutic agent of magnetism was a physical fluid, which resided in the healer. Through the channel of rapport, magnetizers transmitted their potent fluid to the patient, thus correcting the malady through the creation of a better fluid balance within the patient.

Later hypnotists realized how dependent and susceptible patients became during this relationship. It was also soon recognized that rapport and its influence could be extended beyond the hypnotic session in the form of posthypnotic suggestions—that is, patients, who in their conscious state could recollect nothing of what transpired during the session, would act out a demand given during a hypnotic episode. The posthypnotic phenomenon demonstrated the dynamic impact of ideas, through their implantation during hypnosis to their eventual evolution and realization in action. This demonstration quite naturally led to a psychological model of disturbance, in which symptoms were a function of certain ideas. Through the works of the pioneers of dynamic psychiatry, the psychological assumption progressed to the recognition of the influence of subconscious fixed ideas in the development of mental and physical pathologies. Thus dynamic psychotherapy derives from primitive religious and medical practices, with linkages between the cure of souls and exorcism, exorcism and magnetism, magnetism and hypnosis, and hypnosis and dynamic psychotherapy.

Dynamic psychotherapy

It is impossible to know the full evolution of the healing perspective without considering the relationship of dynamic psychotherapy to contemporary social conditions, the articulation of dynamic therapy by Freud, and two adaptions from dynamic therapy—brief psychotherapy and psychoanalytic counseling.

Historical tradition

Therapists are part of their culture as well as contributors to it. The 19th century was alive with many new doctrines: Darwinism, Marxism, biological reductionism, sexology, and others. Such doctrines reflected the basic struggle between the Enlightenment and romanticism: reason versus the irrational, social conformity versus individualism, science versus mysticism, and so on. These doctrines and themes, interacting with the industrial revolution, the growth of cities, and the development of nation-states, helped frame the therapists' outlook: their focus on early development, their interest in biology, their use of psychotherapy to increase awareness, and their beliefs about sexuality.

Early practitioners of dynamic psychotherapy focused on two neuroses, hysteria and neurasthenia. Hysteria, often associated with sexual repression thought to be prevalent in the upper and middle classes during the Victorian period, was mainly a neurosis of women. Neurasthenia was predominantly a neurosis of men caught in the stressful circumstances of the industrial age. Toward the end of the 19th century, patients, as they had done earlier, played an influential role in the development of dynamic psychiatry. For example, it is thought that Freud gained a greater understanding of free association from the case of Elizabeth von R. and of countertransference from the Wolf Man case.

Freud

With Freud, dynamic psychotherapy entered a new era. Among the many sources of Freud's psychological work, one cannot overlook the biological influence in his work from his mentor Ernst Brücke and his friend Wilhelm Fliess. Freud's own personality and illnesses also provided an important contribution. In reflecting on his own neurosis, Freud emerged with confirmations of earlier ideas about the Oedipus complex and the influence of infantile sexuality on the development of neurosis. He and his followers set out to establish these universal truths through the establishment of a classical school with its own organization, publishing house, membership rules, and history. By these means, psychoanalytic theory was consolidated (see Sulloway, 1979).

Psychoanalytic theory continued to evolve through the works and practices of Freud's followers. Many of these contributions raised issues and spirited debates, and in some cases these controversies led to bitter arguments and disrupted relationships.

Brief psychotherapy and psychoanalytic counseling

One issue concerned the increasing length of therapy. In response, Ferenczi (Ferenczi, 1920), Alexander (Alexander & French, 1946), and others helped develop the method of **brief psychotherapy**. Later research (for example Malan, 1963) and practice (Mann, 1973) revealed that most of the essential elements of psychoanalysis could be used in a brief psychotherapeutic format, such as is required in a counseling setting.

Summary

The healing perspective is a transactional process involving a special relationship between a sufferer and a healer. Varying afflictions and therapeutic viewpoints have given definition to this relationship. The spiritual, medical, and early scientific traditions of the healing perspective eventually developed into dynamic psychotherapy. One adaption of dynamic psychotherapy to the counseling context is brief psychotherapy (Budman, 1981), which is of growing interest in the counseling field, especially among new professionals. To these professionals and others, there is an interest in applying psychoanalytic thought to counseling practice (Bordin, 1968).

Approach

Freudian theory, like many theories of human behavior, has received extensive scholarly discussion, and is perhaps more popularly known than any other theory. Consequently, no further elaboration is attempted here but rather a discussion of its basic tenets. (Readers wanting further delineation of the theory see Ellenberger, 1970; Munroe, 1955; and Sulloway, 1979.) However, psychoanalytic theory is discussed in terms of its use in each step of the counseling process. Special attention is given to brief psychotherapy (Malan, 1963; Mann, 1973).

Orientation

Although psychodynamics and psychoanalysis have been used interchangeably, they are distinct. Conceptually, psychodynamics refers to any psychological approach that attempts to explain behavior in terms of motives and drives, while psychoanalysis is only one such system.

Tenets of psychoanalysis (following Malan, 1963)

One of the original observations of psychoanalysis was made by Breuer; that is, hysterical symptoms could be relieved by making the patient reexperience, under hypnosis, painful memories and feelings that were unavailable (*unconscious*) through forgetfulness (*repression*). Freud, increasingly dissatisfied with hypnotism, began using more directive methods (*interpretation*) in unmasking relevant memories (*sexual seduction*) through forcefully suggesting to patients in the waking state that there were things the patient had forgotten and could recover. However,

Freud discovered that many patients struggled mightily against such remembrances (*resistance*). He was able to bypass this difficulty when he began to ask patients to say whatever came into their minds (*free association*) about their symptoms or about their dreams (*dream interpretation*). From these events, he found that the memories or dreams recalled were in symbolized and disguised form; and when he learned how to translate the symbolism, the material was accessible in undisguised form. With more experience, he began to realize that whatever came into the patient's mind had a meaning in relation to past memories or the resistance against them (*psychic determinism*). Moreover, when he focused on the resistances, he discovered that the memories were increasingly available without his having to badger the patient.

The preceding sequence, from hypnosis through suggestion to free association, focuses on Freud's techniques. But a phenomenon appeared that enhanced the more personal dimension of psychoanalysis (*therapeutic relationship*), namely that patients, such as the first case treated by Breuer (Anna O.), began to have intense feelings (*transference*) about the therapist. Freud found that, if he showed patients that these feelings were more appropriate to important persons in their early childhood (*Oedipus complex*) than to the therapist, such feelings could be handled without compromising therapeutic goals.

After Breuer's unsuccessful resolution of his feelings (*countertransference*) about his patient's feelings toward him, Freud realized transference was not something to avoid but could be used as a therapeutic method. That is, transference should be encouraged, especially negative feelings toward the therapist (*negative transference*), since unrecognized hostility is a powerful contributor to neurosis. Memories, especially those concerned with sexual traumas, were regarded as less important, and emphasis was now shifted to the repetition of neurotic childhood patterns in relation to the therapist (*transference neurosis*) and the gradual acquisition of insight and symptom relief (*working through*). Finally, the new kind of relationship with the therapist (*therapeutic working alliance*), through which these neurotic behaviors could be corrected, became the most significant aspect of tranference.

Freud drew from evolutionary theory, biological science, sexology, and the literature and philosophy of humanism to arrive at a concept of mental life. When he spoke about repression and its relationship to the unconscious, he used a topographical viewpoint (unconscious, preconscious, and conscious). When he spoke about the relation between the inner world of drives, including the drives of self-preservation and sex (*eros*) and aggression (*thanatos*), and the external environment, Freud differentiated mental life into the ego, superego, and id. When he spoke about the regulation of psychic forces, he referred to the traditional pleasure/unpleasure principle. When he spoke about different modes of mental functioning, he used terms such as primary process and secondary process. When he spoke of development, he ascribed psychosexual meanings to early physical and socialization processes (for example, oral, anal, and phallic stages, Oedipus complex, latency phase, and others). When he spoke of sexuality, he used the conceptualization frameworks of libido theory and erotogenic zones. When he addressed the question of neurosis, he spoke of anxiety and defense mechanisms. And so on. As can be seen, the concepts are rich, diverse, and ever changing.

Brief psychotherapy

Recently Mann (1973) has discussed many of these psychoanalytic concepts in terms of a particular form of brief psychotherapy. Two features characterize this approach: time limits and goal limits. In Mann's system, the setting of a time limit of 12 interviews has more than practical administrative reasons—it underscores the psychological nature of time. That is, time can be viewed in a developmental way, from the seemingly infinite time of childhood through the limited time of adulthood to death.

As we grow, the process of separation needs to be addressed. College students, for instance, are often confronted with the trials of separating from their parents and developing a personal identity, and brief psychotherapy has proved ideally suited to counseling these students. Through brief psychotherapy, an individual can give up childhood fantasies of unlimited gratification and the self-defeating ambivalences associated with separations and loss and experience separation as a genuine developmental event.

Related to time limits is the limitation of goals. While brief psychotherapy does not attempt to duplicate all the characteristics of long-term psychotherapy, it does emphasize a focused goal stated in psychodynamic terms. This goal, mainly described in terms easily connected to the client's feelings and experiences, usually reflects four basic conflicts in dealing with loss: independence versus dependence, activity versus passivity, adequate self-esteem versus diminished self-esteem, and unresolved grief. Mann's approach has many commonalities with counseling, especially its developmental goal (less encompassing than the goal of personality reorganization through reworking the effects of the past, which is the goal of long-term psychotherapy). In the following sections, each counseling function is explored in terms of the psychoanalytic concepts of brief psychotherapy. As will be discovered, the nature of brief psychotherapy suggests some alterations in traditional psychoanalytic practice.

Establishment

Caricatures of psychoanalytic treatment abound. One concerns the passive role of the psychotherapist. In moving from hypnosis to free association, therapists tended to become increasingly passive. While a passive stance may have been important in the early development of psychoanalysis, such characterizations have led to the assumption that passivity and inactivity are the only appropriate therapeutic stances. On the other hand, it seems from the literature that there are many types of dynamic therapists.

The active role is especially evident in the initial phase of brief psychotherapy. In discussing a treatment plan, the therapist mobilizes positive transference (unconscious expectations of magically undoing past conflicts) by providing a recognition of therapeutic time (a time in which something positive can occur). The assessment of the client's central problem also requires an active therapeutic stance. While clients discuss their current problem, their past, their fantasies and secret feelings (which also provides temporary relief), the therapist confines his or her attention to the central problem through clarification and by questioning its relationship to the information. (As we shall see, this clarifying activity is continued during later stages, through interpretation and corrective therapeutic experiences.) In addition to defining therapeutic time and clarifying the central problem, the therapist also actively supports the client by acknowledging the sincerity and other positive aspects of the client's past attempts to resolve developmental problems.

The specification of the treatment plan stimulates positive client expectations, which stimulates a sequence of positive events. The client then takes a more participatory role and produces material relevant to the agreed-upon problem, including historical material and adaptive reactions. In essence, the client plays out the recurring drama of establishing and terminating a human relationship with a therapist. The difference is that the other participant, the therapist, using a time-limited methodology based on psychoanalytic theory, enables the client to experience positive reactions that lead to a corrective and more mature separation experience.

Conceptualization

Central to brief psychotherapy is the identification of the client's central problem. The therapist encourages the client to talk, obtains information about unconscious conflicts, and relates this information to psychoanalytic concepts regarding the determinants of thoughts, the development of personality, and the expression of self. One method of obtaining the information that lies outside the client's awareness is to use a limited form of free association. The therapist pays attention to the client's emotional expressions of hurt, rage, and so on, and relates these to the client's conscious reason for seeking help, thus making these feelings and fantasies accessible to the client.

After relevant information has been gathered and processed, a close psychoanalytic study of the material will usually yield a theme that began in the past and that remains active in the present. Although themes vary, brief psychotherapy fosters those based on the recurring cycle of separation/individuation.

In practice, one has to decide on how to communicate the central problem to the client. The use of past events, adaptive expression, or character traits is likely to summon resistance and defense. Thus an approach that communicates the central problem in terms of the present painful experience is preferred. In addition, the communication needs to be flexible and general in order to involve the client in the treatment process. As treatment unfolds, the central problem can be further specified and corrected.

An example of the conceptualization process may be helpful. A woman of 24 was single, alone in a university town, and found herself unable to make a decision about her life despite her considerable ability and advanced education. She wanted to pursue a number of options, including a career and a family, but was unable to implement choices. A study of her history revealed that life changed drastically for her at age 12, when her mother committed suicide. The loss of her mother was exacerbated by the recent suicide of her younger sister. One could see the effects of these losses, especially in her adaptive efforts to try to please everyone.

Detection of the central problem is rarely made quickly. In the above example, the central problem was initially stated in a tentative manner: "It seems you are disappointed with the way you are living your life." Such a general theme was easily accepted and led to further elucidation as treatment progressed. As material was produced through therapist/client interactions, an elaboration of the central problem—"You feel inadequate and depressed as a result of your need to please others in order to avoid personal loss"—helped the client establish the connection between significant personal losses and her present depression. The conceptualization guided treatment and directed and limited the client's exploration of her life options.

Intervention

In the first three or four sessions of brief psychotherapy, the therapist, supported by the dynamic set of the client, attends to the central problem. After this, the client's positive feelings and symptomatic relief begin to fade, ambivalences return, and the client withdraws.

The therapist, however, does not follow the client in pursuing problems other than the central one. Resistance appears, decreasing the client's awareness of the central problem and fostering the repetition of unresolved conflicts. The therapist, in response, clarifies this resistance through interpretations of the client's defensive reactions. The linkage between self-defeating behavior in therapy and early childhood experiences is introduced through timely interpretations (most frequently in the later intervention phases, when clients struggle with childhood wishes and dependency and the realities of adulthood). The therapist points out that the feelings of the client experienced earlier with significant persons are now being experienced with the therapist. By being brought into this awareness, the client can begin to feel and know in what ways the past is getting in the way of the present.

Interpretative interventions enable clients to experience a mature relationship by calling attention to resistances and how they take attention away from the main tasks. These interventions are central to the healing process, since the development and working through of a therapeutic relationship cannot be accomplished unless these self-defeating behaviors are exposed and removed.

The following case may provide a useful example. A 19-year-old male university student came to the counseling center seeking help in understanding his rejection by his former girlfriend. In the beginning he had been rather mechanical in recounting his disappointment and lack of understanding; in the last few interviews, he made it clear that he wanted to understand the problem and wanted the therapist to help him understand. This is the eighth interview.

Excerpt	*Commentary*
1. *Client:* I have tried so hard to understand. I don't get it. Why didn't she like me? What is it?	The client seems to have difficulty expressing emotion (1, 3, and 5).
2. *Therapist:* Can you say "I feel angry."	In response, the therapist directs the client to attend and focus on feelings (2–11).
3. *Client:* Sure. Is that it, Doc? I feel angry.	
4. *Therapist:* Say it again.	
5. *Client:* I don't usually get angry.	
6. *Therapist:* Say it.	
7. *Client:* I feel angry.	
8. *Therapist:* Again.	
9. *Client:* I feel angry.	
10. *Therapist:* And again.	

	Excerpt	*Commentary*
11. *Client:*	*I feel angry.* [*Shaking*]	
12. *Therapist:*	Now, go back to your past and identify other instances in which you felt this way.	In excerpt 12, the therapist uses focused free association in order to connect feelings with past conflicts.
13. *Client:*	I feel angry. . . . Let's see . . . I guess I feel this way when I want something and don't get it. [*Pause*] Like always expecting something from someone and never getting it.	
14. *Therapist:*	Can you identify the "someone."	
15. *Client:*	Not really. . .	A little more resistance is encountered (15).
16. *Therapist:*	Have I delivered?	The therapist concentrates on the relationship dynamics (16, 18).
17. *Client:*	I don't know. It makes me uncomfortable to talk about you.	
18. *Therapist:*	You prefer that I stay in my place and talk about ideas rather than the feelings of a human being?	
19. *Client:*	That's stupid. I don't mean that. It's just hard to talk about such things. It has always been hard . . . especially with my dad. There was so much distance . . . and then he died.	The therapist begins to analyze the client's transference (19, 20).
20. *Therapist:*	It seems there is a link between the way you are feeling now with me and	

Excerpt	*Commentary*
your experiences with your father. You expect certain things from me . . . you expected things from your dad. But it doesn't appear that either one of us can deliver—your father is dead and we are approaching the end of treatment.	
21. *Client:* I guess so. . . . What can I do?	In response to the client's avoidance of his feelings (21), the therapist directs the client to engage in focused imagery (22).
22. *Therapist:* Close your eyes. . . . Visualize your dad. . . . Do you have a message for him?	
23. *Client:* [*Shaking*] I . . . miss him. . . . I need him.	

The excerpts reveal a somewhat dependent and intellectualized client struggling to deal with an unresolved relationship with his father. It appears the recent rejection experience has exacerbated this conflict, resulting in a high level of emotionality. In response, the client attempted to stimulate an intellectual discussion about rejection, while the therapist used the therapeutic relationship, free association methods, and interpretations to encourage the expression of feelings.

Evaluation

In the healing perspective, the case-study method is the primary means of substantiating its theoretical propositions. This method involves the gathering of a large amount of descriptive material about a person and the avoidance of dehumanizing abstractions. In addition, during the course of psychotherapy, observations of patients are recorded.

Malan (1963, 1976) and his colleagues conducted a series of case studies at the Tavistock Clinic in London. Experienced psychotherapists treated patients with brief psychoanalytic psychotherapy (10–40 sessions). Malan's studies used full clinical notes, projective test results, and records of a research team's discussions. An examination of this data was conducted, a psychoanalytic interpretation was made, and a plausible set of psychodynamic criteria for each patient's central problem was defined. That is, a clinical judgment, based on the clinical material, was made on how well each patient confronted and coped with his or her central problem without developing new symptoms. These judgments were then summarized in the form of simple ratings.

Although the results of Malan's studies need to be viewed with caution because of design deficiencies, the major findings showed that brief psychotherapy helped in the following ways:

1. Important dynamic changes occurred even in patients with extensive psychopathology.
2. Patient motivation to change correlated with positive outcome.
3. Cases tended to be more successful when transference interpretation became significant early, and the patient's feelings about termination were an important issue.
4. The link between transference and parents was the most important finding.

Many of Malan's findings are congruent with Mann's emphasis on limited dynamic interactions, in which a patient is motivated by time limits and struggles with therapeutic interventions, especially therapeutic interpretations that link early life relationships and current adaptions.

The characteristics of Malan's evaluation strategy are (1) the emphasis on the case-study approach, in which the therapist and the evaluator remain close to the clinical material; (2) the focus on clinical judgment; and (3) the use of psychoanalytic theory to define selection, method, and outcome variables. While Malan's strategy is closely associated with the healing perspective it does not imply that research on brief psychotherapy is restricted to case studies or medically oriented settings. Recent researchers (for example, Gelso & Johnson, 1983) have studied brief psychotherapy that use the procedures of traditional experimental design. While noting such exceptions (Gelso & Johnson, 1983), a healing perspective evaluation of these therapies is more likely to be idiographic, involving an abundance of clinical material and relying on psychoanalytic theory and the experienced analytic clinician to provide meaningful statements.

Professional development

The methods of training psychotherapeutic practitioners are diverse, but most agree about the importance of a personal therapeutic experience and psychotherapeutic supervision.

The therapeutic experience is advocated because it is believed that trainees can appreciate and work with the dynamics and unconscious processes of another person only if they have worked with their own, have reexperienced their conflicts, have freed themselves from self-defeating behaviors, and have experienced resolution. Trainees thus become "clients" and as their therapy progresses, it is assumed they will gain new insights into a therapeutic method through identification with the therapist, discover the existence of their unconscious, and resolve their inner conflicts. Such a therapeutic experience is usually conducted within a particular framework, like psychoanalysis, by therapists who do not serve in a training capacity (although some suggest the therapists become the trainees' initial supervisors, since they are familiar with the trainees' dynamics). In addition, a rather lengthy psychoanalysis is recommended for trainees planning to do psychotherapy for the rest of their lives.

The supervision of the trainee's therapy work by an experienced therapist concerns countertransference problems, the supervisory relationship, and the affective issues raised by the trainee's clients. Although some writers suggest that supervision and therapy are identical, others (Ekstein & Wallerstein, 1958/1972; Kell & Mueller, 1966) point to differences. It is true that many elements encountered in the therapeutic process are experienced in supervision: an affective relationship, change expectations, resistance to change, dependency reactions, unconscious repetitive ways of coping, and the linkage of past and present nurturing experiences. On the other hand, supervision and psychotherapy have different purposes. Problems in therapy are viewed in light of the resolution of inner conflict, while problems in supervision are viewed within the context of helping therapists work with their clients. These purposes, reflecting therapeutic and training goals, do appear to be different, but in practice distinctions may be difficult to maintain. In truth, the focus on the trainee's intrapersonal dynamics varies according to the situation and the theoretical viewpoint of the training.

The process of parallel reenactment provides some insight into therapeutic supervision. In this process, experiences in the supervisor/trainee relationship illuminate experiences in the trainee/client relationship. For example, a dependency experience in the trainee's relationship with a client is likely to stimulate dependency needs and related conflicts in the trainee, which are reenacted with the trainee's supervisor. Such parallel experiences are evidence that the teaching and learning of psychotherapy are not limited to didactics—instruction, information transmission, skill learning—for didactics bypass the powerful affective aspects of the supervisor/trainee relationship and the dynamic patterns of the trainee/client relationship. The heart of the former is the working through of the dynamic patterns experienced in the latter. (Kell & Burow, 1970; Kell & Mueller, 1966; Mueller & Kell, 1972, of Michigan State University, are most often identified with this model of supervision.)

In summary, psychotherapy supervision is a therapy-like procedure that attends to learning rather than psychotherapy. Significant dimensions of trainees' relationships with their clients are recreated in their relationships with their supervisors, from which emerge dynamic patterns of earlier relationships. These patterns are used to understand therapeutic barriers and to stimulate change processes in therapist/client relationships.

Commentary

Many of the factors overlooked in the guiding perspective are given prominence in the healing perspective, including affect, motivation, development, and the therapeutic relationship. Although psychotherapy can be viewed as a product of rationalism, in the sense of bringing into consciousness repressed thoughts and feelings, much more attention is given to unconscious feelings and motivations. In the healing perspective, counseling and therapy do not concern the simple transmission of objective information and the training of the intellect to make wise choices, because history and affect intrude upon the intellect. Moreover, the therapist/client relationship is more than an avenue to therapeutic change; it is in certain respects the treatment.

Affective phenomena and motivational processes deserve more recognition than they receive today. In psychology, cognition is dominant while affect is ignored, subsumed under other cognitive processes, although some recent studies indicate a renewed interest in affect (for example, Zajonc, 1980). The same can be said for historicism and evolutionary theory (see Campbell, 1978). The ahistorical viewpoint discourages a serious appreciation of counseling psychology and a careful evaluation of its research, practice, training, and professional identity. (However, see Wilson's 1975 study, which reminds us that we are persons with biological and cultural pasts.)

Two other factors have a contemporary relevance: time limits and therapeutic relationships. Brief psychotherapy is in tune with the needs of a cost-conscious society, while the therapeutic relationship gives the client a sense of personal worth, often lost in a highly technical world.

Although the healing perspective has made many positive contributions, some issues, especially the psychoanalytic variant, are in question. One criticism is the overemphasis of intrapsychic phenomena at the expense of external variables. Although some argue that Freud did not neglect external variables because he emphasized historical and developmental influences, Freud did not consider social, cultural, and economic factors as causes of current behavior.

Another criticism is the lack of experimental verification. It is doubtful that the healing perspective will ever meet the demands of experimentation, since its terminology and approach do not meet the criteria. The point here is what one will accept as meaningful evidence; those educated in an experimental tradition do not accept the evidence of psychoanalysis as meaningful.

A final criticism is of the time variations within this therapy. Although much of the research is uncontrolled, it does appear promising (see Johnson & Gelso, 1980). Brief psychotherapy can be shown to be practical, but the rationale of psychological time and analytical themes seems to lack verification. In addition, although brief therapy reduces the dependency encountered in long-term therapy, it may enhance another, the expectancy of quick and successful remediation. While the latter is speculative, it does suggest that more theory-based evaluation of brief psychotherapy is needed.

Summary

Counseling function	*Characteristic*
Establishment	Relationship variables and social influence variables are central.
Conceptualization	Assessment of the central problem is framed in terms of unconscious conflicts.
Intervention	Individual psychotherapy involving interpretive intervention is the preferred method.
Evaluation	Case studies are used as evidence.
Professional development	Personal learning through psychotherapy-like supervision is recommended.

Facilitating

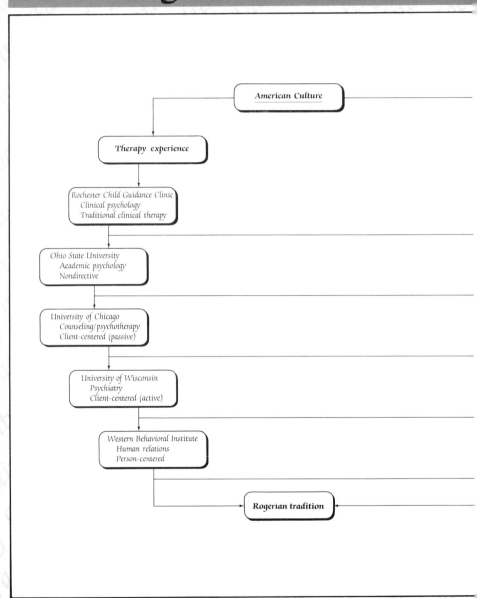

American Culture

Therapy experience

Rochester Child Guidance Clinic
Clinical psychology
Traditional clinical therapy

Ohio State University
Academic psychology
Nondirective

University of Chicago
Counseling/psychotherapy
Client-centered (passive)

University of Wisconsin
Psychiatry
Client-centered (active)

Western Behavioral Institute
Human relations
Person-centered

Rogerian tradition

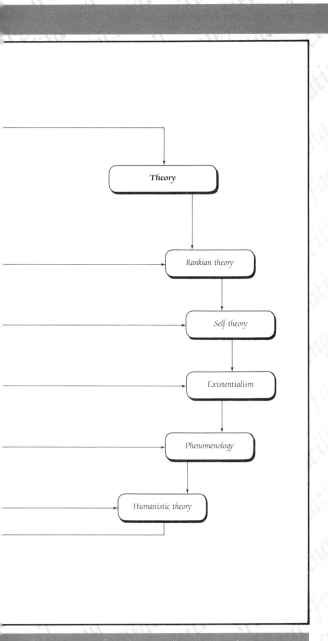

Theory

Rankian theory

Self-theory

Existentialism

Phenomenology

Humanistic theory

4

Facilitating emerged as a helping perspective during the modern struggle between democracy and authoritarianism, which was encountered in the marketplace, in the school, and in the political arena. In the helping fields, an alternative to the directive techniques of guidance and psychoanalysis was proposed, one that did not assume an impairment or other limitation in the client. The directive perspectives, with their assumption of deficient human functioning, elicited directive practices (teaching, guiding, and healing) used by experts who knew, diagnosed, and prescribed. Directive psychotherapists focused on the deficient inner workings of the person, while directive guidance workers focused on a lack of information and problem-solving skills.

Although it would be an error to define the facilitating perspective solely in terms of a protest, it is recognized that this perspective was a reaction to such authoritarian models and practices. Central to the facilitating perspective (also called the third-force approach) is the belief in the self-directing capacity of the individual. In this positive context, the helper relies on client resources without intruding into the client's experience. Facilitating takes on the meaning of enabling, encouraging, or empowering clients in their self-initiated activities. The use of terms such as *nondirective* and *client centered* to describe the facilitating perspective reflect an attempt to avoid the connotations of therapist direction and sick patients. Facilitating implies activities directed at releasing inherent curative powers within the client. Such a perspective is usually identified with the client-centered approach of Carl Rogers.

Historical background

There are many sources for the facilitating perspective, or at least the Rogerian version, but their unifying theme is the importance of self-determination. Such a theme is reflected in Carl Rogers's own experiences.

Carl Rogers: cultural influences

Rogers grew up in the American Midwest in a strict Protestant home. He was nurtured on the Protestant work ethic and the beliefs and myths of the American frontier—for example, that people can make of themselves what they will. As he matured, Rogers reflected the fundamentals of American culture: optimism, pragmatism, and individualism.

Such values led eventually to conflicts with established institutions. In his college years, Rogers emancipated himself from the restrictive religious training of his family. In seminary, he pursued freedom of inquiry beyond even that advocated by Dewey, G. Watson, and Kilpatrick, leading advocates of progressive education. For example, Rogers and others set up a seminar the content of which was composed of their own questions. Although an instructor was scheduled to sit in for administrative reasons, the instructor's participation was contingent upon the group's wishes. Protests against dogma and authoritarianism would continue as Rogers fought battles with psychiatry and behavioral psychology, which limited the self-direction of the client by emphasizing intrapsychic pathology or external control and manipulation.

Rogers's experiences with clients

In his early years (1931–40), Rogers, trained in the traditional approach to clinical psychology that involved a mixture of dynamic and scientific psychologies, used personality testing, diagnosis, and environmental modifications (Rogers, 1939). As he continued to see his clients and interact with social workers in a child guidance clinic in Rochester, New York, Rogers became dissatisfied with traditional approaches and began to experience the client and the therapeutic relationship in new ways. These new experiences were crystallized and expressed in a nondirective approach, much influenced by Otto Rank. In this approach, the counselor eschews all directive techniques while creating a permissive atmosphere through acceptance and verbal clarification in order to enhance client insight. For Rogers, "the *client* . . . knows what hurts, what directions to go, what problems are crucial, what experiences have been deeply buried" (Rogers, 1961, pp. 11–12). Thus Rogers began to look to other theories and methods for confirmations, resulting in continued reformulations of his therapy and theory.

Carl Rogers and Otto Rank

Otto Rank's study of the creative person led him to emphasize the constructive capacities of the individual, or a will to health. In therapy, the therapist provides an interpersonal relationship in which the client is led to self-help. The therapist cannot take responsibility for change, because the central problem is one of will power, of becoming a self-directed individual. Thus therapeutic emphasis is on the therapeutic relationship rather than on the technique. The therapeutic relationship provides a situation in which the client's troublesome behaviors, resulting from inappropriate responses from others, can be experienced anew and changed through interacting with a therapeutic person. Such a person elicits emotional responses and encourages the development of more appropriate behaviors without evaluating past performance.

Rank separated from Freud and traveled to the United States, conducting lecture series and seminars, especially at the School of Social Work in Philadelphia. Later, translations of Rank's work (1929/1945) appeared. Through such exposure and through interactions with social workers influenced by the Philadelphia school, Rogers became familiar with Rankian ideas and saw parallels between them and his own emerging belief in the capacity of the client. Moreover, in the passive therapy of Rank lay the seeds of Rogers's approach.

Formulation and confirmation of Rogers's theory

The expression of the nondirective approach (Rogers, 1942) coincided with Rogers's move to Ohio State University. At Ohio State and later at the counseling center of the University of Chicago, Rogers, at the urging of his graduate students, began to reflect on his therapeutic experiences. The electronic recording of interviews facilitated such reflection and led to research on the therapeutic process. Emphasis on methodology and research characterized this period. In addition, it was becoming evident that the nondirective approach was a technique in search of a theory of personality change. In searching for confirmations of therapeutic insights, Rogers found many parallels in phenomenology (Combs & Snygg, 1959), self-concept research (for example Raimy, 1943), and later, existentialism, especially the works of Buber and Kierkegaard.

Client-centered counseling

These confirmations and research studies led to new formulations of personality change and therapeutic activities. From a nondirective emphasis on insight facilitated by semantic clarification, Rogers moved to a more radical focus on the client's potential. This new focus was influenced by analyses of therapy recordings in which clients repeatedly made self-references. These analyses led to self-concept research and, eventually, to the use of self as an explanatory construct: troubled people had allowed their self-concept to become responsive to outside influences, and so their self-concept was incongruent with their inherent growth-producing factors. Thus they did not express their full potential. This new perspective, reflected in the name change from nondirective to client-centered counseling (Rogers, 1951/1965), led to new counseling practices. Before, counselors had been content to clarify the content of clients' verbalizations; now they responded to explicit and implicit affect, in order to mirror clients' experiential world and help them reintegrate their selves with their inherent potential. Thus counseling practices moved from cognitive clarification to sensitive responsiveness to clients' feelings and their often unrecognized facets of experience.

Counseling with psychiatric patients

Earlier, Rogers had worked in community clinics with adults and children; later he had worked with university students. In 1957, he moved to the University of Wisconsin, where he and other client-centered therapists began offering psychotherapy to hospitalized psychotics. As we have seen, earlier client experiences had led to changes in Rogers's formulations and practices, and now at Wisconsin further evolutions in Rogers's thought and practice took place. One movement was from specific techniques to general therapeutic attitudes (Rogers, 1957). Another was the elaboration of a concept of client change based on the integration of client experiences (Rogers, 1958).

These new practices were tested with a psychotic population but encountered difficulties, leading to further changes (Rogers, Gendlin, Kiesler, & Truax, 1967). Passive therapy was found to be inappropriate for a withdrawn, nonverbal, psychotic patient; more active participation was called for. Counselors began to follow their own advice, relying on their own experiences and expressing them more readily.

Later applications

The Rogerian position has continued to evolve. Its contemporary manifestations have been concerned with the application of the client-centered approach to enhance human-relations abilities of normal individuals in a variety of settings (Rogers, 1969/1982; Rogers, 1961). These applications, especially those concerned with encounter groups (Rogers, 1970), were again influenced by the people with whom Rogers came in contact in his latest moves. In La Jolla, California, Rogers began working with ministers, business people, teachers, and institutions in order to facilitate individual and institutional change. From such experiences, Rogers has expanded his position from personality and psychotherapy to an orientation about life—from a client-centered to a person-centered approach (Rogers, 1977). In this theory of interpersonal relations, a facilitator rather than a therapist fosters the expression and use of inner resources of individuals.

Although there have been many changes in the Rogerian position, these changes do not make Rogers inconsistent. The basic outlook has always been a client-directed approach in which the self-determination capacities of the client are the focus of attention, concern, activity, and acceptance.

Other influences

The focus on Carl Rogers does not imply that other influences are not relevant to the history of the facilitating perspective but that they were important as post hoc confirmations of trends recognized by Rogers.

Other philosophical and psychological traditions—including pheno-menology, existentialism, humanistic psychology, and gestalt psychology—impinge on his thinking, as do the ideas of other theorists, including Lewin, Dewey, Sullivan, Freud, Maslow, and Allport. But Rogers, nurtured within the traditional American culture and shaped by therapeutic experiences, understood the perspective and put it into practice.

Approach

As discussed, Rogers's recent contributions have concerned the development of a person-centered theory, a philosophy of life. We focus here on Rogers's orientation to individual counseling and psychother-apy (see Rogers, 1957, 1958, 1959b). (Rogers's concepts are in *italics*.)

Orientation

The fundamental assumption of the facilitative perspective lies in Rogers's view of human nature. Rogers postulated one motivational force in all forms of life, a force that moves in the direction of inde-pendence, self-regulation, and autonomy, and away from external con-trol (*actualizing tendency*).

From birth onward, the organism regulates behavior by evaluating experiences against the actualizing tendency (*organism valuing process*). As a person develops, some experiences become differentiated, symbolized, and elaborated into a self-concept. As a result, a part of the actualizing tendency becomes a tendency toward self-actualization. As the self emerges, the child develops needs for warmth and love from significant others (*need for positive regard*).

In addition, experiences of being loved and not loved become attached to self-experiences and incorporated into the self-concept (*need for positive self-regard*). These experiences often include the imposition of conditions by significant others; that is, children are told they are acceptable when they behave in accordance with external standards (*conditions of worth*). These imposed restrictions are assim-ilated by children into their self-concepts, creating another regulatory system of behavior, which can conflict (*incongruence*) with the orga-nismic valuing process. For example, say a teacher values his or her abil-ity to create an atmosphere in which students feel free to express their feelings and is frustrated and angry when students don't participate. The more this anger violates a self-image of what a good teacher should be, the more likely the teacher will externalize the anger and blame the students. A person more open to experience (*fully functioning person*) would assume responsibility for his or her own feelings. Such a teacher might say, "I like to express my feelings. I want you to express your feelings. And I am hurt that you don't consider important what I consider important."

With incongruence, self-experiences contradictory to conditions of worth are misperceived, leading to an inaccurate self-concept. Accurate representation and integration of these self-experiences would frustrate the strong and pervasive need for positive self-regard. The person continues to experience, but certain experiences elicit a state of tension (*anxiety*), even though such experiences may not be clearly perceived (*subceived*). In response to subceived discrepancies between the self-concept and experience, a person usually distorts the experience through denial and distortion (*defense*). In sum, incongruence develops because the self-concept is different from the actual experience of the organism. Experiences go on in the individual at all times, but people affected by incongruence turn away from these experiences.

The client-centered method helps people return to the flow of their experiences and reclaim their personal meaning. In facilitating optimal adjustment, the counselor relies on the natural capacity of the client for growth. The fundamental evaluation of humankind in this perspective is good—not bad, not neutral, but good. Under these conditions, coercion is unnecessary, and remedial action, in the sense of adding something to an inherently flawed organism, is not needed. Simply stated, if in a helping relationship the person designated as the helper has helper attributes (*congruence, positive regard, empathic understanding*), then positive change (*inner experiencing*) will take place in the "helpee," resulting in congruence between behavior and inner experience.

Establishment

For Rogers, the process of therapy is synonymous with relational experiencing between counselor and client. Each person in the relationship makes a contribution.

Attitudes of counselor

Counselors' contributions are genuineness, positive regard, and empathic understanding. **Genuineness** implies counselors' sensing and expressing the relevant facets of their own inner experience of the counselor/client relationship, thus providing a reality base that clients can trust. Genuineness means being real, relying on visceral wisdom, not playing a role, intellectualizing, or being defensive.

Positive regard refers to acceptance of the client, valuing the client without judgment, interpretation, and unnecessary probing. Positive regard means a genuine caring, noncontingent and unconditional—not attaching new conditions of worth by manipulating the client to behave in ways approved by the counselor. It tells the client that the counselor completely trusts in the client's resources.

Empathic understanding means that the counselor focuses on the subjective reality of the client's experience. Understanding the client's world is more than listening and reflecting the client's words. It requires that the counselor be immersed in the client's perceptual world and communicate an understanding of that world, some meanings of which may not have been symbolized into the client's awareness. Such empathic communications provide the client an experience of being personally understood.

Capacity of client

The counselor's genuineness, caring, and empathy are based on a trust in **client capacity**. It is assumed that they provide the climate necessary for clients to turn again to their growth processes and remove the barriers. The client who experiences these counselor attitudes may reflect, "The counselor is being real. The counselor likes me. The counselor understands me." These confirmations in turn may lead the client to affirm, "It is okay to be me, although I am changing and not sure what me is or will be in the future."

As this example suggests, the counselor's therapeutic attitudes are not the only contributors to change. The client has influence. First, the client, in seeking help, must sense a need for change; usually it is experienced as anxiety. In addition, the client must experience and perceive that the counselor is genuine, caring, and empathetic. Too often, researchers, counselors, and educators ignore these client contributions, focusing exclusively on the counselor.

Establishment as facilitation

For Rogers, the establishment phase—the development of a therapeutic relationship—*is* the helping process. Thus every person can be a helper to every other person through an interpersonal relationship that expresses a basic respect for the inner resources of the other. The transactions of this relationship are verbal and concerned with the ongoing feeling process. Their aim is to convince clients of their inherent capacity and to show them the incongruence between certain of their experiences and their self-concept. Such helping transactions reflect Rogers's belief that affective responses are key elements in healthy functioning and, in combination with evaluative thoughts learned from others, involved in incongruence.

Although Rogers does not use the concept of social influence, he believes that therapists should help clients recognize their potential and allow it to unfold. In accomplishing this task, counselors rely on their

trustworthiness. Although trustworthiness may be inherent in the helping role, facilitators communicate their trustworthiness through an attitude of genuineness, trusting their own organismic responses. In addition, the facilitator trusts the client's resources. Once clients trust the facilitator and know they are trusted, they can risk expressing themselves.

Conceptualization

Although Rogers, earlier in his career, supported the use of psychometric tests in counseling under limited circumstances (for example, when a client desired testing), his later formulations viewed testing, diagnosis, and other formal problem-identification procedures as interfering with the client's focus on inner experiencing. Tests encourage clients to depend on expert evaluation and deprive clients of experiencing individual responsibility for understanding and improving their condition. Also, diagnostic information might threaten the client, leading to defensive maneuvers and to negative social outcomes. Tests focus on problems, whereas client-centered counselors focus on the person. For these reasons, many client-centered counselors minimize the diagnostic process.

For Rogers (1957), "in a very meaningful and accurate sense, therapy *is* diagnosis" (p. 223). In client-centered therapy, the client makes, experiences, and accepts the diagnosis. Since behavior is a function of perception, the only one who can know the dynamics is the client. This theory, based on the primacy of the individual's perceptual world of experience, assumes that clients will explore areas of conflict as soon as they are able. During therapy the client experiences the consequences of distorted perceptions, experiences more adequate perceptions, and recognizes the relationships between these perceptions. In this way, therapy becomes diagnosis, with the counselor providing the climate in which diagnosis by the client can occur.

In sum, Rogers's beliefs in the primacy of perceptual experience and the self-directing capacity of the individual preclude any external interference with the client's experiential process.

Intervention

Rogers long ago deemphasized techniques in favor of attitudes that facilitate a therapeutic relationship. The essence of these facilitative conditions is the counselor's active involvement. While the main work of the counselor is still to understand the client's experiences and feelings, the newer formulation stresses the expression of the counselor's experience during the human encounter in order to create a living and real relationship.

It is difficult to discuss Rogerian interventions, since they are not separate entities but are interactional processes. In fact, the term "intervention" is not appropriate for what Rogers and other client-centered counselors do. An excerpt from a case history illustrates. In this example, a young mother, trying to integrate career and family obligations, wanted to understand her bad feelings. We begin with the tenth interview.

Excerpt	*Commentary*
1. *Client:* Things aren't right.... I don't feel good about myself.... I mean, I know having a career is good for a woman, for me. But.... [*Silence*]	The client seems to be omitting part of the experience.
2. *Counselor:* "But." There is something else?	In response, the counselor explores the omission.
3. *Client:* Yes. I get the feeling, "oh, you are a bad mother." [*Pause*] Although I know it's ridiculous, I feel guilty, ashamed.	
4. *Counselor:* Although having a career is right for you, on another level, you can't feel good about it.	In excerpts 4 and 6, the counselor's empathic responses attempt to integrate the client's various bits of experience.
5. *Client:* You know, it's total. I can't help feeling defeated. I just have a very down feeling. In my head, the image is superwoman. But I am not home with the kids. I don't have enough time with my husband. [*Pause*]	
6. *Counselor:* You seem to be experiencing different messages. You don't think	

	Excerpt	*Commentary*

you should be feeling guilty about your career, but you do experience feeling bad.

7.   *Client:* Stupid . . .

8. *Counselor:* As I sit here trying to feel what you must be feeling . . . it occurs to me you beat yourself up a lot. I don't mean physically, but with "shoulds." You "should" feel. You "should" do.

In excerpt 8, the counselor discloses his internal sensing of the client's experience.

9.   *Client:* I didn't think about it that way. But I guess I do. It is *me* that is feeling bad.

10. *Counselor:* Right now, you feel very dissatisfied with the person that is you.

In the final excerpt, the counselor provides an opportunity for the client to recognize her feeling, to experience it, and to accept it in this moment.

This example shows a small bit of the client-centered approach. The counselor has established a therapeutic climate and attempts to remove the barriers to client experiencing (excerpt 1) by means of empathic communication (excerpts 4, 6, and 10) and disclosure (excerpt 8). Through such a process, the client becomes aware of her experience (excerpt 9) and it is hoped will use her experiencing as a guide for her life.

Evaluation

The client-centered approach has a strong research orientation. Many factors contributed to the research emphasis: the development of the approach in a university conducive to research, the creativity of client-centered practitioners, and the use of electronic recording. Undoubtedly, Rogers's own predilection for practical and scientific understanding, emerging from earlier interests in scientific agriculture, was a major contributor. This predilection can be observed in Rogers's insistence on studying the raw data of counseling and on describing it without using esoteric jargon. Typically, client-centered evaluation uses the actual events of counseling, conceptualizes general propositions, and tests them empirically with measures developed from counseling practice.

Phenomenological assessment

After many hours of listening to therapy tapes, counselors realized that clients repeatedly referred to self and self-change. This observation led Rogers and colleagues to describe the process of change in terms of changes in the self; that is, a movement from negative feelings about the self to positive ones characterized a successful outcome; the less the movement, the less successful the outcome. In order to check these propositions, some tools were needed to quantify client self-observations. Fortunately, a technology became available when self-theory was growing. Stephenson (1953) supplied an individualized quantitative methodology, called the Q-technique or Q-sort, that permitted an analysis of self-perception before and after therapy. Later, the Barrett-Lennard (1962) inventory of perceived therapist conditions assessed the client's view of the therapeutic relationship.

Content analytic procedures

As Rogers continued to immerse himself in listening to recorded interviews and conducting outcome studies (see Rogers & Dymond, 1954), he published two theory papers that discussed therapeutic conditions (Rogers, 1957) and the process of psychotherapeutic change (Rogers, 1958). Based on propositions contained in these papers and extended in other writings, Rogers and colleagues developed scales to measure these conditions and processes.

The Process Scale (Rogers, 1959a) was based on Rogers's view of personality—namely, that personality is a continuum from rigidity and fixity of perceptions, feelings, and experience at one end to flowingness and changingness at the other end. This continuum was represented in the form of a seven-point scale and was used to locate a client's psychological functioning in seven categories (feelings and personal meanings, manner of experiencing, degrees of incongruence, communication of self, manner in which experience is continued, the relationship and problems, and the manner of relating to others). This scale and its revised versions (for example, the Experiencing Scale) was used to analyze clients' recorded verbalizations over time and to assess the degree of change during treatment.

Scales to measure therapeutic conditions were refined and extended by Carkhuff and colleagues (Carkhuff, 1969) following the original presentation by Rogers (1957) and its development by Truax (1961, 1962a, 1962b). These scales attempt to operationally define the core conditions—genuineness, caring, and empathy—in terms of specific helper qualities, especially the counselor's verbal communications. These scales are often used to rate audiotaped excerpts of counseling sessions.

An evaluation project

A brief description of a research project will provide additional insight into the client-centered approach to research. Rogers and his associates (Rogers et al., 1967) completed a large-scale investigation of psychotherapy with hospitalized schizophrenics. The major purpose was to verify Rogers's theoretical formulations concerning therapist conditions, client process, and therapy outcomes. Specifically, the greater the therapy conditions, the greater the movement of the therapeutic process and the greater the improvement of the client.

Briefly, the design included 14 schizophrenics receiving Rogerian therapy and 14 matched controls receiving group therapy, a traditional hospital treatment. One four-minute tape-recorded sample was taken from every fifth interview for each of the 14 experimental participants and rated on therapeutic condition scales: Accurate Empathy Scale, Unconditional Positive Regard Scale, and Therapist Genuineness Scale. Therapist conditions were assessed not only by judges' ratings of interview excerpts but also by Barrett-Lennard rating scales completed by both therapists and patients. In addition, the recorded sample segments were rated for client process variable (Problem Expression Scale, Exploration Scale, and Experiencing Scale). Outcome measures were administered early (pretest) and late (posttest). The measures included a battery of psychological tests: MMPI, TAT, WAIS, Anxiety Reaction Scales, the Stroop Tests, F Authoritarian Scale, the Q-sort, and the Wittenborn Psychiatric Rating Scales.

The results were complex, but major findings suggest that although different therapist conditions were not associated with differential client process movement, there was some evidence to support the importance of the therapist conditions and process variables in successful psychotherapy. That is, therapist conditions and process variables were higher when there was greater pretest to posttest change.

Summary

The above study is subject to limitations of measurement and controversy. Moreover, it is unclear whether better outcome is a function of a therapeutic therapist or whether a therapist functions better with cases who are in the process of change. On the other hand, it does point out some central characteristics of the client-centered approach to evaluation. First, content analytic procedures using audiotaped therapy sessions and rating scales developed from propositions about therapy and therapeutic change and derived from naturalistic observations of therapeutic sessions are prevalent. Raters use scales measuring therapist conditions and the process of change to describe the relationship between counselor and client. Such procedures represent a major evaluation theme within the client-centered approach—namely, an emphasis on **process**. To Rogers, successive observations over a series of interviews keeps the evaluator close to the raw data. These observations are an appropriate method of evaluation, since they are ongoing and congruent with the change that evolves throughout counseling. In addition to providing outcome information based on the differences between two sets of observations, those made before and those made after counseling, process information provides a trend line over a period of time.

Aside from methodological considerations, the focus of inquiry is also a distinctive feature. In the above study, therapist conditions and the client's experiential process were the dominant focuses. Over the years, client-centered research has expanded on therapist characteristics (Truax and Carkhuff) and client experiencing (Gendlin).

Although the Rogerian perspective may appear to be antiscientific given its phenomenological stance and its sometimes overzealous protests against the psychological establishment, Rogers and his colleagues have historically tried to scientifically validate his propositions about the process of therapeutic change. At the same time, Rogers would consider such scientific knowledge as only one way of understanding and would undoubtedly give more weight to subjective knowledge.

Professional development

Rogers and his associates were one of the first groups to develop brief workshops for the training of counselors and therapists (see Blocksma & Porter, 1947). Training in the facilitative perspective involves (1) experiencing facilitative conditions, (2) teaching facilitative behaviors, and (3) working in a therapy-like group, through which they can explore their difficulties in becoming a therapeutic person.

Experiencing facilitative conditions

The experiential part of the training program is the essential starting point. If trainees do not experience a facilitative atmosphere, it is unlikely that they will function at high levels of therapeutic effectivness. In counseling and therapy, the counselor or therapist provides the facilitative atmosphere. In training, the supervisor creates it, thus modeling facilitative behaviors for the trainee.

The didactic process, occurring within a facilitative atmosphere and focusing on experiential content, was originally conceptualized as graded experiences, including extensive reading in theory; listening to tape recordings of experts; observing live demonstrations; role playing; conducting, recording, and discussing individual counseling interviews; and undergoing some form of therapy. Later Truax and Carkhuff (1967) added significant refinements and technologies to the earlier training procedures and attempted to formally integrate the experiential and didactic components. Their program consists of three stages: discrimination, communication, and action. Within each stage, graded activities are specified.

During **discrimination**, the trainee is exposed to a Rogerian theory of the conditions essential to change. Emphasis is given to the facilitative conditions necessary for self-exploration. Later, Carkhuff (1969) provided an additional theoretical component. As the client self-explores and as the facilitative conditions become more refined, Carkhuff added some action-oriented conditions (confrontation and immediacy), using ideas from behavior modification and social learning. The trainee thus learns to discriminate among levels of facilitation and between facilitation and action. Trainees add to their response repertoire by listening to taped therapy sessions. They refine their discriminative abilities by rating excerpts from these tapes, using scales designed to articulate separate dimensions. Some of these excerpts are transcribed into written exercises and rated by experts, which allows trainees to correct or verify their own ratings.

Teaching facilitative behaviors

Communication training begins when discrimination has been mastered. Focusing on each dimension singly, trainees practice making responses to clients' tape-recorded or written statements. When using tape-recorded excerpts, trainees work in groups, an expert serving as supervisor. Trainees try to communicate to the client at a minimal level of helpfulness before attempting higher levels. When the minimal level is reached, trainees meet in pairs and alternate playing the counselor and client roles. These sessions are recorded for later ratings and discussion in the trainee group. After achieving minimal levels of therapeutic communication during role-played sessions, the trainees are assigned to single interviews with real clients. The focus is still on developing a good therapeutic relationship. Interviews are recorded and brought back to the trainee group for further ratings and discussion.

As the trainee gains experience in facilitative interaction, training proceeds into the development of effective **action** skills. The trainee is instructed in these skills and practices them. (An example of an action skill is systematic desensitization.) When these skills have been adequately developed and demonstrated, the trainee is assigned clients for continuing counseling. These sessions are recorded, and examples are evaluated in a supervisory session or group.

Working in a therapy-like group

Finally, trainees experience a quasi-group therapy or peer cotherapy, to discuss role difficulties and to practice their developing skills in a therapy-like setting.

Summary

Client-centered training is characterized by: (1) a therapeutic context, in which a supervisor offers a high level of facilitative conditions; (2) the integration of didactics and experience, both aimed at fostering appropriate counselor attitudes and behaviors; and (3) a technology, including instruments to measure helpfulness and indexes to assess levels of functioning. Client-centered training has become a focus of research, with researchers using content analytic methods to study counselor performance and client perceptions as a method of assessing training effects.

Commentary

Rogers's facilitative perspective appears very modern. An insistence on naturalistic observations can be seen in the new research strategies that focus on the description of the complex interactions that take place in counseling. These include sequential analysis of verbal interactions (Gottman, Markman, & Notarius, 1977), task analysis of in-therapy client performance (Rice & Greenberg, 1984), and Markov chain analytic methods (Lichtenberg & Hummel, 1976; Neufeld, 1977).

Other Rogerian concepts are relevant to modern models of learning, such as information processing (for example, Wexler & Rice, 1974). Rogers's beliefs in the importance of perception and a proactive stance is similar to the psychology of information processing in which the person is seen as responding to a world of experience actively constructed by the person (see Neisser, 1967). Carl Rogers's discussion of self and its relationship to defensiveness appears to be related to recent research on memory (for example, T. B. Rogers, Kuiper & Kirker, 1977) and a resurgence of interest in the self (for example, Greenwald, 1981). The continued evolution of client-centered theory seems very promising within cognitive psychology. And a major tradition within counseling psychology is identified with Rogers's writings on the processes of the helping relationship and healthy psychological growth. These themes have been extended to a psychological/philosophical value system that has influenced many segments of society.

Numerous criticisms of the facilitative perspective have also been made, including the use of global concepts and faulty measurement techniques. A tendency has also been noted within this perspective to extend Rogers's notions about feelings, subjectivity, and relational dynamics to a point where cognition is only a defense mechanism and gut feelings are wisdom (Strupp, 1976). Both professionals and students have adopted "irrational" approaches to helping, in which undocumented innovations and gut reactions replace critical thinking and scientific study. This extreme does not reflect the penchant for scientific understanding of the original facilitative perspective.

Summary

Counseling function	Characteristic
Establishment	The relationship dimension is central, with little acknowledgement of social influence.
Conceptualization	Formal diagnosis is ignored, while the clients are encouraged to diagnose their own dynamics.
Intervention	Active involvement of the counselor in facilitating a therapeutic relationship is recommended.
Evaluation	Process research, based on naturalistic observations, content analysis, and phenomenological evaluation, is salient.
Professional development	An experiential/didactic program aimed at developing therapeutic attitudes and behaviors provides the training focus.

Modifying

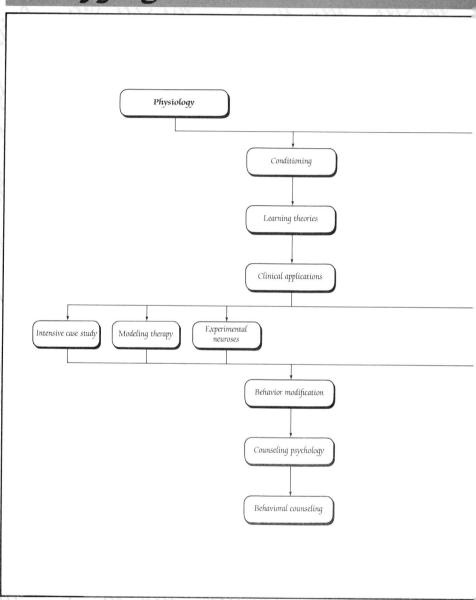

Animal behavior

Deconditioning

Reinforcement therapy

Token economies

The **modifying** perspective is often identified with behavior modification, a modifying approach concerned with changes in the organism caused by environmental factors. Behavior modification has been the subject of definitional controversy. The approach represents a generic goal common to many other helping perspectives, yet includes several behavior-change methods based on seemingly divergent principles and procedures, such as classical conditioning (Wolpe, 1958), operant conditioning (Skinner, 1953), vicarious learning (Bandura, 1971), broad principles of learning (Ullman & Krasner, 1969/1975), clinical approaches of behavior therapy (Lazarus, 1958), and more recent procedures based on cognitive learning (for example, Beck, 1974/1976; Mahoney, 1974; Meichenbaum, 1977; Stone, 1980). Although the modifying perspective lacks an unequivocal definition, one unifying characteristic is a reliance on an empirical methodology in which observations are collected and analyzed, relying on objective and measurable data.

Historical background

The objectivism of the modifying perspective stems from a methodological revolt among disciplines such as biology and psychology, which aspired to establish scientific bases. Using the quantitative approach that Galileo applied to mechanics during the 17th century, Harvey (1578–1615) revolutionized physiology by restricting his biological research to questions that could be solved by experiment and measurement.

Russian physiology

Three later advocates of objective methods in physiology became important contributors to behavior modification. Sechenov, Pavlov, and Bechterev were eminent Russian physiologists deeply committed to objective research in neurophysiology. For example, when a surgical technique was perfected to implant fistulas in the glands of major organs of digestion (stomach, salivary glands, and others), Pavlov and his colleagues were able to collect secretions outside the body and quantify digestive functions. Through their work, especially that of Pavlov and Bechterev, conditioning became a way of objectively investigating biological and motor systems.

In a **conditioning model,** a simple behavior was conceptualized as a conditioned reflex, complex behavior as a series of reflexes. Pavlov showed that these reflexes were established by repeatedly pairing an unconditioned stimulus (food) that elicited a reflex reaction (salivary reflex) with a neutral stimulus (tone), which initially did not elicit such a reaction. After repeatedly pairing food with the tone, the tone alone came to elicit salivation (becoming a conditioned stimulus). This **reflex arc conception** was extended by Bechterev to humans' learned reflexes (for example, by applying shock to the fingertips with various visual, auditory, and tactile stimuli serving as the neutral stimuli). Such an objective approach led experimental physiologists in Russia to abandon vitalistic conceptions and subjectivity and to concentrate on the correlation between external phenomena and the reaction of the organism. This externalistic theme, emphasized by Watson and others, contributed to what was eventually termed stimulus-response psychology.

Animal behavior

The rise of objectivity was not restricted to Russian physiology. Research in animal behavior in England and Germany, stimulated by Darwin, increasingly viewed the responses of animals as a direct function of environmental stimulation rather than a function of consciousness or other anthropomorphic factors. In 1913, John Watson, after reading and hearing about these scientific developments, introduced methodological behaviorism—the scientific study of behavior—to North America. At about the same time, Thorndike and Yerkes began research programs in animal psychology based on laboratory experimentation.

Thorndike employed the same objective methods as Pavlov but studied a seemingly different kind of learning. Instead of focusing on stimulus characteristics and how various stimuli come to elicit inherent reflex responses, Thorndike centered on the acquisition of responses that were instrumental; for example, animals escaping from a puzzle box in order to secure food. For Thorndike, learning became connecting—connecting responses to stimulus conditions through the impact of the consequences of behavior. Animals in Thorndike's puzzle box explored various escape alternatives in a trial-and-error fashion. Observations from repeated trials indicated that random movements and errors decreased and consistency of successful performance increased.

Thorndike's work can be seen as a precursor of objective psychological study like Pavlov's, but unlike Pavlov, Thorndike was part of the old, subjective tradition and described outcomes in terms of subjective states and satisfying or annoying consequences. The works of Pavlov and Thorndike influenced the development of the conditioning paradigm and, along with the methodological formulations of Watson, the expansion of the objective study of psychology. Such expansion resulted in a productive research tradition in the psychology of learning in North America, represented by the work of Watson, Thorndike, Guthrie, Tolman, Mowrer, Hull, Spence, and Skinner, who has been perhaps the single most influential learning theorist.

Skinner's contributions to behavior modification have been substantive and methodological. At the substantive level, he, in a manner similar to Thorndike, shifted the focus in learning from classical to operant conditioning through his programmatic animal research on the impact of diverse aspects of reinforcement under controlled conditions. From such laboratory investigations, Skinner described and elaborated many basic principles of operant conditioning: reinforcement, punishment, extinction, and stimulus control.

Methodologically, Skinner resolved to establish descriptive relationships between behavior and environments without appealing to internal constructs. In carrying out the program, termed **experimental analysis of behavior,** many methodological innovations were introduced, including the Skinner box, automated electrical laboratories, and the study of responses of the individual organism over extended periods of time.

Clinical applications

The preceding experimental work laid the foundations for behavior modification, but little of the work was applied to clinical situations. The transition from laboratory research to clinical applications began with the work on experimental neuroses, conditioning and deconditioning of emotional reactions, and the development of operant procedures within clinical and educational settings.

Experimental neuroses

The discovery of experimental neuroses happened in Pavlov's laboratory. One of Pavlov's experiments exposed a dog to two stimuli, a circle and an ellipse, with conditioned salivation occurring in the presence of the circle, only. As the ellipse was altered, it increasingly resembled a circle, resulting in a difficult discrimination. After a few weeks under this difficult condition, the dog's usual calm behavior was changed—it struggled, became agitated, barked, and attacked the equipment. Moreover, the dog's performance of the conditioned response decreased even under the gross discrimination conditions experienced earlier. Such a breakdown of conditioning coupled with increased emotional reactions was termed experimental neurosis.

The work on experimentally induced neurosis was extended by Masserman (1943), who added procedures for treating neurotic behavior and integrated experimental research with psychoanalytic theory. Various extensions eventually led to important therapeutic methods (systematic desensitization) and useful paradigms (shock avoidance) for exploring abnormal behavior, such as despondency and learned helplessness.

Classical conditioning

In their classic study, Watson and Rayner (1920) suggested that learning could account for humans' fear reactions. This suggestion was based on their conditioning study of Albert, an 11-month-old boy. A white rat, which elicited little fear from Albert, served as the neutral stimulus. The rat was presented to Albert with a loud noise (unconditioned stimulus), resulting from a hammer striking on a steel bar, which elicited a startle response from Albert. After a number of trials, the rat was presented alone (conditioned stimulus), causing Albert to fall over, cry, and crawl away. Stimuli such as a rabbit, cotton, and wool, which previously caused no fear reaction, also began to elicit a fear reaction, indicating some generalization from the rat.

Although the demonstration was considered an application of classical conditioning, the actual procedures (the loud noise was contingent on Albert's reaching for or touching the rat) follow a response-contingent procedure, such as punishment. Whatever the explanation, the use of learning principles to alter behavior stimulated clinical applications of conditioning procedures: Jones's (1924) treatment of fear reactions by direct conditioning, Mowrer and Mowrer's (1938) treatment for enuresis, and Wolpe's (1958) desensitization work.

Operant conditioning

In 1953, Skinner and Lindsley (Lindsley, 1960) extended the use of operant conditioning to psychotic patients under laboratory conditions (for example, plunger pulling associated with various reinforcers and reinforcement schedules). They called their applications behavior therapy. Bijou and coworkers at the University of Washington extended operant research to children, both normal and retarded.

An early application of operant techniques with clinical populations was the development of a reinforcement system to alter patients' behavior. Teodoro Ayllon at Saskatchewan Hospital in Canada used positive reinforcement and punishment to reduce patients' interruptions of nurses, violent acts, and psychotic talk. The work was extended to Anna State Hospital in Illinois by Ayllon and Azrin, leading to token-economy systems, in which total environments were planned in order to motivate a larger number of patients. Bijou, Baer, Wolf, and Risley applied operant techniques, including token programs, at the Rainer School (University of Washington); later, the latter three helped initiate a center for applied operant research at the University of Kansas.

Conceptual and empirical advances

As clinical applications increased, conceptual and empirical attempts were made to provide a general theory of behavior. These attempts were an alternative to the medically and psychoanalytically dominated approach to psychopathology. Dollard and Miller (1950) attempted to conceptually unite learning (Hull), psychopathology (Freud), and modern social sciences. In England, Eysenck and coworkers at Maudsley Hospital argued for the importance of experimental psychology in clinical practice. In addition, Eysenck's (1952) pessimistic review of the psychotherapy literature and his subsequent polemics against the psychoanalytic model have outlined for many behavior modifiers the inadequacies of traditional psychotherapy.

Such arguments led M. B. Shapiro (1966), head of the clinical section at Maudsley, away from traditional assessment approaches and batteries of psychological tests. He replaced these procedures with methods that would facilitate the research responsibility of the clinician, such as an intensive case study of the individual over time.

In the early 1950s, learning concepts were providing a fresh perspective on psychotherapy. In one learning concept, **verbal conditioning** (for example, Greenspoon, 1962), the verbal behavior of an interactant was altered by following specific responses with contingent events. Truax (1966) analyzed a tape recording of one of Carl Rogers's therapy cases and discovered that the empathy and warmth of his comments were contingent upon specific client responses. Rogers, of course, is an advocate of nondirective counseling.

Up to this point, conditioning had been the major learning paradigm. A second learning paradigm, called **social learning,** or modeling, although mentioned at the same time as conditioning by some investigators, was articulated later than conditioning (Bandura & Walters, 1963; Miller & Dollard, 1941), especially by Bandura (1969). In the social-learning paradigm, a social model demonstrates the desired behavior. Acquisition of new responses occurs through cognitive processing without overt practice or reinforcement. However, reinforcement can affect subsequent performance.

An early clinical application of social learning was conducted by Jones (1924). After selecting children (aged 3 months to 7 years) who displayed fear reactions to various situations (being left alone, being in a dark room) and objects (loud noise, frogs, white rats), Jones used several methods suggested by Watson and Rayner to reduce these reactions. Social modeling was a success: the child displaying a fear reaction to a particular object was placed in a situation with that object and with fearless children, who approached and played with the object. When the fearful child began to imitate the other children, his or her fear was reduced. Modeling therapies have been extended to anxiety reduction (Bandura, Grusec, & Menlove, 1967; Bandura, Jeffrey, & Gajdos, 1975), social skills training (Bellak & Hersen, 1979), and various cognitive-control procedures (Bandura & Whalen, 1966; Stone & Noce, 1980).

This section provides only a brief glimpse of the development of behavior modification. (Kazdin, 1978, has written a comprehensive history.) In the early stages, behavior modification took on many of the characteristics of a protest movement. In order to establish their discipline, behavior modifiers emphasized a scientific approach, stressing the differences between behavior-change methods based on experimental psychology and the medically oriented treatment of psychotherapy. Behavior modification is now in an atheoretical stage, which emphasizes the development and evaluation of methods of change.

Behavioral counseling

A behavioral approach in counseling psychology was first promoted publicly by Krumboltz (1965) of Stanford University, although others also called for the application of learning principles to counseling-like situations (Bandura, 1961; Michael & Meyerson, 1962; Shoben, 1949). In a series of conceptual articles (Krumboltz, 1964, 1965, 1966a) and at a conference devoted to the implications of experimental procedures and learning theory for counseling (Krumboltz, 1966b), Krumboltz outlined the major features of behavioral counseling. These features included firm commitments to the application of learning theory, the use of diverse methods, and the adoption of experimental methodology to guide counseling.

These commitments were first realized through a series of studies on decision making conducted by Krumboltz and his students (Ryan & Krumboltz, 1964; Krumboltz & Schroeder, 1965; Krumboltz & Thoresen, 1964; Krumboltz, Varenhorst, & Thoresen, 1967). The procedures were reinforcement counseling and model reinforcement counseling, derived from verbal conditioning and social learning, respectively.

Expansion of a behavioral approach to counseling was abetted by the emergence of major behavioral journals *(Behavior Research and Therapy, Journal of Applied Behavior Analysis, Behavior Therapy, Journal of Behavior Therapy and Experimental Psychiatry)* and publications (Bandura, 1969; Eysenck & Rachman, 1965; Franks, 1969; Goldstein, Heller, & Sechrest, 1966; Hosford, 1969; Kanfer & Phillips, 1970; Krumboltz & Thoresen, 1969, 1976; Mager, 1962; Thoresen & Coates, 1980; Ullman & Krasner, 1965; Wolpe & Lazarus, 1966; Yates, 1970) that helped establish the behavioral approach in clinical settings. Behavioral research continues to flourish through new journals *(Behavior Modification, Cognitive*

Research and Therapy, Behavioral Assessment, and *The Journal of Behavioral Assessment)* and annual series *(Advances in Behavior Therapy, Annual Review of Behavior Therapy,* and *Progress in Behavior Modification),* in addition to individual texts.

Today, behavioral counseling is viewed as a major helping perspective with its own special interest group (for example, Counseling Special Interest Group of the American Association for the Advancement of Behavior Therapy) and journal *(Behavioral Counseling).*

Approach

Three types of learning have been discussed: classical conditioning, operant conditioning, and social learning. The outline of the modifying perspective below emphasizes their common characteristics and the determinants of behavior.

Orientation

The modifying perspective does not yield a simple history nor a single definition. It is probably more useful to consider behavior modification in terms of two basic common themes with associated characteristics: (1) a commitment to the scientific method; and (2) an externalistic model of human behavior based on the psychology of learning (which differs fundamentally from the traditional internalistic model of mental illness, based on disease and intrapsychic conceptions of medicine and dynamic psychiatry).

Behavioral counselors, committed to an applied science of counseling, use specificity and experimental evaluation to assess, treat, and conduct research and training. Client progress is continually monitored so it can be objectively evaluated. While all behavioral methods are not based on strong scientific evidence, it is assumed that all behavioral treatment methods are derived from or at least consistent with the content and method of experimental science.

In following their scientific commitments, behaviorists have developed an alternative model of abnormal behavior. In chapter 3, mental illness was said to function like a medical disease. A person suffering from an emotional disorder was "sick" and could be restored to "health" only by treatment of the "internal dis-ease," such as unconscious conflicts resulting from the past or from biochemical imbalance. In protest, behaviorists have conceptualized psychological disorders in terms of externalistic determinants, labeled antecedents and consequences. Behavior occurs in between these determinants. Behaviorists use various learning theories, including classical conditioning, operant conditioning, and social learning, to determine the role of antecedents and consequences in maintaining the client's problem behavior.

Adoption of a behavioral model has major consequences for the interpretation of the development of client problems. For example, the treatment focuses on present behavior and external determinants, without assuming that problematic behavior is symptomatic of something else. Terms such as "healthy" and "sick" are seen not as names for intrinsic behavioral differences but as labels of social judgments made by health professionals about the appropriateness of behaviors on certain occasions at given places. In addition, adoption of a behavioral model has implications for the assessment and treatment of problems, to which we now turn.

Establishment

Unlike some other helping perspectives, the modifying perspective emphasizes the development and evaluation of specific treatment effects. Moreover, it appears that many behavioral techniques can be administered by many kinds of helpers (Leitenberg, 1976) or can be self-administered, or automated (for example, Lang, Melamed, & Hart, 1975). Measurable procedures, self-administered methods, and tape-recorded programs led to a lopsided preoccupation with treatment procedures. As a result, the essence of behavior therapy appeared to be a set of specific techniques, while the helping relationship was deemphasized and relegated to a nonspecific influence. Mechanistic metaphors—social reinforcement machine, behavioral engineer, behavioral programmer— replaced humanistic descriptions of the counselor.

But, while the modifying perspective puts less stress on the client/ therapist relationship than other perspectives (at least in textbooks and case studies), this does not necessarily lead to mechanistic therapy. Recent concepts of behavior therapy and research evidence attest to the importance of relationship variables (Goldfried & Davidson, 1976) and the humaneness of behavior therapy (for example, O'Leary, Turkewitz, & Taffel, 1973; Sloane, Staples, Cristol, Yorkston, & Whipple, 1975). Although many behavior therapists remain skeptical about the significance of relationship variables, these variables are given serious consideration.

Three facets of the therapeutic relationship have been given special attention in the behavioral literature: social influence, problem analysis, and treatment.

Social influence

The counselor's role in the therapeutic relationship in terms of social influence usually takes the form of preparing the client for therapeutic change and instigating those activities considered beneficial. Preparation means structuring the therapeutic experience for the client, and structuring includes a learning-based orientation to the presenting problem, presentation of the treatment rationale, development of therapeutic expectancies, and specification of the therapy experience. Although structuring is conceptualized as an influence process, it does not imply that counselors force their behavior-change attempts on clients. Such an authoritarian approach would undoubtedly lead to client resistance to the therapeutic regimen.

In preparing the client, behaviorists pay special attention to the development of expectancies. It has long been recognized that a client's positive expectations for improvement enhance client motivation (Frank, 1961/1973). Behavior counselors often have clients with pessimistic attitudes. These counselors respond by citing clients with similar problems who have achieved success or by showing why clients' past therapeutic activities were ineffective and why the present approach is different. Of course, structuring initial therapeutic successes may be the most effective method of developing client optimism.

Many clients enter treatment with expectancies about the treatment procedure. Most behaviorists agree that neglect of these expectancies can impede progress and contribute to premature termination of therapy. Two variables seem related to the development of client treatment expectancies. The first is how well the counselor describes what will take place during therapy. The second is the client's perception of behavioral therapy. Clients whose expectancies are at odds with a behavioral approach and clients who, coming from other therapeutic experiences, find behavioral therapy novel may be skeptical after preparation. It is best for counselors, early on, to understand these clients' viewpoints and to communicate their acceptance of them. The counselors can then gradually introduce a behavioral explanation or procedure as an alternative that, despite its seemingly simplistic or mechanical nature, has proven to be very effective. If these efforts prove ineffective, referral becomes probable. But they are preferable to authoritarian attempts at changing attitudes.

Although the above discussion may suggest some Machiavellian tendencies, behaviorists prefer, for scientific reasons if not ethical reasons, to deal with social influence as openly as possible.

Problem analysis

The establishment of the therapeutic relationship provides an opportunity for problem analysis by providing a sample of client behavior and an opportunity to learn how the client may react outside the therapeutic setting. It also provides an occasion for counselors to establish client trust. In response to clients' disclosure of their problems, counselors convey a caring attitude through traditional therapeutic communication (warmth, empathy, and so on) and also may disclose personal information linked to the therapeutic situation in order to help clients clarify their own experiences. Of course, behaviorists recognize that clients' self-report data are not necessarily congruent with information from other sources, but interviewing and observing relational behavior in the therapy session are major methods of obtaining information about controlling factors, especially when these factors may not be easily observed in the natural setting.

In addition to obtaining information, counselors can give information, helping clients establish more appropriate goals through reconceptualizing the problem from a behavioral perspective or by selecting indirect goals that will lead to treatment goals. Behavioral explanations attribute emotional difficulties to faulty learning experiences, which can be corrected, instead of to a disease or psychological trait. Such reconceptualizing often reduces unnecessary anxiety and enhances self-esteem. In helping clients select indirect goals, counselors might reduce depression (treatment goal), for instance, by teaching more effective interpersonal skills, or alleviate shyness (treatment goal) by teaching more effective communication skills.

Treatment

Although many of the previously discussed components of establishment have some therapeutic influence (for example, expectancies, attributions, data gathering), their influence is primarily instigational. While the following activities can also be instigational, they are viewed here as interventions; that is, the treatment variables are the relationship variables, themselves. Although the instigational/intervention dichotomy is arbitrary, it seems to reflect the descriptive literature on behavior therapy.

Behaviorists construe the direct therapeutic influences of the relationship differently from traditional psychotherapy. In the latter, it is believed that therapeutic communications, verbal and nonverbal, enable the client to experience self-worth. Behaviorists believe they provide counterconditioning, modeling, and social reinforcement experiences. Thus the therapeutic relationship in itself can help clients reduce their anxiety through counterconditioning and provide counselors opportunities for modeling and for reinforcing appropriate behavioral and cognitive coping strategies.

Summary

Despite the strong emphasis behavior counselors place on procedure, the client/counselor relationship is an important therapeutic dimension, although construed in a conceptual framework more conducive to experimental verification. The framework often adopted is a social-influence model, in which the role of counselors is to mobilize clients to undertake behavioral tasks. Mobilization often occurs through therapeutic transactions intended to reduce anxiety, induce expectancies, model coping strategies, and enhance the social power of the counselor. Each of these transactions is viewed as occurring within a context of social influence, in which attractiveness-enhancing skills are communicated by an expert. Ideally, clients are collaborators in this process, but behavioral descriptions tend to focus on counselors as the dominant interactants, while the role of clients is that of apprentices in problem solving—learning to conceptualize and communicate in a more specific language.

Conceptualization

Many behavior modifiers use a simple ABC model to describe the assessment process. The behavioral counselor identifies the problem behavior (B) before analyzing the antecedent stimuli (A) and the consequences (C). Early formulations used operant terminology and external variables in defining the assessment model. More recent formulations emphasize that internal, external, and ecological variables can be represented. Consideration is also given to events that occur simultaneously with the problem behavior.

An example

A behavioral counselor confronted with a university student complaining of learning problems would seek information about a number of variables. Assessment of developmental history might reveal motor and neurological involvement as potential antecedents. An evaluation of the student's thought patterns associated with studying might reveal immature and self-stimulating cognitions that interfere with effective learning. An ecological study of the student's learning and living environments might find a restrictive atmosphere, in which little choice is perceived, resulting in the student's reactance and consequent reduction in effort. The study environment might be distracting. The student might be neglecting a balanced lifestyle of nutrition, activity, and rest, resulting in a lack of energy and concentration. The counselor would then investigate the pattern of events that followed the learning problems, perhaps finding them to be significant contributors to problem maintenance, such as attention from significant others reinforcing the student's complaints about school failure, or the student's focusing attention away from personal responsibility.

The ABC model does not imply a simple or narrow data base. The variables that entered the assessment model above are broadly defined and range from simple external reinforcers (attention) to lifestyle (nutrition and so on) and ecological variables (learning environment). The hallmark of behavioral assessment is its emphasis on scientific procedures, in which observable behaviors and their situational determinants are of greatest significance (in contrast to other approaches, which treat behavior as a sign of some underlying trait or disease).

Characteristics of behavioral assessment

Five characteristics define the nature of behavioral assessment.

Language.   Behavior therapists see problems as problematic *behavior.* As a result, they carefully describe, in concrete terms, what a client does in various situations, eschewing inferences about personality traits. Inferential statements cannot be avoided, but behaviorists believe that descriptive and concrete statements foster better understanding of problems than abstract generalizations about personality.

Relation to individual treatment.   Behavioral assessment not only fosters understanding of the problem, but it provides necessary information for the development of treatment programs. According to behaviorists, traditional assessment is obsessed with the classification of mental disorders, resulting in the production of psychological reports and case files without necessarily linking diagnosis to treatment. For the behaviorist, assessment and treatment are closely linked, each influencing the other. One suggested way of evaluating a behavioral-assessment strategy is to ask what the counselor would do differently in treatment as a result of obtaining additional assessment information. If the counselor would do little differently, then the assessment needs to be redesigned so as to contribute to the development of individually tailored treatment.

Current level of functioning.   The assessor may obtain information about the past development of problems, but the critical data concern present functioning.

Continuation throughout treatment.   Behavioral assessment is not composed of discrete episodes before and after treatment but is continuous.

Multioperational approach.   Areas of functioning, such as motor, physiological, and cognitive, are assessed by multiple methods, such as the interview, client self-monitoring, direct observation, role play, and self-report inventories and questionnaires.

The following example highlights some of these characteristics.

	Excerpt	*Commentary*
1.	*Client:* I feel very uptight a lot of the time.	
2. *Counselor:*	When you feel uptight, what do you experience?	The counselor helps the client become more specific (excerpt 2).
3.	*Client:* A feeling of anxiety. Like when you feel something bad is going to happen.... It's difficult to describe.	The client seems to have difficulty in specifying the concerns (excerpt 3).
4. *Counselor:*	So you know the feeling, but it's tough to put into words.... It's like being uneasy because something is going to happen that you don't like.	Instead of pushing for specifics, the counselor attempts to build rapport (excerpt 4).
5.	*Client:* Yes.	
6. *Counselor:*	Can you be more specific about this feeling? For instance, what is going on inside of you, physically?	The counselor helps the client focus on relevant dimensions. In excerpt 6, it is physical (somatic/ motor/physiological). In excerpts 10, 12, and 16, situations are the focus. In excerpt 22, it is cognition.
7.	*Client:* Well . . . let's see. My heart pounds, like it's going through my chest. I feel my hands shake.... My muscles tense. My mouth is dry, and it is very difficult to speak or concentrate. I feel like a wreck.... It's not always like this; sometimes it isn't so bad.	
8. *Counselor:*	I see. Sometimes it's intense, other times you are less anxious.	

Excerpt   *Commentary*

9. *Client:* Right.

10. *Counselor:* How about those tense times? Tell me about those times when you feel like a wreck.

11. *Client:* Let me see. . . . I guess it's when I feel I have to perform. I feel overwhelming pressure to perform.

12. *Counselor:* Give me a concrete example.

13. *Client:* That is hard to do. . . . I can remember when I was younger. School grades and sports were real important for my parents. I sure felt the pressure to do well. In fact, I used to panic or get sick over a test or during a soccer game.

14. *Counselor:* Let me see if I understand. It seems that school and sport performances upset you and that somehow this was connected to your parents' expectations.

15. *Client:* Yes.

16. *Counselor:* I want you to close your eyes for a moment. I want you to visualize an event from these times, let's say a soccer game. Can you do this?

17. *Client:* I'll try. . . . OK.

18. *Counselor:* As you see this soccer game, do you see yourself?

Excerpt   *Commentary*

19.   *Client:* Yes.

20. *Counselor:* Do you experience some
of those tense feelings?

21.   *Client:* It's not the same, but I
can sense them.

22. *Counselor:* Stay with this experience
for a moment. What is
that boy—you—thinking
about?

23.   *Client:* Uh . . . I guess . . . I need
to do well. I better make
a goal. Dad would be
proud if I score. Some-
thing like that . . .

24. *Counselor:* I want you to come back
to your present situation.
In the next week I want
you to list situations that
occur that upset you and
to record the situation,
your thoughts, and your
reactions.

The above example focuses on specific physical, cognitive, and behavioral information. Past information was used but in conjunction with
understanding the present (excerpt 24). Although the clinical interview
was used here, the counselor included an additional assessment procedure (excerpt 24). Of course, the counselor hoped the material gained
from these procedures would point to the appropriate treatment
procedures.

Intervention

Most textbooks on behavior modification describe a number of behavioral methods in a straightforward fashion, but ignore the complexity of
treatment selection. In order to provide a more adequate understanding of the intervention process, a problem will be used to illustrate the
various procedures and problem conceptualizations associated with
various behavioral methods.

The problem, taken from the example excerpted in the previous section, concerns the social/evaluative anxiety experienced by a young man who previously felt parental pressure about his performances in school and sports. The methods that follow are only representative, not exhaustive. Some methods could be conceptualized differently. Some methods, including modeling and other cognitively based procedures, are subsumed under other methods (also see chapter 6).

(Before we go on to the various intervention methods, it is necessary to stress the link between intervention and assessment. Comprehensive behavioral analysis is a continuous process, yielding information about the critical controlling variables on which counselors base changes in intervention methods until goals are reached.)

Systematic desensitization

Relaxation has been used to facilitate birth (Lamaze, 1958) and to foster health (Schultz & Luthe, 1959). Recently its relation to meditation and other eastern practices has been studied (D. Shapiro, 1980). In the behavioral tradition, relaxation training has been most identified with Wolpe's systematic desensitization method.

The counselor viewed the anxiety attested to by our uptight client as **conditioned anxiety.** Using a classical conditioning model, the counselor linked the client's anxiety to evaluative situations—school and sports performance. To help this client reduce his anxiety, the counselor helped him learn a different response to evaluative situations. Anxiety reduction occurs through a process called reciprocal inhibition, a **counterconditioning procedure** in which an incompatible response is systematically and gradually paired with anxiety-producing situations. Typically, the incompatible response for desensitization is muscle relaxation.

Systematic desensitization entails three steps: relaxation training, hierarchical construction of a stimulus situation, and pairing a representation of the stimulus situation with relaxation.

Relaxation training.   The behavioral counselor in the example above presented relaxation to the client as a skill to be learned, an educational experience, the components of which were described and modeled by the counselor and practiced at home by the client with audiotapes or manuals. Several methods of relaxation training are available (see Goldfried & Davidson, 1976). Many self-control variants of relaxation have also been developed: coping skills (Goldfried, 1971); anxiety-management training (Suinn & Richardson, 1971); and cue-controlled relaxation (Russell & Sipich, 1973). But regardless of the way the client was trained to relax—muscle relaxation, sensory awareness, yoga, or hypnosis—the important consideration is that the client was able to relax when requested.

Hierarchical construction of stimulus situations.   As relaxation training progressed, the counselor and client (through continuous assessment) selected the situation to desensitize. This was not easy for our uptight client. He may have been afraid of all evaluative situations or just situations that involved authority figures, such as parents, teachers, or the boss on the job. Once a useful description was selected (such as evaluative situations that included authority figures), the counselor helped the client choose a situation and identify the concrete components that seemed related to his anxiety. An upcoming final exam had stimulated the client's concern about performance. The client then told the counselor about his past emotional reactions to events before examinations, such as studying, talking to others, and talking to his professor. From this discussion and other sources (the counselor, significant others), the counselor collected 10 to 20 events symbolic of the situation. The client then rank ordered these events according to anxiety experienced (see Goldfried & Davidson, 1976; Marquis & Morgan, 1969).

Pairing a representation of the stimulus situation with relaxation.   In his imagination, the client moved up the hierarchy of symbolic events, from the least anxiety producing to the most, while in a state of relaxation. (Previous to this, the counselor had assessed and helped develop the client's imaginal ability so that he could imagine vividly.) If progress had been disrupted, the client would have returned to a lower event and attempted again to achieve vivid imagery in a relaxed state. Continued disruptions may suggest a need for revision of the hierarchy for renewed relaxation training.

Social-skills training

Of course, anxiety does not automatically dictate desensitization procedures. Sometimes a person's anxiety is related to a **skill deficit.** For example, the problems of the uptight client appear to be related to a lack of self-assertion with authority figures.

Procedurally, social-skills training involves cognitive learning, behavior rehearsal, and practicing the new skills in real-life situations. During the cognitive learning phase, the uptight client recognized his need to learn assertion. Then he learned about assertive behavior (that is, component skills) through reading and social modeling.

Following this, the client rehearsed assertiveness **(behavioral rehearsal).** This procedure, depending on ethical considerations and the anxiety level of the client, may be cognitive rehearsal, role playing, or some other form of simulated rehearsal. During this procedure, feedback and coaching provided the client with information about the appropriateness of his behavior. The counselor assumed the role of a high-pressure parent with whom the client practiced asserting his need to live his own life ("I don't want to *run* my life or have others run my life, I want to *live* my life").

In the final step, the client applied his new skill. Applications can be carried out as homework assignments between counseling sessions. Self-observations during these *in vivo* applications serve as a framework for counseling discussions. (For more on the social-skills approach see Bellack & Hersen, 1979.)

Reinforcement

The previous methods are aimed at modifying client behavior. But perhaps it is the life situation of our uptight client (overly demanding parents) that needed to be modified. The client found himself in an **unresponsive environment,** one which did not support him regardless of his efforts. His parents' standards permitted little reinforcement. **Operant training** provided for environmental change. Initially, consultation attempted to facilitate cooperation with the change agents—the parents. The parents' help was solicited in supporting their son's endeavors without suggesting responsibility for his anxiety. The counselor prepared parents by giving them information about reinforcement concepts in laymen's terms, practice through role-played examples, and restructuring (see also chapter 6). Parents need support as they try new ways of acting, and the counselor can provide this support. In addition, the client reinforced his parents' supportiveness of him. This reciprocal support helped maintain appropriate behavior on the part of both parents and client. In fact, the use of reinforcement procedures may necessitate the counselor's ceasing to view the individual as the client and focusing on the environment.

Summary

The list below shows the three behavioral interventions used for our client along with the problem each was to solve and the procedure used.

- Systematic desensitization: *problem*—conditioned anxiety; *procedure*—counterconditioning
- Social-skills training: *problem*—skill deficit; *procedure*—behavioral rehearsal
- Reinforcement: *problem*—unresponsive environment; *procedure*—operant training

There are many other behavioral intervention methods, but the intent here has been to simply illustrate the modifying perspective's approach. The choice of treatment method follows a scientific model, with the target behavior as the dependent variable. Once the controlling variables have been identified, a treatment program is selected and becomes the independent variable. Thus the counselor and client conduct an experiment in which the treatment is modified according to ongoing evaluation.

Evaluation

A central characteristic of the behavioral approach is its commitment to scientific method, measurement, and evaluation. Behaviorists' contributions to the analysis and evaluation of treatment outcome range from single-case and between-groups methodology to laboratory-based evaluation of treatment methods.

Single-case design

Behaviorists have provided a methodology for studying the individual case without sacrificing experimental concerns. A major feature of single-case research is repeated assessment of client behavior before treatment, providing a baseline assessment of the problem. (In traditional research, the no-treatment control group serves as the baseline.) Repeated observations over many baseline and treatment conditions provide data for the examination of systematic discontinuities between these conditions. Before examining various designs, it may be helpful to illustrate the logic of the single-case methodology.

Wark (1976) provides an example of single-case methodology from his work with adult students at the University of Minnesota. According to Wark, adult students reported an inability to concentrate on studying because of a tendency to daydream and think about other things. In response, Wark and others (Fox, 1962) emphasized stimulus control. In this approach, students come to see concentration as a habit to be formed by associating study with particular locations, times of day, and specific stimuli. The associations are built up and protected by studying in only these situations. When interfering internal responses occur, such as daydreaming, students are taught to leave the study situation in order to dissociate distractions and the study area, thereby maintaining the association. Figure 5-1 illustrates the decrease in distracting thoughts for a typical student when standing up, turning around, and leaving the study area.

This is an example of an ABAB, or reversal design. In this design, a period of baseline observation (A) preceded the implementation of treatment (B) (stand, turn, and leave). As the daydreams became less frequent, the treatment was withdrawn in a return to baseline procedure (A). As daydreams began to increase, treatment (B) was reintroduced. Systematic discontinuities between baseline and treatment conditions give evidence about the effectiveness of treatment. Although the reversal design is a prototype of single-case methodology and overcomes some

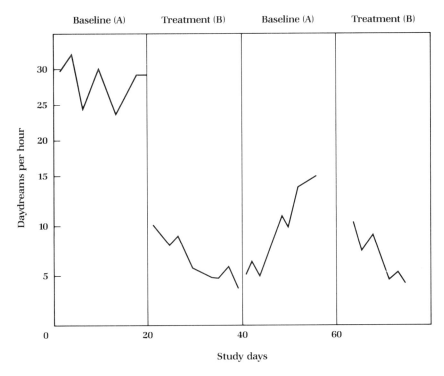

Figure 5–1   Simulated example of reduction in a student's daydreaming as a function of treatment (standing up, turning around, and leaving the study area)

limitations of simple AB designs, it also has deficiencies. The effects of treatment may disappear at the return to baseline, which raises practical and ethical questions.

Another single-case design is the multiple-baseline design, a variation of which is multiple-baseline design across behavior, in which different responses are identified and assessed over time (providing a baseline for comparison purposes). Treatment is then applied to each response, one at a time. Baseline conditions remain in effect for all other responses. If response modification happens only when specifically treated, evidence for treatment efficacy is provided.

The most important characteristics of the single-case design are careful specification of variables, continuous measurement of the individual, and adoption of explicit criteria. Of course, single-case researchers have been criticized for problems in generalization, in assessment of interactions between the client and the treatment variables, and in evaluation of the results. In response, single-case researchers have recommended systematic replication and statistical analysis of single-case data (Box & Jenkins, 1976; Gottman & Glass, 1979; Kazdin, 1976; Neufeld, 1977; McCain & McCleary, 1979).

Between-group design

As an alternative to studying clinical issues in the field, where it is difficult to conduct controlled and ethical research with sufficient numbers of appropriate therapists and clients, many behaviorists bring together well-defined problems and treatments into the controlled conditions of the laboratory. Although such analog procedures may not reproduce the total clinical situation, they do provide some standardization of treatment without the methodological or ethical issues of a clinical study. For instance, laboratory approaches have enabled Bandura and colleagues to assess particular phobias and fear reactions, to evaluate treatment techniques, and, more recently, to develop theories regarding the mechanisms involved in therapeutic success (Bandura & Adams, 1977; Bandura, Adams, & Beyer, 1977).

Evaluation of treatment

One strategy used to evaluate the effectiveness of treatment compares a treatment's effectiveness to appropriate control groups and to other treatments. This strategy is usually called an outcome strategy, or comparative outcome strategy. Recently, behavioral researchers (for example, Kazdin & Wilcoxon, 1976) have stressed the importance of empirically demonstrating that placebo-like control groups are controlling for potential factors, such as treatment expectations, satisfaction, and plausibility, that are nonspecific to treatment effectiveness.

After treatment outcomes have been satisfactorily evaluated, including maintenance and follow-up studies, other strategies are used to analyze and isolate the components of a promising treatment. A **dismantling strategy** takes specific components of a multicomponent treatment and systematically eliminates one component at a time, assessing the decrement in treatment effects. A **constructive strategy** uses a building-block approach, in which a single treatment component is established through previous outcome research, and additional components are added to see if there are associated increments in treatment effects.

In an investigation concerned with students' study behavior, Richards (1975) assessed the impact of two self-control procedures—stimulus control and self-monitoring—as additional components to a typical treatment for college students' study behavior. Constructive strategy was used, with combinations of self-control procedures added to typical study-skills advice. All treatment groups were compared to no-contact and no-treatment controls. This strategy yielded four treatment groups (study-skills advice, study-skills advice plus stimulus control, study-skills advice plus self-monitoring, and study-skills advice plus both stimulus control and self-monitoring) and two control groups (no contact and no treatment), with the no-treatment control group serving as an attention-placebo group, since they received questionnaires on study habits.

One hundred and eight college students participated (90 volunteers, 18 nonvolunteers), with experimentals receiving treatment via biblio-therapy (handouts). Students were separated into two blocks based on their scores on the midterm psychology exam (taken previous to treat-ment). There were nine high-scoring students and nine low-scoring stu-dents in each treatment and control group. Eighteen nonvolunteer students served as the no-contact control.

The impact of treatment was assessed on the following dimensions: the final-exam score in the psychology course, the final grade in the psy-chology course, a multiple-choice exam developed by the counselors, a posttreatment evaluation questionnaire, and self-monitoring data. Results indicated that self-monitoring was an effective treatment, and that detailed study-skills advice seemed to be a minimum prerequisite for study-behavior change, since the no-treatment control procedure failed to modify behavior.

This study illustrates several characteristics of good behavioral research: careful specification of treatment, objective measures, and intensive treatment-evaluation strategies. Time-series data that included outcome and component analyses were collected for the self-monitoring groups. Final-exam scores and course grades helped define the differential effects of treatment. An attention-placebo control group and comparative and constructive research strategies were also used. Also, the researchers did not provide evidence about long-term effects or generalize across courses, nor was it clear whether they regarded the no-treatment group as equivalent to the other groups in terms of expec-tations and other nonspecific influences.

Professional development

The behavioral training approach is derived primarily from operant con-ditioning and social learning. The application of these two streams of behavior modification to training and supervision has resulted in two developments: a training technology and a conceptual framework of the helping process.

Training technology includes: (1) didactics (for example, specific instructions, programmed manuals, readings, guided discussion); (2) modeling via direct observation, videotape, and audiotape; (3) behav-ioral rehearsal through role playing or some other form of simulation; and (4) feedback through supervision and performance-specific infor-mation. Training might also include guided practice with immediate and delayed feedback; but the instruction, modeling, practice, and feed-back routine is representative of most behavioral training.

The conceptual framework breaks the helping process into separate skills, which can be taught as single units and later integrated into unique therapeutic styles. The specific skills depend on types of programs, including programs to train parents, teachers, and social workers.

In counseling and clinical psychology, **microtraining** (or microcounseling) has integrated technology and the conceptual framework into a systematic format for teaching the basic helping skills (see Ivey & Authier, 1978). Microtraining comprises the following steps: (1) videotaping a brief (5–15 minutes) baseline interview with a role-played client or a volunteer client; (2) reading a programmed text or other material that describes the skill or skills being taught in the session; (3) viewing models demonstrating both effective and ineffective actions, with discriminative cueing; (4) viewing the baseline interview and receiving feedback and reinforcement; (5) observing supervisor or peers as they model responses and rating these responses; (6) role playing a client with a role-played counselor who is practicing the target skills; (7) rehearsing the skills with others, who provide feedback; and (8) videotaping a second interview to determine the effectiveness of training and the need for further training.

As well as being a powerful methodology (Ford, 1979; Kasdorf & Gustafson, 1978), microtraining has led to the identification of those interview skills that lead to effective counseling. These microskills, assumed to be applicable to widely different problems, have been organized into successive steps: attending behavior (eye contact, body language, and verbal following); communication skills (open and closed questions, encouragers, paraphrase, summarization, and reflection); influencing skills (focusing, directing, interpreting, self-disclosing, instructing, advising, and confronting). The counselor structures the interview and integrates these microskills into a therapeutic style, using different patterns of skills for different situations and different clients.

Thus microtraining helps trainees identify, apply, refine, and integrate specific helping skills. Supervision focuses on these skills rather than on the therapeutic relationship, which they see as providing an environment conducive to learning, not as the central source of change.

Although behavioral training has proven effective, there are questions about professional training that reduces the complex therapeutic process to technology (input) and discrete skills (output) and that neglects mediational processes (see Stone, 1980). How does a counselor fit the bits of counselor skills into a coherent identity and therapeutic style that reflects emotional self-understanding? Furthermore, how are these bits integrated and connected to various patterns of client behavior? These criticisms and questions might be applicable to microtraining as a comprehensive training program. But as the initial component of a broader training program, microtraining has been effective.

Commentary

Scientific methodology is a central and definitive characteristic of the modifying perspective. The scientific process of inquiry, however, can become scientism, a distortion of scientific inquiry in which the multidimensionality of the external environment is reduced to a few elements. A person is regarded as a recipient of stimuli and a producer of molecular responses rather than an active and constructive participant and processor of information, capable of a whole range of complex overt and covert behaviors. Dynamic, multidimensional, and reciprocal interactions between the person and the environment are reduced to static, unidimensional, and unidirectional phenomena. Such reductionist distortions limit the content of research and clinical practice. Other criticisms of the modifying perspective concern ethics, significance of behavior change, and a limited applicability.

Much of the debate between the so-called behavioral and nonbehavioral camps has been polemics and posturing, but it is partly an attempt by behaviorists to convince their colleagues and the public of the scientific legitimacy—if not supremacy—of their therapeutic model. While such motivation is praiseworthy and probably conducive to the development of research and practice, the same motivation could also lead to an orthodoxy that rules out any research question, treatment, or clinical problem that does not accord to some outmoded model of science.

Summary

Counseling function	Characteristic
Establishment	Relationship and social influence variables serve as adjuncts to behavior-change methods.
Conceptualization	Scientific procedures are used to link observable behaviors to situational determinants.
Intervention	A wide range of empirically validated behavioral methods are used.
Evaluation	Rigorous scientific evaluation is conducted through the use of single-case designs or treatment-research strategies.
Professional development	A behavioral curriculum emphasizing skill training is recommended.

Restructuring

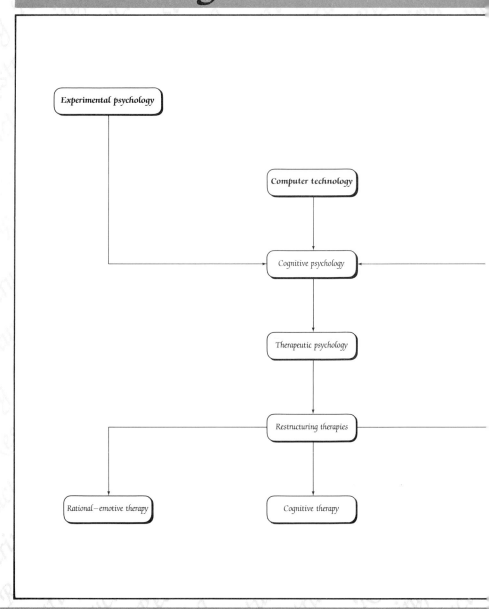

Psychological testing

Coping skills

The reemergence of cognition in therapeutic psychology during the 1970s and 1980s has led to the **restructuring** perspective, which is a convergence of behavioral methodology and cognitive theory.

The cognitive renaissance has led to a reinterpretation of experimental psychology, giving new meaning to perception, learning, and motivation. In the area of perception, for example, Miller (1956) related the old problem of apprehension span to information theory, describing the difference between a bit of information and a chunk of information (a bit being the standard unit of information theory and a chunk, a larger unit; the amount that can be recognized and retrieved in short-term memory). His descriptions within the context of information theory helped stimulate renewed interest in higher mental processes.

Cognition has also affected other areas of psychological study. Developmental psychologists have again become interested in Piaget (Piaget, 1970) and have extended their interest in cognitive development to moral development (Kohlberg, 1969) and social cognition (Shantz, 1975). Social psychologists are using subjective reports (for example, Cacioppo & Petty, 1981) and are writing about attributions and their influence on human affairs (Heider, 1958; Kelley, 1967). Personality psychologists have begun to reconceptualize personality in social-learning terms (see Bandura, 1969; Mischel, 1973), emphasizing the role of central-mediational processes in human experience. Emerging interest in the self in its social context (for example, Gordon & Gergen, 1968) and in the self as a knowledge structure (Greenwald, 1981) also underscore the cognitive trend in personality psychology. Researchers in the areas of psycholinguistics (Chomsky), sleep and dreams (Dement), imagery (Singer, Paivio, Shepard), hypnosis (Orne, Barber, Hilgard), and others have used a cognitive emphasis. While cognitive psychology is not a complete psychology itself, it is certainly reshaping the discipline. And cognitive reformulation has also affected therapeutic psychology.

Historical background
Reemergence of cognitive theory

Even during the heyday of behaviorism there was cognitive work being done in psychology: Bartlett's work on remembering and thinking, Freud's and Jung's contributions to dynamic psychology, Kohler's animal research into insight, Binet's development of an intelligence test, and Tolman's work on intervening variables (cognitive maps) in learning research. At the same time, ideas and theories grow within social contexts; renewed interest in cognition emerged along with the development of modern computers. Although computer analogies of human thinking may be inadequate, computer technology stimulated the growth of information theory as an alternative to behaviorism.

In addition, the testing movement, brought about partly by societal needs for the rational allocation of human resources during war and economic depressions, focused attention on cognitive abilities. Although some of these tasks were undertaken in the psychology laboratory, psychometrics developed outside the mainstream of experimental psychology.

Finally, in reaction to behaviorism, humanistic psychology developed, which emphasized human values and enriched the models of human functioning by its internal focus, which stresses purpose and personal meaning.

Cognitive theory and therapeutic psychology

In clinical psychology and psychiatry, Kelly (1955), Rotter (1954/1973/1980), Frank (1961/1973), and Beck (1974/1976) are leading spokesmen for a cognitive approach. In dynamic psychology, the ego and its processes have emerged as a salient topic (for example, Hartmann, 1939/1958/1964; Kohut, 1971). One of the most influential spokesmen for cognitive therapy is Albert Ellis. His view of the role of irrational thoughts in emotional distress have become a central focus of cognitive restructuring therapies (for example, Beck, Rush, & Kovacs, 1975; Meichenbaum, 1973).

Client-centered therapy (Wexler, 1974) and behavior-modification strategies have also been reassessed according to an information approach. In behavior-change strategies, clinical applications based on attribution (Kopel & Arkowitz, 1975), imagery (Singer, 1974), problem solving (D'Zurilla & Goldfried, 1971), self-control (Goldfried & Merbaum, 1973), biofeedback (Shapiro & Schwartz, 1972), and others reflect a convergence of cognitive and behavioral methodologies. (However, the recent emphasis on cognition has not gone unchallenged; see Wolpe, 1978.)

Cognition theory and behaviorism

The reintroduction of a cognitive orientation has occurred at the same time the use of performance-based treatments has increasingly been recognized as a powerful methodology for behavior change. These cognitive and behavioral trends have converged, giving rise to the restructuring perspective, which stresses the reciprocal impact of cognitive processes and environmental variables. While interaction is stressed, the approach to human understanding is constructive, and people are viewed as actively construing their experiences.

The restructuring perspective is diversified and has avoided formal conceptualization. Although its applications have not been demonstrated across a broad range of clinical populations, it suggests specific ways of carrying out the counseling process.

Approach
Orientation

Although the restructuring perspective uses input and output events similarly to the modifying perspective, the restructuring perspective places a heavy emphasis on hypothetical processes between input and output. These processes are the active processes of experience, although the degree of active construction of environmental events varies. Many different mediators have been used in cognitive psychology, including constructs from computer science, linguistics, perception, and cybernetic theory. In experimental psychology, the overall strategy has been to develop structural theories of mental events through the use of temporal measures to determine the time course of information processing and to isolate processing stages and subsystems (for example, Posner, 1978).

More germane to our interests is the application of a cognitive approach to therapy. Here the emphasis has been on identifying and correcting information-processing deficiencies and focusing on the enhancement of generalized-response strategies. The works of Ellis and Beck represent the cognitive-deficiency viewpoint, and the coping-strategy literature (see Stone, 1980) focuses on response strategies.

According to the **cognitive deficiency viewpoint,** performance dysfunctions and subjective distress result from central-processing deficiencies. For instance, Ellis believes that irrational ideas (for example, that adults need to be loved by everyone for everything they do) cause and sustain emotional disturbance and maladaptive behavior, while Beck lists specific cognitive deficiencies (for example, overgeneralization) in the development of emotional disorders. Many other cognitive distortions have been suggested, including inappropriate attributions, expectations, self-instructions, and others. Whether the deficiencies are content-based irrational ideas or cognitive distortions, the therapeutic focus is on procedures designed to improve information processing. These procedures have been commonly termed cognitive restructuring, rational-emotive therapy (RET), attribution therapy, and cognitive therapy.

Another viewpoint assumes that people with **broad mediation strategies** are better able to cope with stress. The focus here is on methods to develop the client's generalized-response strategies, which often involve cognitive processes. This focus is different from that of early behavior-modification research, which relied on simple motor-learning models of skill development and emphasized discrete, situation-specific responses. The coping-skills literature emphasizes broad mediation strategies.

The task of relating the restructuring perspective to counseling psychology is in its initial stages (see Stone, 1980). What follows is an exploration of the contribution of the restructuring perspective to the counseling process.

Establishment

Although previous perspectives differ in the importance attached to the counseling relationship, it is typically described as an affective experience based on positive attitudes and feelings. Through the relationship, the client is led to emotional understanding and maturity.

In the restructuring perspective, the counseling relationship is thought to serve a cognitive function. This perspective does not deny the importance of the relationship nor its affective dimension but does suggest that an overreliance on affective experience may blind us to the cognitive-processing implications of relationship counseling. Wexler (1974) has done some original conceptualizing in this area and much of the following discussion is stimulated by his work.

From the restructuring perspective, relationship-enhancement methods can involve four cognitive-processing functions: an attentional function, an organizing function, an evocative function, and a social-influence function.

Attentional function

Counselor statements summarizing client statements reflect client experience and focus attention on those expressed aspects of client experience. Counselor statements that do not follow the client's verbal expressions tend to introduce other material and, in so doing, divert attention away from the client's experience. Such a description is similar to a client-centered discussion of reflective communication, where the emphasis is on reflecting client feelings. But within the restructuring perspective, the attentional functions of such communications are stressed in addition to the affective functions.

Organizing function

Counselor statements interpreting client statements facilitate cognitive processing by helping clients organize their experiential information in new ways. These interpretations offer clients new frameworks for elaborating, differentiating, and integrating experiential information. The organizing function parallels the depth-of-processing approach to memory in cognitive psychology (Craik & Lockhart, 1972), in which material that is enriched by elaborated processing is remembered. Perhaps clients who are helped to organize and elaborate their experiential information through counselor interpretations can deal with their problems in a more constructive way, since self-information is more accessible and meaningful.

Evocative function

Counselors' empathic communication, rich language (active verbs, vivid adjectives, metaphors), and imagery evoke clients' processing of self-relevant information and enable them to relate facets of their experience in more meaningful ways. Preliminary evidence shows that counselor expressiveness affects the richness of client verbalizations (for example, Wexler & Butler, 1976) and that this enriched self-exploration affects therapeutic outcome (Rice & Wagstaff, 1967).

Social-influence function

The social-influence function includes the development of a well-structured treatment approach, creation of favorable outcome expectancies, and the maintenance of helper credibility. This function is based partially on cognitive processes and is directed at negative cognitions often associated with client demoralization.

During initial contacts, client self-referent thinking is often pessimistic and self-deprecating, involving self-doubt, worry, and apprehensiveness. These negative experiences can interfere with treatment plans and reduce compliance and new constructive actions by the client. Social-influence strategies can disrupt such negative preoccupations by redirecting the attention of the client to competing cues. Optimistic treatment rationales often divert clients' attention away from dysphoric inner states—pain, depression, and pessimistic ruminations—and enable them to engage in treatment more effectively by reducing their resistance to therapeutic guidance, maintaining their motivation during difficult treatment stages, and enabling them to try new behaviors.

Another cognitive feature of social influence is the way clients construe the influence methods. In the past, many social-influence researchers relied on external resources—instructions, setting, credentials, jargon—to establish an appropriate therapeutic set, and neglected clients' activity in preparing for treatment. But external-influence tactics are cognitively assessed by clients in terms of credibility, relevance, and personal costs. If clients see therapeutic guidance as self-serving, unrelated to their history, or as requiring competencies beyond their capabilities, then social-influence attempts will not succeed.

Conceptualization

The restructuring perspective emphasizes internal cognitive processes in assessment and therapy (see Merluzzi, Glass, & Genest, 1981), although a concurrent collection of self-report and behavioral data is usually undertaken to avoid the temptation to study cognition in isolation.

The assessor's interest in cognition arises from the mediational assumptions of the restructuring perspective. The mediational view assumes that knowledge of reality is mediated knowledge—information transformed by the sensory system—and interpreted by other complex systems. These complex systems can be viewed in two ways: (1) as information processing (sensory store, short-term memory, long-term memory), which can be studied using time measures to describe the individual system; and (2) as products or cognitive structures resulting from past experience and human development. The restructuring perspective has focused on the latter, which includes irrational beliefs and dysfunctional internal dialogues.

Targets of assessment

Negative self-referent frameworks are characterized by self-preoccupation and negative self-information. These knowledge structures are hypothesized as mental structures (for example, schemata, scripts, templates, prototypes) that lead to cognitive distortions, emotional disturbances, and behavioral maladjustment. Although other assessment targets concerned with cognition have been explored—cognitive abilities, cognitive constructs (Epting, 1984; Neimeyer & Neimeyer, 1981), prototypical categories (for example, Buss & Craik, 1980), and self-efficacy expectations (Bandura & Adams, 1977)—a negative self-reference ideology seems persuasive (see Meichenbaum & Butler, 1978). This negative set is associated with a great variety of performance deficits— depression, low stress tolerance, and social-skill inadequacies. A negative-thinking pattern has been observed in many different populations, including unassertive females, unsuccessful athletes, depressed patients, and low-creative individuals.

Another assessment target is clients' **generalized competencies** that are relatively stable over time and situations. Some of these cognitive competencies have to do with generalized problem solving (Stone, 1980). Others, such as plans and psychological knowledge, have more to do with metacognition—the awareness of cognitive processes and products and the way they operate.

Strategies of assessment

Cognitive assessment depends heavily on **self-report methodology.** In the modifying perspective, clients are asked to keep records about circumstances surrounding maladaptive behavior. In the restructuring perspective, clients keep records of circumstances surrounding their thoughts and the frequency of such thoughts. For example, depressed clients may record thoughts associated with their depression episodes, including negative feelings and environmental events.

There are a number of other self-report formats. Clients might describe their cognitive experience through interviews, think-aloud procedures, thought listings, projective techniques, postperformance videotape reconstructions, and self-report inventories. For example, a nonassertive client was continually passive during counseling sessions, although there were nonverbal indications that a lot of activity was going on internally. Probes by the counselor concerning the client's passivity seemed to get lost in the translation or they biased the client's response by leading him to superficially confirm the counselor's assumptions. To gain cognitive information from this passive client, a counseling session was videotaped. When it was played back to the client, he was asked to report his cognitions while observing his in-session passiveness. The videotape reconstruction method provided the necessary retrieval cues (while reducing counselor bias) for the generation of cognitive material. These stimulated recollections could lead the client to attend to self-inhibiting thoughts and the external circumstances and affective reactions associated with them.

Self-report inventories or think-aloud procedures could also be used for problem solving. Clients could rate their typical problem-solving responses in terms of various dimensions (Heppner & Petersen, 1982), compare their problem-solving strategies with others judged to be competent (Goldfried & D'Zurilla, 1969), or describe verbally their thoughts as they solve a problem (Goor & Sommerfeld, 1975). The videotape reconstruction method, in conjunction with counselor probes, could gather information about psychological strategies in order to assess the client's understanding of what occurred during a problem-solving session. Perhaps this metacognitive information might indicate some strategy deficiency or lack of social knowledge.

To avoid improper generalizations, cognitive assessors anchor cognitive data to specific performances in specific situations relevant to human conditions. They do not ask people to report about themselves in general, nor on broad, nonspecific dimensions, nor in situations involving overlearned skills in which cognitive information may be less relevant.

Despite the growing popularity of cognitive assessment, limitations need to be recognized. Distortions can occur during self-observation, encoding, storage, retrieval, and reporting. As Nisbett and Wilson (1977) indicate, self-report data do not automatically yield valid causal statements about behavior, although they can reflect access to private cognitive experiences. Whether the data will be relevant to the diagnostic enterprise is a question of validity.

Intervention

The popularity of cognitive therapy is partly attributable to its procedural flexibility. The restructuring perspective subsumes a diversity of methods, since different therapists conceptualize their clients' cognitions differently. Yet the restructuring perspective has a common goal based on the belief that distress is a disorder of thinking. Treatment therefore always stresses modification of clients' thinking.

The restructuring therapies of Ellis (rational-emotive therapy), Beck (cognitive therapy), and Meichenbaum (self-instructions), although similar, convey distinctive emphases. All of these therapies emphasize the role of cognitions in psychological distress. They use cognitive and behavioral methods to generate positive thoughts and behaviors, which lead to new cognitive structures and effective coping behavior. For Ellis, the focus is on irrational beliefs. Beck's restructuring approach focuses on faulty thinking styles (for example, faulty inferences, exaggeration, dichotomous reasoning, and overgeneralization), while Meichenbaum attends to the negative thinking revealed in self-referenced internal speech and ineffective coping skills. Procedurally, Ellis relies on rational analysis, imagery, and logical persuasion for the identification and remediation of irrational beliefs. Beck uses cognitive-behavioral methods in helping clients gather data with which to recognize and test the validity of their faulty assumptions. Meichenbaum uses tasks, self-report methods, and think-aloud procedures to increase clients' awareness of their self-defeating ideology and skill deficiencies. Meichenbaum also uses an educational format for instructing the client in adaption enhancement and coping skills.

Rational-emotive therapy

Rational analysis is Ellis's major procedure. In essence, Ellis teaches clients to analyze their situation in terms of the event (A), subsequent self-verbalizations (B), and the consequences (C) of these self-verbalizations. Clients learn this analytic procedure to sensitize themselves to the effect of their own irrational thinking on their lives. A client may learn about irrational beliefs through reading material (for example, Ellis & Harper, 1975, *A New Guide to Rational Living*) or counselor modeling and instructions. During consultation, counselors may challenge the clients' statements or persuade them about the relationship of inappropriate behavior and irrational beliefs through the use of humor, rational disputation, imagery, and logic.

After rational analysis has been learned, clients are given assignments to practice at home (see Goodman & Maultsby, 1974). They are instructed to record the objective facts of an event, their self-verbalization about the event, and their associated emotional reactions. Clients review these records in light of the rationality criteria learned earlier, underlining irrational statements and inappropriate emotions, refuting the statements and replacing them with more appropriate descriptions.

Cognitive therapy

Beck uses many of the same methods as Ellis but puts more emphasis on behavioral methods (activity schedules, graded tasks), which he sees as opportunities for gathering data to test clients' assertions in a scientific manner. That is, if a lonely client asserts that no one likes her, her task might be to gather data from others to verify the assertion. The client may find that some people don't even know her, which is different from not liking her. (Ellis, on the other hand, may simply point out the illogic of the assertion by asking "How can you know the feelings of everyone in the world?")

Self-instructions

Meichenbaum emphasizes the provision of coping skills. For instance, Meichenbaum's stress-inoculation training (Meichenbaum, 1977; Meichenbaum & Jaremko, 1983) teaches clients direct actions (collection of information, relaxation) and cognitive-coping methods (using negative self-statements as a cue to positive self-statements, such as "Relax, you're in control") in dealing with stress reactions. Through the acquisition of new behavioral skills and internal dialogues, clients develop new cognitive structures and effective coping behaviors.

An example

A woman, middle-aged, well-educated, and suffering depression over her recent divorce, came for counseling. At first, she wanted to know how to get her husband back. After a while, she realized the futility of pursuing that goal, yet remained depressed over her prospects. The excerpt below reflects this stage.

Excerpt	*Commentary*
1. *Client:* I keep experiencing bad feelings. . . . I see pictures, like in a dream. I see myself across the bridge . . . on the other side. No one else around!	Although the restructuring perspective primarily uses verbalizations, it is clear from excerpts 1 and 11 that images can convey cognitive information.
2. *Counselor:* Do you have any idea what that picture means?	In excerpt 2, the counselor probe conveys the cognitive emphasis by requesting the personal meaning of the mental picture.

Excerpt	*Commentary*
3. *Client:* No. It's so peaceful, but makes me feel uneasy.	
4. *Counselor:* Sometimes it's difficult to understand our own reactions. Remember how you practiced attending to your thoughts and emotions the last few weeks. . . . Let's try it with this mental picture you have about the bridge.	In excerpt 4, the counselor indicates that oftentimes our internal thoughts are inaccessible unless attended to through practice.
5. *Client:* OK.	
6. *Counselor:* Can you imagine the bridge scene? Close your eyes . . .	Again the use of imagery is used as a retrieval cue for internal cognitions and emotional reactions (excerpts 6–11).
7. *Client:* I'll try. . . . Let's see. . . . Yes. It's more faded, but I can make it out. . . . Just like before . . . a *long* bridge. No one around. Very peaceful. There. There I am, over on the side, huddled in a corner.	
8. *Counselor:* OK. Hold the scene. What thoughts occur to you?	
9. *Client:* I am safe. . . . But that bridge. . . . It suggests a crossing, but I am scared. It's safe here . . .	
10. *Counselor:* Why are you scared to cross the bridge? What might happen?	
11. *Client:* I don't know. I have another image of being beneath the house in the dark, of not wanting to come out in the sunlight.	

	Excerpt	*Commentary*
12. *Counselor:*	I am wondering. . . . What must be going on? Why must you hide out? What could you be telling yourself to avoid crossing the bridge or coming out from under the house? Is there any parallel here between these pictures and your own reluctance to rejoin life?	The counselor in excerpts 12, 14, and 16 is requesting the client to attend to unrecognized assumptions.
13. *Client:*	Well, I am ugly . . . now.	
14. *Counselor:*	Were you always ugly?	
15. *Client:*	No. . . . Since the divorce. I am . . .	
16. *Counselor:*	It seems to me you're saying something to yourself like "I am divorced, therefore I do not exist; or if I do, I am a deformed or bad person." In terms of your mental pictures: "I can't cross the bridge or leave the house because of my ugliness. No one wants to be with a divorced person."	
17. *Client:*	Well, isn't that true?	
18. *Counselor:*	Tell me. How can we find that out?	In excerpt 18, the counselor moves the client to consider an evidential basis for her attitude about being a divorced person.
19. *Client:*	To find out . . . I would have to cross the bridge, leave the house!	

Excerpt	*Commentary*

20. Counselor: I know. . . . One way we
can move on this is for
you to complete a task
during next week . . .

In this brief exchange, the counselor focused on the client's cognitions about divorce through the use of imagery, prior work in rational analysis, probes about personal meaning and thoughts, and undoubtedly, as the last exchange indicates, a homework assignment, perhaps to ask a friend for lunch or to set up a job interview.

Coping skills

Meichenbaum's coping-skills approach provides an alternative restructuring procedure. The divorced woman could have been taught active relaxation skills (Goldfried, 1971; Paul, 1966; Suinn & Richardson, 1971), cognitive-coping skills for problem solving (Mendonca & Siess, 1976), stress-reducing cognitive strategies for distraction (Mischel, 1973), misattribution (Storms & Nisbett, 1970), and how to refocus attention from the self to the task (Wicklund, 1975).

Coping-skills training consists of three phases: education, rehearsal, and application. In the educational phase, clients are provided conceptual frameworks for understanding their reactions. Counselors who use the theoretical framework of objective self-awareness (Wicklund, 1975) would tell self-conscious clients how chronic self-focus leads to self-evaluations, negative feelings, and internal attributions by personalizing external events that have little relationship to them, the clients. Following the conceptual presentation, these clients would begin to monitor their self-statements, observing their tendency to personalize events ("The picnic was cancelled because of rain. It is all my fault for planning the picnic on a stormy day").

In the rehearsal stage, these clients would be taught coping skills: relaxation, cognitive reappraisal, self-instructions, and selective attention. To develop reappraisal skills, clients could be given events from everyday life and asked to gather information to authenticate depersonalized ways of viewing them. For instance, the self-conscious client who blamed himself for a picnic cancellation due to bad weather could be instructed to observe how other events, unrelated to him, were also cancelled. These observations could lead to a realization that he was not responsible for the storm. Decentering self-instructions ("Relax, you are not responsible") could be modeled and practiced. Clients could be asked to describe situations in a distancing manner (as if they were weather forecasters) to facilitate an external orientation. Throughout the rehearsal stage, clients would be given homework assignments to practice these skills.

After clients had become proficient in coping methods, they would be exposed to analogue or real-life stressful situations, in which they would apply their skills. For these self-focused clients, low ego-threatening tasks (such as selecting heads or tails on a coin toss) could be used, followed by a brief interview to analyze clients' verbalizations. A low frequency of first-person pronouns may indicate the efficacy of coping-skills training in reducing personalization.

Evaluation

Evaluation from the restructuring perspective, as from the modifying perspective, relies on rigorous experimentation, especially comparative treatment-outcome strategies. In the past, researchers were so concerned about being scientific, they put undue emphasis on defining the experimental situation solely in terms of experimenter-defined or rater-defined categories. In such a situation, research participants were seen as pawns.

However, the cognitive emphasis within the restructuring perspective has broadened outcome research. It views research participants as active. The meaning participants place on experimental manipulations contributes to an understanding of outcome and validates treatment procedures. Cognitivism has also given rise to renewed concern about theory-relevant research, because of its own theorizing tradition.

An example will help us see the impact of a cognitive emphasis on treatment-outcome research. Rush, Beck, Kovacs, and Hollon (1977) compared treatment with cognitive restructuring (Beck, Rush, & Kovacs, 1975) to treatment with pharmacotherapy (imipramine), using 41 unipolar, depressed outpatients, who were randomly assigned to one of the two groups. All patients satisfied the criteria of a depressive syndrome across self-report inventories (Beck Depression Inventory; MMPI), clinical ratings (Hamilton Rating Scales), and history (depressive episodes, suicidal ideation, chronicity, hospitalization). They met none of the exclusion criteria (for example, schizophrenia and poor response to tricyclic antidepressants). Treatment for both groups averaged 11 weeks. They were treated by 18 therapists across disciplines who had some experience in pharmacotherapy but little in psychotherapy (a majority were psychiatric residents with a few predoctoral clinical psychologists and psychiatrists). The therapists received brief training in cognitive therapy. The pharmacotherapy sessions included evaluation of medical side effects and supportive therapy.

Results indicated that depression and anxiety were significantly reduced in both groups. However, cognitive therapy produced significantly greater improvement on both self-ratings and clinical ratings of depression. Treatment gains were maintained at three-month, six-month, and twelve-month follow ups (Kovacs, Rush, Beck, & Hollon, 1981). These gains were not substantially affected by the inclusion or exclusion of dropouts in the analysis. In fact, dropout rate was significantly higher with pharmacotherapy than with cognitive therapy. Finally, 68% of the pharmacotherapy group but only 16% of the cognitive therapy group reentered treatment for depression.

These findings are truly impressive, especially because of the features of the study. First, patients were selected using multiple measures. The syndrome was checked against many types of information. The inclusion criteria (for example, past psychotherapy failures but no history of a poor response to antidepressants) provided safeguards against treatment bias, although it might be said the experimenters were biasing selection against their own therapy program.

Second, the use of random assignment, published protocols, numerous therapists, and treatment checks is persuasive evidence about treatment validity. It's unfortunate that treatment expectations, contact time, nonspecific effects, drug dosage, and lack of blind raters cannot be ruled out as alternative explanations. On the other hand, the selection of pharmacotherapy as a comparison method is commendable, since tricyclic antidepressant drugs have been shown to be quite effective in comparison to other treatments.

Third, relatively inexperienced therapists briefly trained in cognitive-behavior methods used cognitive restructuring effectively.

Fourth, the therapeutic setting (the mood clinic at the Psychiatry Department, University of Pennsylvania) was associated with cognitive therapy, so these results need cross-validation at other institutions.

Professional development

Although the restructuring perspective has not generated formal training models, it suggests that traditional psychotherapeutic and behavioral training have neglected trainees' cognitive activity and professional development. Cognitively oriented educators have suggested that thinking is relevant to training (see Hirsch & Stone, 1982; Richardson & Stone, 1981; Stone, 1980; Stone & Kelly, 1983).

Cognition and practice

Cognitive structures can interfere with training. Beliefs about competence, for example, can overwhelm trainees with self-preoccupations and emotional reactions, taking their attention away from clients and from their own therapeutic impact. If trainees' beliefs about the helping role conflict with the training approach ("These helping skills are simply not my *natural* way of helping people"), trainees may resist the program or question their ability to assume a helping role. Trainees' perfectionistic demands on themselves ("I must make *no* errors." "I must not lose control." "I must not feel angry, anxious, or bored with this client. I must help this client.") and their associated emotional reactions (anxiety, anger, hopelessness) also interfere with training.

Trainees' cognitions do not necessarily lead to negative consequences. When appropriately addressed and worked through, they can be beneficial. Restructuring procedures can be used to work through these cognitions. The first task of the restructuring process is to help trainees recognize their self-statements. Next, they are instructed about the nature of coping, relating it to expectations of mastery. Trainees can use a videotape reconstruction method (the interpersonal process recall method in Kagan et al., 1967) to think aloud about the counseling session. Physiological behavior during the counseling session can be videotaped along with the counseling session itself, and both played back on a split screen. With such juxtaposition of information, trainees can recognize and label connections between thoughts, physiological reactions, emotions, and behaviors.

Training groups can be used to learn active relaxation skills. Group training also provides trainees opportunities to model and practice coping strategies and to express their beliefs and test new ones in a supportive atmosphere.

Cognition and theory

The training implications of a cognitively oriented perspective are not restricted to practice. The theory-building tradition of cognitive psychology has renewed interest in theory, philosophy, and cognitive approaches in the curriculum. Cognitive theory can stimulate the reconceptualization of career counseling (Keller, Biggs, & Gysbers, 1982), clinical judgment (Strohmer, Haase, Biggs, & Keller, 1982), relationship conditions (Stone, 1980; Wexler, 1974), and supervision (Loganbill, Hardy, & Delworth, 1982).

Commentary

The discussion to this point has been positive. But it should be understood that I am classified within this perspective. I would like to reemphasize that the data are promising but incomplete and that the definitions and techniques are diverse but too broadly conceptualized for rigorous evaluation.

A basic problem, although not unique to this perspective, is conceptual. For example, what is cognition? How are cognitions related to emotions? In what situations do cognitive processes play a substantial role and in what situations do they not? The flexibility afforded by fluid terminology can easily lead to uncritical acceptance and exaggerated claims. Critical scrutiny is at the mercy of the shifting sands of indefinite terms.

Another problem is that enthusiasm for cognitive variables tends to obscure the effectiveness of behavioral procedures. Cognitions do not function independently, although some enthusiasts seem intent on replacing performance-based treatment methods with the verbal-interview method. Some cognitive assessors naively assume that a cognitive deficiency in a pathological group automatically has etiological and treatment significance. These findings are usually correlational but do not necessarily imply treatment significance. For instance, if Beck is accurate that negative cognitions have causal significance in depression, these cognitions may be of etiological importance but may not be responsible for maintaining the depressed mood. Because of the reciprocity among cognitive, emotional, and behavioral processes, it is unclear that deficiencies in one domain must dictate the treatment content. That is, self-efficacy (a cognitive variable) appears to be influenced more by performance (a behavior variable) than by verbal therapy.

Current interest in cognition also tends to obscure an understanding of emotions. Can irrational behavior be reduced to simply not understanding logic or problem solving? Should the teaching of new ways of thinking to clients be restricted to cognitive learning methods? Are cognitive procedures necessary for mechanical self-talk to evolve into meaningful internal communications? Are relationship conditions reducible to information functions?

These questions and discussion points suggest that the restructuring perspective is somewhat less than messianic. Until conceptual and methodological issues are resolved and the treatment programs extended to other clinical populations, the restructuring perspective remains only a contender for being *the* perspective.

Summary

Counseling function	Characteristic
Establishment	Relationship and social-influence variables serve cognitive functions.
Conceptualization	Cognitive processes are emphasized in assessment.
Intervention	Performance-based treatments are used to influence a client's cognitive process.
Evaluation	Theory-relevant research and cognitive-data collection are highlighted.
Professional development	Cognitive development of trainees is a major focus.

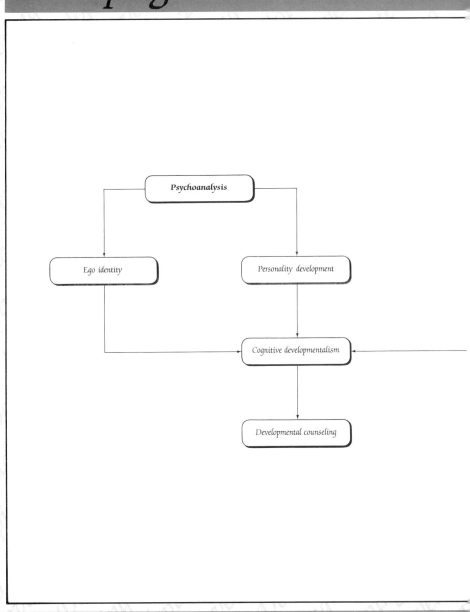

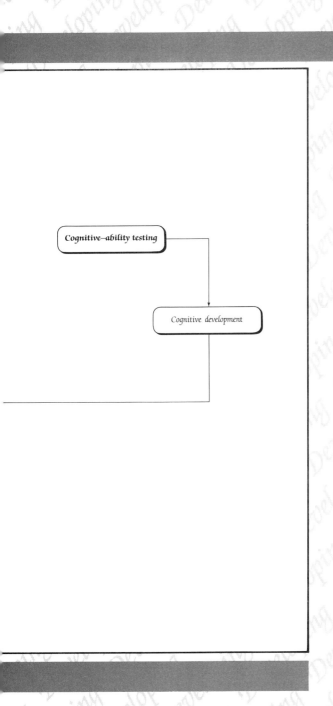

7

One characteristic that has differentiated counseling psychology from other clinical professions has been its concern with human **development**. In particular, this developmental concern has focused on careers (Crites, 1981; Super, 1964) and education, especially higher education (Parker, 1978).

Although fostering development has been a major helping perspective for counseling-related professions, development has lacked a clear definition. Many modern helping perspectives emphasize actions in the here and now. But when the emphasis shifts to examining how behavior is different from one point in time to another, we are considering a developmental point of view, which is concerned with the properties of change over time.

Internalism versus externalism.   Historically, the question of whether the stimulus for change comes primarily from within or without the person has defined the thinking about development. Those stressing the importance of the internal stimulus look to innate ideas, human instincts, and libidinal drives to explain change. According to an internal conception of change, everything is preformed at birth and merely unfolds or evolves with age. The internal factors are prepotent, while the environment is the context in which the processes of internal regulation and spontaneous maturation occur. Representatives of internalism include psychoanalytical thinkers (Jung), educational philosophers (Rousseau, Pestalozzi, and Froebel), and psychologists (McDougall and G. Stanley Hall).

In marked contrast, the external position minimizes internal contributions of the individual while emphasizing the role of the environment in determining developmental outcomes. Lamarckianism, reflecting the importance attached to environmental exposure, assumed that acquired characteristics were transmissible to offspring. More modern representatives of externalism include behaviorism and other forms of cultural and social determinism. To a degree, the humanistic movement can also be seen as emphasizing external determinants; that is, given nurturing conditions, the developmental potentialities of a person are unlimited.

Although these distinctions are better conceptualized as extremes on a continuum—nature versus nurture—the differences are not always so clear-cut. Increasingly, most developmentalists, while endorsing different emphases depending on the kind of developmental outcome, agree that the interaction of the person and the environment stimulates development.

Structural change.   Another defining characteristic has to do with the nature of change. Most developmentalists are concerned with structural changes in the organization and patterning of thought and behavior over time. These structural changes are conceptualized as different from changes resulting from learning. Learning is a quantitative change in behavior or information, whereas development is a qualitative, organizational change that is conceptualized either in sequential patterns, called stages, or as continuous over a life span.

In general, the developing perspective assumes that a person grows to be effective through healthy interactions between the growing self and the environment. These interactions differ in type, rate, and direction of change, depending on the function.

Cognitive developmentalism

In counseling, three approaches to development have been used: life span (Buehler, 1933); ego identity (Erikson, 1950/1963); and cognitive development (Harvey, Hunt, & Schroder, 1961; Kohlberg, 1969; Loevinger, 1976; Perry, 1970; Piaget, 1970; Selman, 1980). The life-span approach, which is not of central interest here, was used by Super (1980) in his theory of career development. The ego-identity models and the cognitive-developmental approach have been applied to counseling (Blocher, 1966/1974); career development (Blocher & Siegal, 1981; Jepsen, 1979; Knefelkamp & Slepitza, 1976); supervision (Loganbill, Hardy, & Delworth, 1982); and student development (Parker, 1978). The latter two models will be used to exemplify the developing perspective, with cognitive development and ego-identity literatures providing, respectively, the guidelines for the design of the counseling process and the articulation of counseling goals.

Cognitive-development models have come to be known collectively as cognitive developmentalism, a structural approach that is not a single theory but includes many models of development. All models, however, use a constructivist explanation of personality and a stage approach to development. The constructivist position proposes that people actively process and interpret external stimuli through their cognitive structures, thus making behavior a function of mediated external stimuli, rather than of raw external stimuli. In a sense, people create assumptions and propositions about the world (called cognitive structures), which help them perceive, organize, and evaluate events.

The stage approach to development implies an invariable sequence of stages, which are defined by distinct and qualitatively different cognitive activities. Each stage builds on, incorporates, and transforms the previous one and prepares for the next one, resulting in a hierarchical organization. Generally, higher stages of cognitive development represent increasing levels of differentiation and complexity and decreasing levels of egocentricity and categorized thinking.

From cognitive developmentalism, developmental counseling obtains a structural model of the way thought processes develop and influence other aspects of personality. A counselor can use the model to relate the developmental status of a client to counseling processes. The transition from the structural model to content, however, is unclear. A primary source for understanding the content of development, particularly for counseling adolescents and young adults (traditional users of counseling services), is the ego-identity literature. Most of the literature describes self-development as psychosocial stages associated with developmental tasks, such as the task of achieving an identity.

Approach

A number of cognitive-developmental theories and ego-identity models have been written about. In this section, the cognitive developmental theory of Harvey et al. (1961) and the ego-identity approach of Erikson (1968) provide general guidelines. Specifically, Hunt's conceptual level (CL) approach (Hunt & Sullivan, 1974), Loevinger's ego-developmental model (1976), and Chickering's (1969) refinement of Erikson's description of developmental themes for the young adult are used.

Orientation

Environmental structure

The conceptual level (CL) matching model (Hunt, 1971) coordinates personal and environmental dimensions and relates the developmental status of the client to the counseling process. Conceptual-level theory was formulated within a person/environment theoretical context (Lewin, 1936), with strong emphasis on the reciprocal impact of the person and the environment. Originally formulated within a developmental theory of personality (Harvey et al., 1961), CL is viewed as a personal variable, reflecting development of cognitive complexity and interpersonal maturity. The sequence of CL development is increasing interpersonal maturity (from an immature, unsocialized stage, through a dependent, conforming stage, to an independent, self-reliant stage) and increasing effectiveness in processing information (from recall and a categorical view of knowledge to analysis and synthesis of knowledge and a pluralistic perspective). Harvey and associates believe that individuals possess many domain-specific conceptual systems, each with its own sequence of development. For instance, a person may have a simplistic view of women's role in society ("Women's place is in the home"), but a more complex and pluralistic view of world affairs ("Each country has a valid point, but the underlying theme seems to be security").

Since its original formulation, the authors have developed more specific versions and extended CL theory to social psychology (Harvey, 1967), information processing (Schroder, Driver, & Struefert, 1967), and education (Hunt, 1971). Hunt's extension has come to be known as the CL matching model, which specifies the environmental arrangements most appropriate for a person's immediate needs (contemporaneous) and growth (developmental). This approach is based on the principle that low CL people (dependent and deficient in generating their own concepts) profit from a highly structured environment and high CL people (self-reliant and capable of generating alternatives) profit from low structure or are unaffected by structure.

In developmental terms, matching is finding the appropriate environment for clients to progress to the next developmental stage. For example, for unsocialized and dependent people to become socialized and dependent, they need to understand and identify with the cultural rules. The matched environment for progression to the dependent, socialized stage would be a highly structured one.

Developmental content

Although the CL matching model helps to structure the counseling process to fit the client's needs, it does not help select content. The stage-related goals of independence and maturity do not suggest which tasks will help people reach these goals.

A primary source for developmental content, particularly for the college-age person, is the work on **ego identity** of Erikson and Chickering. Erikson's (1950/1963) overall aim was to chart the universal stages of personality development, using historical information about intrapsychic dynamics, social situations, and the relation between them. He hypothesized eight stages. These stages represent the maturation-like unfolding of a genetically transmitted plan of personality. Associated with these stages are major crises. To progress in an adaptive manner, a person must adequately resolve each crisis. Early life crises are primarily due to conflicts between biological desires and reality. The source of conflict increasingly shifts from biology to sociology, as a person addresses questions of what kind of person to be, whom to interact with, and what to do.

Using Erikson's work as a starting point, Chickering (1969) enhances understanding of the identity stage by specifying themes that occur during the normal development of the young adult. These developmental themes include competence, emotional awareness, autonomy, theoretical identity, tolerance, intentionality, and integrity. **Competence** means ability in intellectual, physical, and manual skills as well as in social interactions. **Awareness** means an alertness to affect. **Autonomy** means being independent while accepting the reality and value of interdependence. **Theoretical identity** means an inner consistency of values, emotions, and beliefs. **Tolerance** builds on the other themes and is evidenced by social interest and spontaneous acceptance of individual differences. **Intentionality** means clarifying occupational, avocational, economic, and other life goals. **Integrity** means having a belief system that guides behavior. Once the relevant developmental theme has been established, the CL matching model would guide the structure of the counseling program.

Establishment

Like counselors in other helping perspectives, developmental counselors see helping relationships as contributing to the growth of both client and counselor and consider the traditional relationship conditions and social-influence factors as important in counseling. But developmental counselors also stress the developmental nature of the relationship itself. They assume that both client and counselor grow and develop in stages and that the relationship, too, grows and develops.

The therapeutic relationship is not an event but a process, with a beginning, a middle, and an end. All relationships, of course, do not go through the same process, since some relationships never develop fully. The beginning (initial) phase and the middle (developing) phase are discussed below.

Initial phase

The beginning phase, as with most other relationships, focuses on the development of trust between the participants. Developmental counselors, like most counselors, convey facilitative attitudes and use a supportive approach in establishing a therapeutic relationship. During this phase, many clients resemble a low-CL participant, concerned about the nature of counseling, searching for the right way to do things, and dependent on the counselor for advice.

The developmental counselor, sensitive to the client's developmental needs for structure and autonomy, can use Hunt's model for encouraging autonomy within a normative structure. The counselor can structure the counseling experience by using social influence—describing the developmental nature of therapeutic relationships and outlining developmental expectations ("Since a large part of people's stress has to do with the unfinished business of growing up due to unfulfilled relationships, my hope is that our relationship will help you accomplish your tasks").

To encourage client autonomy, counselors might allow the client flexibility in answering questions. And they can encourage clients to tell their own stories and explore their own reactions to the developing therapeutic relationship.

Developing phase

Since the relationship is viewed as developing over the entire counseling experience, the middle phase often includes assessment and intervention. The counselor becomes increasingly sensitive to developmental themes and the client's developmental status. The ways in which clients relate to the counselor give clues about their developmental history and past relationships with significant people.

Suppose a young man talking to a young male counselor presents his most amusing self. The counselor might frequently inquire of himself as well as of the client "What is the problem here?" The counselor is aware from previous sessions about the client's intimacy needs. When he realizes that the client's jokes and charm has disarmed him and kept him from knowing the client except in the most superficial sense, the counselor understands that the client's amusing but empty manner must also prevent the client from meaningful encounters with others. The counselor can then use the developing relationship to help the client learn about his intimacy needs in a safe environment.

Conceptualization

The developmental counselor views client problems as psychological experiences related to unfinished developmental tasks, rather than as pathology. This developmental view has been one of the major distinctions between counseling psychologists and clinical psychologists.

Formal assessment methods

Sentence completion.   A procedure widely employed in cognitive-development research is a verbal-projective technique called sentence completion. Generally, the sentence stems permit an almost unlimited variety of endings ("When I am in doubt . . ." "What worries me . . ." "My ambition . . ."). Sentence stems are formulated to elicit responses that are relevant to the theoretical framework under study. Loevinger and her associates (Loevinger, Wessler, & Redmore, 1970) undertook to measure ego development from the responses to the Washington University Sentence Completion Test. Responses were classified as presocial and symbiotic, impulsive, self-protective, conformist, conscientious, autonomous, and integrated. At the presocial end of the scale, illustrated by infants, individuals are incapable of self-conceptualization. As children develop into adolescence, they gradually form stereotyped, conventional, and socially acceptable self-concepts. With increasing maturity, they leave behind stereotypical concepts and begin to develop differentiated and realistic self-concepts. Although these integrated people may not appear as well-adjusted as conventional people, they are aware of their peculiarities and accept themselves.

Paragraph completion.   The Paragraph Completion Test (Schroder et al., 1967) was designed to assess levels of conceptual complexity in the interpersonal and uncertainty domains. Sentence stems represent structure ("Rules . . ."), conflict ("When I am criticized . . ."), and uncertainty ("When I am in doubt . . ."). The client completes six stems by writing at least three sentences for each of them. Sentence completions are scored according to their structural properties (how a person thinks). Responses are scored (for example, Hunt, Greenwood, Noy, & Watson, 1973) according to their conceptual complexity and self-conceptualizations. Low scores (0, 1) represent a lack of alternatives, categorical thinking, and self-preoccupation, and high scores (2, 3) indicate conceptual complexity, integration, and self-responsibility.

Assessment procedures for personality, aptitude, and behavior could be organized into tests to assess relevant populations in terms of Chickering's tasks.

Informal assessment methods

Interpersonal transactions between counselors and clients can provide information about clients' developmental status—the completion or impairment of past developmental tasks—and the risks in correcting it. The following exchange between a female counselor and a male college student provides an example.

Excerpt	*Commentary*
1. *Counselor:* It seems you were about to tell me something. Something that hurts.	
2. *Client:* Yes. . . . You know, I am thinking about being a psychiatrist or someone who helps people.	
3. *Counselor:* Yes, I do remember your saying that.	
4. *Client:* Well . . . I was invited to join a group. You know, like group encounters, where people come together and talk and share things.	
5. *Counselor:* Uh-huh . . .	

	Excerpt	*Commentary*
6. *Client:*	Last week . . . Well . . . it just came apart. . . . I never knew I could be so hurt. . . . I cried.	Pathologically oriented therapists might say that the client experienced regression (excerpt 6) and does not have adequate defenses.
7. *Counselor:*	You lost me. What happened last week that hurt you so much?	
8. *Client:*	In the group . . . last week. Some people were giving me feedback, people I admire. . . . Well . . . they said . . . I was rather unfeeling and distant. What they meant was, I was a cold fish.	Client statements 8, 10, and 14 may indicate to a developmental counselor what the client wants and needs; namely, the capacity to give and receive affection. These client statements can lead to inferences about the degree of impairment and the approximate age at which development was incomplete.
9. *Counselor:*	And that hurt . . .	
10. *Client:*	Hell, yes. I know I have trouble with feelings. It's hard for me to accept affection or to give it easily. But to think I want to care for people . . . and others see me as a fish. . . . I don't get it! . . . I am so inadequate.	
11. *Counselor:*	I am trying to sense what it was like for you to hear that feedback . . . that you were cold . . . unfeeling . . . inadequate.	
12. *Client:*	[silence]	

Excerpt	*Commentary*
13. Counselor: You said that affection was difficult for you.	Since the focus is on developmental needs rather than the pathology of regression, the counselor asks questions about earlier relationships (excerpts 15, 17); for instance, the destructive impact of parental relationships on the client's feelings about himself as someone who can be supportive and loving.
14. Client: Yes, I guess so.	
15. Counselor: When did you realize this difficulty?	In excerpt 15, the counselor attempts to learn the time of the client's incomplete development, which will affect how the counselor will work with him.
16. Client: Oh, I don't know. . . . Can't we blame my parents?	
17. Counselor: Well. . . . Let's see. How did you feel about them? How did you express your feelings?	
18. Client: Come on! I was just kidding. . . . I loved my folks, but we didn't believe in all that hugging stuff. It was just understood.	In the last excerpt, the counselor learns about early experiences with parents that were unfulfilling and that may have blocked this client's affective development.

Intervention

Orientation

Cognitive-developmental theory suggests that development follows a particular process and sequence. Developing individuals pass through stages on their way to the highest stage of functioning. Thus, if one knows where the person is along the developmental path, then one could assign tasks and a specific way for them to be accomplished. The developing perspective lends itself to the design of intervention suggested in Erikson's and Chickering's work.

Unfortunately, most cognitive-developmental theories are descriptive rather than prescriptive, resulting in difficulties as one moves from theory to intervention. Furthermore, most developmental applications have been in instruction (for example, career-planning courses: Touchton, Wertheimer, Cornfeld, & Harrison, 1978; developmental instruction: Widick & Simpson, 1978) and student development (for example, workshops in life planning, text anxiety, and academic skills: Hurst, 1978), rather than counseling. The instruction-oriented nature of developmental applications requires a somewhat different approach in describing interventions. First, the focus of the service delivery will be on a target group rather than on a single individual as in most counseling work. In this example the target group is adult women students rather than traditional college-age students. Second, the description of the intervention will not be restricted to one intervention per se but will offer interventions adapted to developmentally different individuals. Finally, the intervention program proposed here has much less support from history, theory, and research than do many interventions discussed in this book and thus is best thought of as a proposal exemplifying the developmental perspective. Similar programs have been developed and evaluated positively; for examples see Widick and Simpson, 1978. These programs and others (Knefelkamp & Slepitza, 1976; Knefelkamp, Widick, & Stroad, 1976; Touchton et al., 1978) give substance and guidelines to the following proposal.

One intervention program

Ego-identity models have identified vocational development as important in clarifying a personal identity. Developmental counselors on university campuses could build a program based on vocational development (which lies within Chickering's framework, and which he calls *clarifying purposes*). Others also identify career issues and vocational development as salient developmental experiences (Cross, 1971; Yankelovich, 1974).

Having identified the issue, counselors would identify the target group. One possible student subgroup, which is increasing in number (Van Dusen & Sheldon, 1976), is adult women who wish to reenter the job market. Cognitive developmentalism would define their goal as career development, moving from a simple, categorical view of women and their role in society to a complex, pluralistic view, in which women accept responsibility for their identity.

In developing an intervention (say a course or workshop on career development) to meet the needs of these women, counselors realize (through the Paragraph Completion Method or other procedure) that the women fall developmentally into two groups. One group thinks categorically about the role of women in society, believing there is one right role for women and those who differ are wrong. Homemakers may believe their place is in the home, feminists may believe the professions are the only path to follow, and others may believe that salvation is in education.

Women in the other group recognize diversity and conflicting viewpoints but are overwhelmed by possibilities. The old rules and regulations have lost their meaning. These women (returning middle-aged women, young mothers, single parents, and others) are confronted with making their own way in a world that offers a wide array of options, some involving conflicting commitments.

The differences between these two groups in cognitive complexity require different approaches, in which instructional environments are matched with developmental status (developmental instruction, or developmental counseling in a counseling context). Learning environments are designed to stimulate individuals to think in increasingly more complex ways. In stimulative matching (plus-one staging), clients learn at a level they can understand (support) but then are exposed to harder tasks (challenge), which lead to conceptual conflict and dissonance. A repeated sequence of support and challenge promotes greater cognitive complexity and development (see Day, Berlyne, & Hunt, 1971).

Each group will need different supports and challenges. Women in the categorical group need to be exposed to a variety of views on women's roles. They could be asked to read excerpts from books about women's midlife experiences and occupational reentry (for example, Sheehy's *Pathfinders*). They could interview community women who have made unusual career choices. But the diversity in their program needs to be carefully selected, sequenced, and presented to provide a structure for guidance.

Women in the diversity group do not need exposure to diversity but need to integrate varying factors and resolve them. These women could focus on the common dimensions of the various career paths they discover in their reading and interviews. These dimensions might include time, ability, work demands, and a personal definition of a working woman. The workshop for these women should be less structured than the workshop for the categorical group. They need fewer guidelines and should be given more responsibility for what they read and whom they interview. The process of finding common dimensions and resolution should emerge inductively from group discussions about each woman's decision and its consequences. For example, after reading about and interviewing a diverse group of women, a woman may decide that she wants to have a professional career. Her peers then may force her to integrate the realities of time, family responsibilities, and economics into this decision.

Women in each group are helped toward a higher order of cognitive processing. The workshop for the categorical women is designed to enable the members to appreciate the diversity of options. The workshop for the cognitively more advanced women is designed to reveal common factors within diversity, which need to be personally addressed and resolved. Each workshop should be evaluated for its effect on the women's development, career activities, and satisfaction. Developmental progress could be based on responses before and after the workshop, using measures of development like those of Hunt, Loevinger, and Perry. Evaluation of career activities might use an indicator of information seeking, such as career library use (see Krumboltz & Thoresen, 1964). The women's satisfaction with the workshop could easily be assessed by questionnaire.

Evaluation

Applied research in psychology and education has been concerned with two problems: selection and evaluation. The issue in selection has been the search for predictors of successful performance. Evaluation measures the effectiveness of alternative methods by experimental procedures.

Reflecting Lewinian and Darwinian thinking about organism/environment relations, the developing perspective is not interested in selection (selecting the clients who best fit existing counseling procedures) or evaluation (the best counseling method). But, along with Cronbach (1975), developmentalists would like to unify correlational and experimental psychologies, so that the primary issue is optimal match between the client and the treatment. An educational approach that emphasizes person/environment interactions has been called **aptitude/instructional treatment interactions,** or ATI. Here, ATI is broadly defined to include variables other than those in traditional educational settings (for example, attribute replaces aptitude).

A study by Stein and Stone (1978) is an example of ATI research in counseling. The authors assessed the impact of the CL matching model in a university-counseling context. An ATI design (2 × 2), with an individual characteristic (CL) and a counseling interview (structure), was used. The verbal and self-report effects of matching client's CL (high and low) to the interview structure (low and high) were evaluated in an initial interview. It was predicted that high-CL clients in a low-structured interview and low-CL clients in a highly structured interview would respond better (talk longer, self-disclose more, express greater satisfaction) than mismatched clients (high with high and low with low). Some of the positive aspects of this study included theoretical validity (use of theory to relate individual difference to treatment variables; and use of multiple measures to incorporate different sources and methods), internal validity (random assignment and empirical checks of the treatment conditions), and external validity (use of more than one interviewer).

Results of the study supported the matching model, but this support was primarily from self-report measures of satisfaction (low-CL clients were satisfied with high structure; high-CL clients were satisfied with low structure). Verbal measures reflected differences among the CL groups congruent with CL theory (in low-structured interviews, high-CL clients talk more and express more self-awareness than low-CL clients). Of course, verbalization could be a more parsimonious explanation: clients who like to talk (high CL) are more satisfied in situations in which they can talk more (low structure). Or perhaps the expected interactions between CL and structure were masked by a too-structured and time-limited experimental situation.

But beyond the rigor, the particular findings, and the remaining questions, this ATI counseling study reveals the heart of the developing perspective: the relationship between the person and the environment. The traditional question of which method is best would not have been easily answered, since treatment averages would have yielded little information. Here, the traditional question has been modified to ask, best for whom? Client's CL interacted with counselor's structure in predictable ways, suggesting that counselors may want to adjust their interventions to client differences in order to capitalize on the strengths and preferences of each kind of client.

Professional development

As would be expected from a developmental point of view, development is a key concept in professional training and supervision. Some writers use a generic-developmental stage or learning theory (Hogan, 1964; Littrell, Lee-Borden, & Lorenz, 1979; Stone, 1980). Others rely on cognitive developmentalism (Berg & Stone, 1980; Loganbill et al., 1982; Stoltenberg, 1981). But they all share the assumptions that counseling psychologists develop through distinct qualitative stages and need a changing environment during their apprenticeship in order to move toward higher-order functioning.

Supervisory approaches differ in the content models they use to explicate their approaches. Some rely on Hunt (Stoltenberg, 1981), while others (Loganbill et al., 1982) integrate ideas from many cognitive developmentalists—Chickering, Erikson, Loevinger, Perry, Kohlberg, and Harvey et al. Loganbill and colleagues identified stages, borrowing from the works of the cognitive developmentalists, and discussed supervisory issues based on Chickering's ideas. The authors elaborated a scheme in which a trainee's competence, emotional awareness, autonomy, identity, respect for individual differences, goal setting, motivation, and ethics go through the stages of stagnation, confusion, and integration.

Most training programs approved by the American Psychological Association attempt to move a trainee from an apprentice to master practitioner (see Hogan, 1964) through a hierarchy of practical experiences organized by training level: prepracticum, practicum, advanced practicum, and internship. Advancement through these levels should reflect increasing competence and independence. From a developing perspective, competence and independence would be fostered by developmental supervision, in which supervisory experiences would be adapted to the needs of the trainee. Within each training level, developmental supervisors would arrange supervisory experiences that would move trainees from dependence to independence and from simple to complex.

Perry's and Hunt's formulations suggest three stages of development: dualism (stage 1), relativism (stage 2), and commitment (stage 3). Stage 1 is characterized by dependence and categorical thinking ("one right way"). Stage 2 reveals some flexibility, but trainees at this stage are overwhelmed by options. The disorienting experience of diversity leads to dependence/independence conflicts (for example, premature closure or meaningless eclecticism). Although trainees at stage 2 can discriminate options, their thinking never moves to a higher order of integration and personal commitment. On the contrary, trainees are so busy seeking options that practice involving decisions and commitments suffers. In stage 3, trainees function independently and integrate information from a diversity of sources, enabling them to make personal decisions.

In table 7-1, trainees' statements illustrate their characteristics at each stage within the four levels of training. Supervisors support and challenge these characteristics in order to move the trainee on to the next stage. At the prepracticum level, the focus of support and challenge is on developing basic communication skills. Practicum supervision is concerned with the improvement of sensitivity to client dynamics. Advanced practicum supervision seeks to establish conceptualization skills. The internship outcome is about learning to use personal experience within the context of supervising a practicum student.

Commentary

The developing perspective has made at least two major contributions to general psychology—an understanding of change and of individual differences.

Table 7–1   Trainee characteristics and supervisory responses at four levels of professional development

Level of professional development	Trainee statement	Supervisory support and challenge
Prepracticum Stage 1.	"That's not my natural way of helping. This is too mechanical."	*Support:* Provide a structured skill-learning environment, like micro-counseling. *Challenge:* Expose trainee to a diversity of communication skills.
Stage 2.	"There are so many things that I could do. How do I decide what to do?"	*Support:* Provide a supportive atmosphere in which alternatives can be explored. *Challenge:* Encourage trainee to explore counseling style by analyzing tapes in order to discover actual skill use.
Stage 3.	"I feel comfortable in a counseling situation. I have come to recognize that I use these skills, the skills don't use me."	
Practicum Stage 1.	"I am using the skills. What do you mean 'Pay attention to the client's experience'?"	*Support:* Expose trainee to structured encounters with clients, using filmed situations. *Challenge:* Ask trainee to respond to diverse client dynamics through filmed simulations (for example, Interpersonal Process Recall method, Kagan et al., 1967).

Level of professional development	Trainee statement	Supervisory support and challenge
Stage 2.	"That counseling session was a buzz . . . Too many things going on."	*Support:* Encourage trainee to explore reactions to different clients. *Challenge:* Help trainee articulate intuitive models (internal gyroscope) by analyzing previously recorded physiological reactions to filmed clients (see Kagan & Schauble, 1969).
Stage 3.	"My sense of the client. . . . It seems the client doesn't want to get too close to me."	
Advanced practicum Stage 1.	"The client is obviously neurotic as hell. He doesn't want anything from me. I don't understand your idea of client pull. I just don't think there is a commitment there."	*Support:* Provide trainee with a structured outline for client conceptualization. *Challenge:* Expose trainee to a diversity of conceptualizations (Millon, 1981; D. Shapiro, 1965).
Stage 2.	"There are so many ways to view this client. I like eclecticism; it gives me so many possibilities."	*Support:* Assign trainee to write reports and present cases from more than one point of view. *Challenge:* Encourage trainee to adopt a personalized perspective.
Stage 3.	"Shapiro's concept of rigid thinking style, in his book *Neurotic Styles*, makes sense to me about this client."	

Table 7–1 (Continued)

Level of professional development	Trainee statement	Supervisory support and challenge
Internship Stage 1.	"I don't understand it. This practicum student does not do what I tell her to do. She resists my suggestions."	*Support:* Provide a supportive group atmosphere. *Challenge:* Explore personal reactions in group setting.
Stage 2.	"I can recognize her approach to her clients. I recognize our differences. Hell, I recognize everybody's approach. I just don't know my own reactions."	*Support:* Establish a trusting relationship with intern. *Challenge:* Challenge intern to attend to own internal assessment capabilities.
Stage 3.	"When she resists my suggestions, that's a signal. I feel it. I find myself asking 'What is she telling me?' I finally recognized that I like to tell people what to do."	

The developing perspective reasserts the active nature of humankind. Change is not simply quantitative, consisting of the continuous accumulations of skills, habits, and other specific and observable behaviors stamped by the environment. For developmentalists, change is qualitative. It occurs in the psychological structures that underlie behavior and is actively participated in by the person. Such structural changes are not continuous nor simple but are discontinuous and have unique structural characteristics at different, separate points in life.

Professional psychology's traditional reliance on global descriptions of clients and treatments (uniformity myths) and theory-outcome evaluations (which treatment is best?) neglect individual differences. Cognitive developmentalists point out that therapists and counselors have been so preoccupied by unconscious processes, feelings, or specific behaviors that they have neglected cognition and its developmental modes of action. Developmental counselors adapt treatment to the developmental needs of clients and conduct research on individual characteristics in conjunction with alternative treatments.

There are negative aspects, also, to developmental counseling. Constructs of individual characteristics and environments are vague or concentrate on a few dimensions that are easily assessed but that are not sufficiently complex or relevant. The literature on developmental counseling is based more on theory and description than on data, which suggests that stage theory and developmental instruction are still hypotheses.

Perhaps a more important problem has to do with the traditional idea of development as progression and increasing complexity. This unidirectional viewpoint neglects bidirectional and multidirectional perspectives. For instance, observations of human behavior indicate the possibility of developmental regression in moral thinking (Kohlberg & Kramer, 1969) and cognitive development (Werner, 1957). In therapy, regression in the service of the ego can be quite functional in times of crises.

This unidirectional thinking combined with psychology's penchant for typologies unfortunately leads to value-laden and culture-specific descriptions. Individual differences in cognitive styles have been used, like traits in more traditional models, to categorize and characterize people. In many studies, these characterizations take on some of the negative aspects of diagnostic labels and seem related to the black-hat/white-hat thinking expressed in cartoons and John Wayne movies. Although many developmentalists claim that, while the underlying structures are universal, content differs by culture, their client descriptions and treatment goals are related to the rational ideals of western civilization. The developing perspective, like most helping perspectives, is as yet not fully developed.

Summary

Counseling function	Characteristic
Establishment	Use of relationship conditions and social influence are linked to the needs of relationship development.
Conceptualization	Assessment of cognitive development is emphasized.
Intervention	Interventions adapted to client developmental needs are stressed.
Evaluation	An evaluation approach focuses on attribute-treatment interactions (ATI).
Professional development	Supervision matches trainee needs at each stage of professional development with appropriate supports and challenges.

Influencing

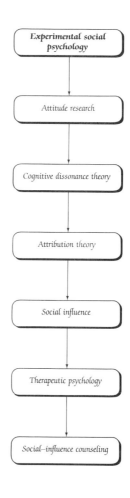

Experimental social psychology

↓

Attitude research

↓

Cognitive dissonance theory

↓

Attribution theory

↓

Social influence

↓

Therapeutic psychology

↓

Social–influence counseling

8

The use of **influence** in helping has a long and distinguished history—from religious healing to more scientific healing practices. Within most healing practices, the helper tries to change the sufferer through ritual, or magic, or perhaps more "scientific" means. The interactional process of one person (the helper) attempting to alter the actions, attitudes, or feelings of another (the sufferer) has come to be identified as social influence.

The term *social influence* may stimulate visions of Machiavellian agents of change making specific demands, and social-influence counseling does attempt to help clients by changing their thoughts, feelings, and actions. On the other hand, social influence is involved in all human discourse. Social-influence counseling does not mean that counselors impose restraints on clients where none existed before but that new and effective controls are offered in the place of those that have badly regulated clients' behavior in the past. The question is not whether influence occurs but rather by whom, by what methods, and for what purposes.

Social influence is not restricted to a particular orientation. Rather, it is a conceptual framework that may account for the effectiveness of diverse counseling methods in a variety of theoretical perspectives. It focuses on the features of human interactions that contribute to social influence (the *how* of change) rather than what the therapist says and does (the *what* of change).

Historical background

The idea that counseling methods should be examined in terms of their influence process and independent of their content was documented by Frank (1961/1973). Frank, a student of Lewin, used his background in experimental social psychology and experience in social-persuasion research to analyze primitive and modern healing practices. His use of experimental studies of persuasion was one of the earliest attempts to interpret the therapeutic process in terms of social influence.

Of course, the development of the social-influence perspective can be traced through many traditions. The **Lewinian tradition** focused on the interrelatedness of the person and the environment and was promulgated by Kurt Lewin's students, including Festinger (cognitive dissonance), Cartwright (social power), Kelley, Thibaut, and Schacter (attribution), and Back (attraction).

Another tradition, and a significant contributor to social influence, is the **attitude research** conducted by Carl Hovland and his group at Yale University (Hovland, Janis, & Kelley, 1953). Most of this research focused on persuasive communications and the way variables (for example, source, message, recipient, channel) affect the learning of the message and the consequent attitude change. Reviews of social-psychological research (McGuire, 1969) implicate these perceived communication variables as important determinants of social influence.

Within a short time, many writers were applying social-psychological concepts to therapy, especially Festinger's (1957) **cognitive-dissonance theory.** Goldstein and colleagues attempted to reformulate and clarify the therapeutic relationship in terms of interpersonal attraction (Goldstein, 1971). Bergin (1962) completed the first analogue study applying cognitive-dissonance theory to therapeutic phenomena. Levy (1963) developed a theory of psychological interpretation based on cognitive-dissonance theory. And Goldstein, Heller, and Sechrest (1966) summarized similar research findings and challenged the counseling and psychotherapeutic professions to apply principles and findings from social psychology to counseling and psychotherapy.

With a background in social psychology derived from the teachings of Elliot Aronson and Karl Weick, Strong reasserted the **influence-process view** of counseling (Strong, 1968) and linked this view to experimental research in counseling settings (Strong, 1971).

Approach

The social-influence approach discussed here is based on Strong's proposals, since they are advanced within the framework of counseling. In comparison to the other perspectives in this book, the social-influence perspective may be the only one elaborated within a counseling context (see Zytowski & Rosen, 1982).

Strong and his associates (Strong, 1978; Strong & Claiborn, 1982) have broadened Strong's influence view of counseling (Strong, 1968) by incorporating other theories besides internal consistency (for example, communication theory). Since chapter 9 deals with communication theory, this section focuses on Strong's work based on cognitive-consistency theory.

Orientation

Cognitive-consistency theories, of which Festinger's theory of cognitive dissonance is prominent, suggest that related attitudes held by an individual tend toward internal consistency. If individuals are exposed to information that produces an inconsistency among these attitudes, then one or more of the attitudes will change to enhance consistency. Some argue that cognitive inconsistency is stressful and its resolution is stress reducing. Others (Bem, 1967) argue that cognitive consistency may not motivate change at all. That is, self-observation of counteratti-tudinal behavior leads to changed attitudes. Whatever the role of emotional arousal, some counseling theorists endorse cognitive consistency as framework for counseling.

For instance, Strong sees counseling as an ongoing influence process of stimulating and resolving cognitive inconsistencies. Counseling intervention (regardless of content) provides discrepant information, which results in dissonance and demand for resolution. Clients can resolve the dissonance by (1) changing attitudes in the direction advocated by the counselor, (2) discrediting the counselor, (3) discrediting the issue, (4) changing the counselor's opinion, and (5) seeking others with supporting attitudes.

Strong (1968) proposed that counselors promote change in the target attitude and reduce the number of alternatives by arranging influence conditions during the interview. Based on opinion-change research from social psychology (Hovland, Janis, & Kelley, 1953), Strong suggested a two-stage model of counseling. In the first stage, counselors increase their social power (perceived expertness, attractiveness, and trustworthiness) and clients' dependency and involvement. In the second stage, counselors use their powers and influence to implement interventions designed to reveal discrepancies, create cognitive inconsistencies, and promote client change.

Before I describe the specifics of Strong's stage model, it is necessary to stress the importance of **client subjectivity** in the social-influence process. Social power (Strong & Matross, 1973) is dependent on clients' judgment of the match between their needs and their perception of counselors' resources—expertness, attractiveness, and trustworthiness. Counselors' influence is not simply a matter of professional attire, academic degrees, physical attractiveness, self-disclosure, and provision of information. Rather, the way clients process this information and their resultant inferences are central. Clients respond not only to the objective characteristics of social-influence situations but also to personal involvement.

Establishment

The influence view of counseling offers very little in the way of unique communication skills or relationship-building methods. To be sure, Strong endorses the traditional conditions of therapeutic understanding, genuineness, and warmth. In the establishment phase, counselors demonstrate sincere interest through reflective and empathic communications, initiating the influence structure in which needy clients reveal actions, ideas, and feelings to counselors whom they perceive as having expertness, attractiveness, and trustworthiness. These communications between the needy (clients) and the resourceful (counselors) foster dependency relationships in which clients become increasingly involved. They perceive the counselors as powerful, which enhances counselors' social influence.

In the initial encounters, counselors control the interview and clients are taught how to be clients, exploring problems with an interested and concerned person. Through these explorations, counselors enhance their social power by arranging influence conditions—expertness (office setting, attire, jargon), competence (structuring, rationale), attractiveness (self-disclosure and accurate empathy), and trustworthiness (interest in clients' welfare).

Schmidt and Strong (1970) and Strong and Schmidt (1970) have provided evidence of the cues and behaviors associated with expertness in a counseling-like situation. The following expert and inexpert introductions and the behaviors associated with each is from Strong and Schmidt (1970).

Expert: The person you will be talking with is Dr.—, a psychologist who has had several years of experience in interviewing students. Now, if you would step this way (p. 83).

Inexpert: We had originally scheduled Dr.— to talk with you, but unfortunately he notified us that he wouldn't be able to make it today. In his place we have Mr.—, a student, who unfortunately has not had interviewing experience and has been given only a brief explanation of the purpose of this study. I think he should work out all right, though. Now, if you would step this way (p. 83).

The *expert* was attentive and interested in the subject (S). He looked at the S, he leaned toward him and was responsive to the S by his facial expressions, head nods, posture and so on. He used hand gestures to emphasize his points. The *inexpert* was inattentive to the S. He either did not look at the S, or he gave him a dead-pan stare and was not reactive to him. He either did not use gestures, or his gestures were stiff, formal, and overdone. While the *expert* performed with an air of confidence, the *inexpert* was unsure, nervous, and lacked confidence.

The *expert* was organized and knew what he was doing. He structured the interview by suggesting possible topics and where the S might begin. He described the task to the S, and explained that his own role in the interview was to facilitate the S's discussion. The *inexpert* was confused and unsure of where to begin. He offered only minimal help to the S and did not clarify his role in the interview (p. 82).

From these descriptions, the initial structure of counseling is evident: the client is initially to assume a dependent role and the counselor is to assume control.

Conceptualization

Strong has not written extensively on diagnosis but seems to have adopted **causal-attribution theory** in addressing the conceptualization function (Strong, 1978). For Strong, assessment of the nature of the cause is important. The key is to identify causes that are amenable to change. To put it another way, events or problems whose causes are outside the personal influence of the client are useless targets. The emphasis is on discerning personal causes under clients' control. For example, a clinically distraught young man suffering from procrastination tells the counselor of his miseries. He describes his anger at others for disturbing his work. He describes other people as always "needing him." As counseling proceeds, it becomes obvious that little can be done about the behavior and needs of others but much can be accomplished with this client's attitudes ("people always need me") and behaviors (choice of workplace).

Recently Strong (Strong & Claiborn, 1982) has downplayed traditional diagnosis ("The problematic behavior does not have to be identified to be changed," p. 59) because it relies on an outdated paradigm. Traditional diagnosis seems to be preoccupied with elaborate schemes of intrapsychic dynamics and linear causality, while recent developments in family-system theory have focused on **interactional** and circular causality. As a result, Strong emphasizes the pattern of behavior a client "pulls" from the therapist. Kiesler and colleagues have developed a measure relevant to interactional psychology. The Impact Message Inventory (Perkins, Kiesler, Anchin, Chirico, Kyle, & Federman, 1979) is a method of assessing common evoking styles. The IMI indexes the affective, behavioral, and cognitive reactions of one individual (counselor) to another (client). The inventory is related conceptually to circumplex models of interpersonal behavior (Leary, 1957; Lorr & McNair, 1963) that yield interpersonal categories (for example, competitive, nurturant) based on the underlying dimensions of affiliation (love/hate) and status (dominance/submission).

Intervention

The first phase (establishment and conceptualization) is preliminary to the change phase. In the change phase counselors have maximum effect on clients' cognitions and behaviors due to the influence accumulated in the prior phase. The heart of the social-influence view is behavior modification. Using the attitude-change model, interventions are conceptualized to meet clients' goals through the creation and resolution of cognitive inconsistencies. **Discrepancy** is the central ingredient.

That is, in addition to discrepancy-inducing interventions (for example, recognition of irrational ideas, insight into psychological defenses) is feedback, which makes clients aware of discrepancies between their interaction patterns and their expected effects on others.

Interpretation

Strong (Strong, Wambach, Lopez, & Cooper, 1979) endorses Levy's (1963) view of interpretation as "an alternative frame of reference or language system" (p. 7) used to change the meaning of clients' problems, making these problems amenable to change. Too often, clients have defined their problems in a way that doesn't allow change.

The relationship function of interpretation is also important. Counselors' positive remarks about the clients' evaluations can change the clients' perceptions and experience. The conceptualizing function of interpretation is conveyed by counselors' remarks to clients about causal relationships and personal responsibility. These interpretations can lead clients to process information differently, increasing personal involvement.

One interpretive intervention uses paradox, or contradictory communications. In counseling and psychotherapy, contradictory messages ("Only you can decide about what you are going to do"; "Certainly you need to consider your education") facilitate therapeutic change through spontaneous compliance. To foster compliance, clients are induced to adopt the behavior counselors desire, allowing clients to believe the change comes from deep within their personalities, not from counselors' demands or clients' willpower. In other words, the clients misattribute the change to spontaneous internal causes. Rogers's system exemplifies a spontaneous-compliance situation. Rogerians often present desired behavior to clients through counselor self-disclosure, modeling, and verbal reinforcement ("I like you much more when you are quiet and reflective"). Rogerians emphasize to clients the necessity for them to assume responsibility for their lives and propose that the agent of change is the deep core of the clients' personality.

Other contradictory messages discourage symptomatic behavior by providing unexpected feedback. Counselors encourage clients to discuss their symptoms but refuse to react in expected ways; that is, supporting clients or giving pathological labels to their symptoms. The violation of clients' expectations frustrates their use of symptoms in maintaining relationship control. To regain control, clients abandon the nonproductive behaviors (symptoms) and search for effective behavior. When they hit upon the effective behavior, they will then attribute it not to the unresponsive counselor but to their own spontaneous adjustment to the unexpected situation.

Directives

Some counselors' communications direct clients to behave in particular ways, often in paradoxical situations. The effects of directives depend on their intention, whether to invite compliance or defiance. For instance, counselors' demand for clients to perform their symptomatic behavior can lead to refusal because the situation becomes paradoxical. The demand that persons do what they already are doing alters the attribution process; namely, external directives question the clients' arguments about the uncontrollability and intrinsic nature of their behavior. Compliance reduces the clients' control over their symptoms while enhancing the social power of the counselor. On the other hand, defiance is an admission of the internal reasons for the symptomatic behavior.

Illustration of interpretation and directives

A number of verbal tactics can be used to induce discrepancy and stimulate change. The following case involves a middle-aged divorcee with three children. She was raised in a small town and educated in Catholic boarding schools for girls. After her divorce from her husband of twenty years, she moved to a large city and experienced difficulty in socializing and being spontaneous with people. The excerpt below begins with the second session.

	Excerpt	*Commentary*
1.	*Client:* Why is it so hard to be spontaneous? I try so hard, but I always fail. . . . What do you think?	In excerpts 1 and 2, the initial structure of the counseling relationship is demonstrated. Excerpt 1 reveals that a dependency relationship ("What do you think?") has been created in an earlier interview.
2.	*Counselor:* Well, the first sense I get is not so much thinking, but a feeling . . . a feeling of frustration . . . of trying hard . . . of failing . . . and more hard work.	In excerpt 2, the counselor uses reflective communication in showing interest in the client.

		Excerpt	*Commentary*
3.	*Client:*	Yes. . . . I am frustrated. It seems the harder I try to be sociable . . . at ease with people . . . the more difficult it becomes.	In excerpt 3, the client reveals a self-defeating pattern: one cannot be deliberately spontaneous.
4.	*Counselor:*	Perhaps we could learn more about your lack of social spontaneity. . . . Perhaps a little experiment . . . Yes . . . If you could, for your next social encounter, elaborately plan the encounter . . . commit it to cards and read from it . . . we might be able to collect instances of thoughts and feelings that keep you from being spontaneous *[pause]* No . . . That may not be a good idea.	In excerpt 4, a number of verbal tactics are used. A homework assignment containing a directive (symptom prescription) is contemplated. In addition, the counselor has adapted the directive to the client's dependency strategy. The counselor attempts to reduce the distance between them by suggesting that he is not without his frailties ("that may not be a good idea").
5.	*Client:*	Oh . . . I don't know. It sounds worth trying.	Moreover, as demonstrated in excerpt 5, the client is more likely to undertake assignments and make internal attributions if the external influence is kept low-key.
6.	*Counselor:*	Well, why don't we think about it. In the meantime, you can simply attend social encounters and avoid meeting anyone new.	In excerpt 6, the counselor has used the paradoxical tactic of suggesting the client go slow ("think about it"; "avoid meeting any-

		Excerpt	*Commentary*
			one new'') to reduce client's anxiety about solving the problem immediately and to enhance treatment progress and internal attributions.
7.	*Client:*	OK.	
8.	*Client [a week later]:*	I think I made some progress. I was more aware of talking to people, but I didn't feel pushed to meet new people as you suggested— although I did meet some new people, nonetheless. I felt pretty good about that.	
9.	*Counselor:*	I am pleased. But I don't want us to go too fast. *[pause]* I've thought about our experiment. . . . It may not be very important.	Excerpt 9 repeats the go-slow tactic and the distance-reduction approach.
10.	*Client:*	I've thought about it, also. . . . I want to try it.	Excerpt 10 reveals the client's intentions and implies the transition from dependency (''What do you think?'') to personal responsibility (''I want to try it'').
11.	*Counselor:*	Well . . . if you think it is worth it. . . . I am not so sure. . . . Well . . . let's give it	

Excerpt	*Commentary*
a try. *[Client and counselor go over specifics of the experiment.]*	
12. Client [a week later]: I have my journal here. I didn't do very well. Also, I was too tired to write out all my anticipated encounters. . . . As I considered our experiment, I don't understand it. However, I had an outstanding week. I was complimented. . . . I met new people. I have a date next week. . . . There still is more to come. . . . Can you believe my daughter said, "Gosh, mom, you are getting it together." God, our best communication in three years!	Excerpt 12 shows the effect of the paradoxical directive. The client failed to meet the requirements of the counselor's directive (symptom prescription to be deliberate), but experienced new social encounters with enthusiasm.
13. Counselor: I don't know what to say. I guess my experiment didn't work too well. I would suggest that the great amount of progress made this week probably precludes much progress for the next few weeks. Thus . . .	Finally, in excerpt 13 the counselor points away from counselor's responsibility and at the same time reduces pressure on the client for the upcoming weeks. Both of these tactics set the stage for further improvement and equip the client for self-initiated change.

In the preceding example, the counselor suggested an extreme elaboration of planned social encounters which, given the client's symptom, does not seem desirable. However, the counselor was not seeking more elaborate planning but was influencing the situation through paradox so that the client would take responsibility for her old social behavior and initiate new social behavior. In essence, paradoxical interventions invite clients to take control by changing undesired behavior to desired behavior through their own internal characteristics. The paradoxes do not force the client to change but reveal opportunities.

Summary

Counselors build social power and client dependency so that they can introduce behavior-change strategies during the intervention phase. Counselors propose changes to clients that make the relationship incongruent and induce discrepancy into the clients' psychological world. As the interventions become effective, these discrepancies decrease and clients experience responsibility.

Evaluation

One of the most developed research topics in counseling psychology is Strong's social-influence view (see Borgen, 1984; Zytowski & Rosen, 1982). At least 60 studies have been completed, followed by two major reviews (Corrigan, Dell, Lewis, & Schmidt, 1980; Heppner & Dixon, 1981). Most of this research has focused on the events that influence clients' perceptions of counselors, especially their expertness, attractiveness, and, to a lesser degree, trustworthiness.

Considerable evidence supports the hypothesis that perceptions of expertness and attractiveness are enhanced by using appropriate cues (objective evidence of education) and behavior (therapeutic communications, self-disclosure). Behavior seems more robust than objective cues (Murphy & Strong, 1972; Scheid, 1976). Perceptions of expertness and attractiveness have been found to enhance counselor influence in specific conditions (Strong & Dixon, 1971), but the evidence is mixed. Recent research has focused on the impact of discrepancy-inducing interventions such as interpretations (Claiborn, 1982; Claiborn, Crawford, & Hackman, 1983; Claiborn, Ward, & Strong, 1981; Lopez & Wambach, 1982; Strong, Wambach, Lopez, & Cooper, 1979). Most of this research suggests that discrepancy, apart from any particular theoretical context, is an important variable.

All this research relies on a common method, the **analogue** (see Strong, 1971). Using an analogue, social-influence researchers hope to reduce alternative explanations through experimental control but still capture the essential processes of counseling. The results may increase understanding of the counseling process, although generalization of these results is not easily addressed (see Heppner & Heesacker, 1982).

A research example (Claiborn, Crawford, & Hackman, 1983) shows the recent emphasis on intervention research. College students experiencing negative emotions were exposed to three verbal treatments representing three levels of intervention discrepancy: (1) listening—low discrepancy, (2) congruent interpretation (summarizing clients' material in the counselors' words)—semantic discrepancy, (3) discrepant interpretation (presentation of an alternative causal framework)—propositional discrepancy. The experiment consisted of a brief counseling analogue (two interviews) with an emphasis on experimental rigor.

Assessment was based on the hypothesis that discrepancy interventions serve two general functions: establishment of the therapeutic relationship and the reconceptualization of clients' material to enhance clients' self-control. All three treatments contributed to the establishment of a counseling relationship, as assessed by a revision of the Barret-Lennard Relationship Inventory (Mann & Murphy, 1975). The two interpretative interventions facilitated participants' control over their negative emotions more than the listening condition (as measured by the Client Beliefs Inventory). The discrepant interpretation treatment enhanced self-control. Finally, all treatments reduced negative emotions, with discrepant interpretation the most consistently effective (Beck Depression Inventory; Beck, 1967).

This example illustrates two characteristics of the influence perspective: use of a metatheoretical approach, in which content and procedure are reconceptualized to reflect the influence process used (discrepancy); and use of analogue to capture these influence processes. Of course, the research described above is not without its flaws. Critical comments, since they are germane to the social-influence enterprise as a whole, are in the Commentary section.

Professional development

Little has been written about the way the interpersonal-influence process approaches professional development. Some writers (for example, Heppner & Handley, 1981) seem to argue that the training process is comparable to the counseling process: Supervisors first increase their influence through the enhancement of trainees' perceptions of supervisors' expertness, attractiveness, and trustworthiness. Second, supervisors use this influence to bring about desired changes in trainees. As experts, supervisors can encourage trainees to study certain material and to rehearse certain patterns of actions toward the end of broadening their therapeutic repertoire. In later stages, these directives may be paradoxical, so that noncompliance leads to desirable outcomes—internal control and a reevaluation of therapeutic decision making. Of course, the above is all conjecture, since social-influence writers have not explicitly examined professional development.

Commentary

As should be clear, the social-influence model of counseling is in transition. It began with traditional social psychology and recently has integrated communication theory. But in spite of its state of flux, the influence perspective has made at least three contributions to the field of counseling.

Contributions

The social-influence perspective, in its reliance on social psychology, has underlined the importance of **psychological theory** in counseling and research. Too often, practitioners, researchers, and students do not comprehend the meaning of the old saying "There is nothing so practical as a good theory." In a field that wrestles with anti-intellectual tendencies (for example, the substitution of bodily wisdom for scholarly wisdom), conceptualizing is a valuable contribution. This conceptual framework—a metatheory, really—provides an understanding of existing strategies across a range of theoretical orientations.

Another contribution is the articulation of the counseling process as an **influence process.** Counseling is not simply an honest human experience between two persons but an occasion for strategic responding through which the counselor stimulates client change. A third contribution is **analogue research,** which provides a somewhat controlled environment within which questions related to counseling can be answered with reasonable confidence.

Criticisms

It is interesting that each contribution listed above raises contentious issues. The borrowing of influence from social psychology has stigmatized counseling with connotations of a game. Terms like power, control, and strategic tactics suggest manipulation by counselors, who know what is best for clients, within a relationship that is supposedly interactional. Does the term *interactional* simply designate the familiar relationship between a "healthy" counselor and a "helpless" client? Such a question suggests that counselors' influence may not be the only process going on.

Another theory-related issue has to do with the reliance on clients' phenomenology. The focus on clients' attitude change has led to a preoccupation with outcome, one consequence of which is the neglect of how influence occurs. How do clients process discrepant information? Some researchers (see Petty & Cacioppo, 1981) suggest that cues for expertness and attractiveness are salient when persuasion is based on issues that are not the participants' primary concerns, while persuasion based on relevant issues and active, cognitive involvement leads to attitude persistence.

Another question concerns clients' cognitive processes evoked by transactions with counselors. Do all clients perceive counselors in the same way? What perceptual processes, schemas, or cognitive styles are responsible for variations in their evaluations of counselors and in their responses to discrepancy? Interpersonal-influence research needs to include process dimensions and attitude-research variables such as message and recipient characteristics. This latter variable is important if social-influence interventions are going to take individual differences seriously.

Outcomes relying on clients' self-reports raise questions about the impact of influence intervention on behavior change. The few influence studies that have incorporated behavior-change assessment used the subject's self-reported behavior change (Dell, 1973; Hoffman & Spencer, 1977) or behaviors requiring minimal commitment from the subject (Heppner & Dixon, 1978). Perhaps behavior change requiring subject's commitment cannot be expected in an analogue situation. This is a generalization problem. Many analogue studies involve brief contacts (one or two sessions) and unrealistic conditions (unattractive counselors); moreover, some do not involve necessary counseling conditions (face-to-face interviews). Recently, researchers have been testing the social-influence model in more appropriate experimental situations (Strong et al., 1979) and in actual counseling situations (Heppner & Heesacker, 1982, 1983). But the question of the clinical usefulness of social-influence interventions remains.

Summary

Counseling function	Characteristic
Establishment	Relationship variables establish a social-influence structure.
Conceptualization	Causal-attribution theory specifies causes amenable to change. Traditional diagnosis has been replaced with inter-

Counseling function	*Characteristic*
	actional approaches from family-system theory.
Intervention	Procedures are adaptions from attitude research and family therapy. Discrepancy is a key factor in stimulating client change.
Evaluation	Experimental methods from social psychology are often employed, especially the analogue.
Professional development	Social-influence processes are given prominence, although little has been written on training.

Communicating

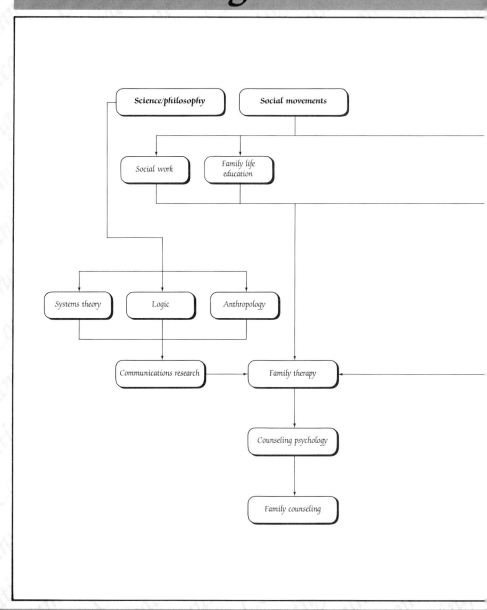

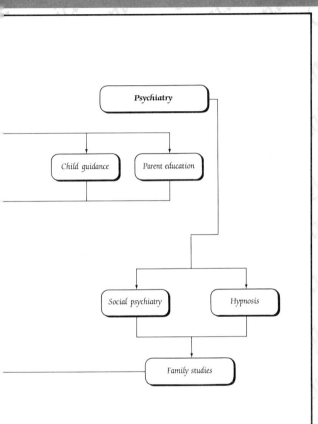

Psychiatry

Child guidance

Parent education

Social psychiatry

Hypnosis

Family studies

9

Communication appears to be involved in all perspectives. In traditional counseling and psychotherapy, **communicating** is understood as clarifying, making real, and helping clients understand their problems. In most helping perspectives, communication occurs within the constraints of a clinical model. The individual client is the locus of the problem, and the problem is caused by an imperfection in the client's genes or biochemistry or intrapsychic development.

Family therapy views communication in a broader context, resulting in new analogies and models. In these models, communication is seen not as linear, from counselor to client, but as circular, among everyone present (family and counselor). This focus represents a shift from the individual's personality to the individual's context, and from the content of communications to communications about communications (metacommunications).

Thus the communicating perspective, emerging from the family-therapy movement, is more than a different approach to counseling. It is a different way of looking at behavior. It can be described as communications research on interpersonal relationships of people in ongoing groups and represents a transition from psychiatry and psychology to social science.

Historical background
Social setting

There are many precursors to the family-based perspective. As with other helping professions, family therapy developed in response to social needs. Early influences on family therapy include other movements based on social need—social work, family-life education, child guidance, and parent education. In addition, a social perspective gained popularity in mental-health disciplines (social hygiene) and psychiatry (Adler, 1939; Sullivan, 1953/1968).

These early influences provided a family focus that was to receive particular attention after World War II. After the war, with families reunited or newly established, problems arose involving marital discord, divorce, juvenile delinquency, and breakdowns in intergenerational relationships. Many helping professionals continued to work with the individual to solve these problems, but others began to consider family relationships and transactions. Borrowing from earlier social movements and extrapolating from other disciplines, researchers and clinicians developed new ways of thinking about and treating problems, focusing on family relationships. Psychiatrists such as Ackerman, Lidz, Wynne, Bowen, Nagy, Whitaker, and Jackson became interested in family study as a result of their exposure to families of schizophrenics.

The Palo Alto group

Family therapy began in the early 1950s in a dozen places among many different researchers and clinicians. Although many differences exist and many changes have occurred, the Palo Alto group (Bateson, Haley, Weakland, Jackson, and Satir) and their work on family-communications theory provide an excellent overview of the historical and conceptual foundations of family therapy.

The Palo Alto group owes much of its existence and conceptual heritage to Gregory Bateson, who assembled the group and gave it direction. Bateson, an anthropologist and philosopher, received research grants to study communication patterns in a number of situations. He later focused on families of schizophrenics in the Palo Alto Veterans Administration Hospital. As an anthropologist, Bateson had been influenced by Franz Boas and his concern for cultural understanding of human experience. Bateson did field work in the South Pacific and elsewhere, studying the social systems of various animals and human cultures (Iatmul culture in New Guinea). In those studies, Bateson joined with his engineer-turned-anthropologist colleague, John Weakland. They began to understand the infinite variety of human experience through an understanding of the context in which a particular behavior occurred.

As a philosopher, Bateson was interested in general-systems theory (Bertalanffy, 1968), cybernetics (Wiener, 1948/1961), communication theory (Shannon & Weaver, 1949), and logic (Whitehead & Russell, 1910). From these interests in systems and communications flowed some of the major working assumptions of the Palo Alto group. All human behavior was viewed as communication, and human beings were seen as systems and parts of larger systems.

The logical model

One communication aspect that fascinated Bateson and the Palo Alto group was paradox, such as the classic "I am lying" paradox (it is true only if it is false and false only if it is true). Bateson formulated an understanding of paradoxical communications as communications at different logical levels. There is the evident content of the paradoxical statement ("I am lying"), and there is a qualification of content ("I expect you to believe what I say to you"), or metacommunication. When meta-statements are made clear, paradox is transformed into contradiction between the levels of logic.

This logical model, encompassing a levels analysis of communication, provided a foundation for the Palo Alto approach to family therapy. Jay Haley, a communications specialist, became interested in Frankl's (1960) work on paradoxical intention and the ingenious work of Milton Erickson (see Haley, 1973), a hypnotherapist, specializing in paradoxical interventions. Later, a paradoxical approach would become the trademark of the Palo Alto group.

The initial Palo Alto group (Bateson, Weakland, and Haley) applied the logical model to various situations (humor, popular movies). Later, Don Jackson, a psychiatrist with clinical experience with schizophrenics, gave a lecture at the Palo Alto Veterans Administration Hospital on family homeostasis, which Bateson attended. After that encounter, Jackson joined the Palo Alto group, which began to apply communications research to clinical problems. These clinical applications generated one of the most discussed papers in psychiatry (Bateson, Jackson, Haley, & Weakland, 1956). The paper, focusing on pathological communications within families, announced the double-bind theory (that is, distorted communications are created as a result of responding to contradictory messages).

The Mental Research Institute

Jackson extended these clinical applications through presentations at American Psychiatric Association meetings, publications (Jackson, 1957), and the establishment of the Mental Research Institute (MRI). Meetings with other family therapists resulted in a journal *(Family Process)* and the recruitment of other clinically oriented family therapists (for example, Satir). In the early 1960s, others joined MRI (Riskin, Watzlawick, Haley, Weakland) and expanded research (Riskin & Faunce, 1970), publications (Watzlawick, Beavin, & Jackson, 1967), training (Satir), and practice (Brief Therapy Center). In the ensuing years, the MRI continued to work in the areas of communication, family systems, and larger social systems (see Bodin, 1981).

During this time of expansion and growth, people associated with the Palo Alto group went their separate ways. Jackson died in 1968. Satir became involved in the human-growth movement and eventually became the first director of the Esalen Institute at Big Sur, California. Haley and Weakland joined MRI after the close of the Bateson projects. Later, Haley left MRI to join Minuchin and Montalvo at the Philadelphia Child Guidance Clinic, and in 1976 Haley left for Washington, D.C., to establish his own family-therapy institute with his wife, Cloe Madanes.

Approach

Strategic therapy has evolved from and represents the concepts of communications theory. In the strategic approach to family therapy (Haley, 1964, 1973, 1976), counselors initiate action during treatment and design a particular approach for each problem. Although this approach is yet to be fully integrated into counseling, it is influencing counseling writers

(Ivey & Simek-Downing, 1980; Strong & Claiborn, 1982) and appears to be growing in popularity among counseling psychologists.

Orientation

Most of the general concepts presented earlier apply to the strategic approach, including (1) contextualism, (2) systems thinking, (3) circular causality, and (4) levels of communication. Fundamental to communication theory is the idea that communication defines the nature of a relationship; that is, individuals interrelate through communication. Moreover, such communication has different levels of meaning.

In addition to these fundamental concepts, Haley stressed the role of power in relationships. From his observation of families and his exposure to experimental social-psychology literature on coalitions in small groups, Haley became interested in the power tactics of families. To Haley, the central issue is control. The struggle is not to control the other person but to control the definition of the relationship. Thus symptoms do not reflect intrapsychic conflicts but interpersonal events—the tactics used in defining the relationship. For example, a husband refuses to attend social events because he suffers from severe social anxiety. He does not acknowledge that he controls his wife's social life, since his refusal is blamed on his extreme shyness, over which he has no control. The wife faces a dilemma: she cannot acknowledge that he is responsible for her lack of social experiences, since that is due to his shyness; but for the same reason she also cannot refuse to let him control her.

To Haley, symptoms are a strategy for dealing with people and reflect an improperly functioning family organization. As a family therapist, he takes responsibility for changing the family organization, relying heavily on directives or tasks, often of a paradoxical nature, to counteract families' maladaptive efforts to solve their control issues. He uses an active, goal-directed, brief-treatment approach, focusing on changing specific problematic behaviors. The strategic approach is not intended for use over a long term, nor does it necessarily involve insight, resolution of intrapsychic conflicts, or growth experiences. It follows a careful and systematic plan analogous to a medical approach: first, establish control (the doctor is in charge), then diagnose, then resolve the problem (fix the broken bone).

Establishment

The issue of control is the central focus in the establishment of a therapeutic relationship. Although it is assumed, if not stated openly, that most strategic counselors rely on traditional relationship and social-influence skills in order to relate to their clients in a humane and influential way, the important issue is for the counselor to gain control of the relationship. One major control issue concerns who is to be involved in treatment. Unlike individual psychotherapy, family counseling does not typically involve a single individual but all parts of the system (grandparents, school), and even if an individual is seen alone, the problem is conceptualized as involving at least two or more people.

One strategy for obtaining power in the therapeutic relationship is the use of **paradoxical tasks.** In the establishment phase, the counseling setting implies change, but the therapist may not ask for change. If clients who are not requested to change obey, they have allowed someone else to be in control and to make the rules. If they disobey, they have reduced their symptoms and may have regained a sense of their own control. It is argued that nondirective procedures enable clients to continue to control others and the counselor with their symptoms, and the use of persuasion leads to clients' attempts to change, followed by their resistance and failure, and eventually the defeat of counselor control.

Another strategy used to enhance a counselor's potency is **positive interpretation.** Blame and criticism elicit resistance from family members, so the pejorative labels are made positive—"hostile behavior" becomes "concerned interest." "Problems" are "family stumbling blocks," a term indicating that problems are shared rather than belonging to a single individual. Whatever positive-interpretation tactic is used, the family's symptomatic behavior is redefined to become understandable.

The structure of the counseling process is straightforward. Counselors assume responsibility; they are the experts and they determine all aspects of the counseling process. Clients are assumed to be aware of their problems but unable to solve them. The transactions between counselors and clients focus on tasks that enable counselors, through strategic problem solving, to change families' behavior with or without their awareness. Change is brought about by interaction rather than by insight, interpretation, or catharsis.

Conceptualization

As in most problem-solving approaches, emphasis is given to problem identification, although Haley has rejected traditional models of assessment. For Haley, individual problems are **system problems,** symptoms of dysfunctional power arrangements within an improperly functioning family organization rather than signs of personality disorganization. Individual symptoms are viewed as adaptive responding rather than as irrational or maladaptive. For example, a bright boy's continual failure in school is viewed as a symptom, an adaptive response to his father's lack of employment. In the context of his family life, the boy's symptom may be necessary to family stability at a time when the father needs protection. Recently, Haley (1977) has emphasized sequences of behavior that circle around the problem. He describes these sequences in terms of family organization. In a family composed of a problem child, one overinvolved parent, and a less concerned parent, the child acts out his problem, elicits alternate anger and forgiveness from the overinvolved parent and somewhat less concern from the other parent. This results in recurring feelings of exasperation by the overinvolved parent and continuing marital fights about discipline.

The interview is the main procedure for gathering information. It is composed of four stages, during which problems are identified for change. During the social stage, counselors observe the family interaction and try to get all members to participate (perhaps asking the youngest child the first question "Why are you here?"). During the problem stage, counselors ask each family member about the problem. In the interaction stage, counselors stimulate family interaction through therapeutic acts. For example, the counselor may want to see if the father and the daughter can relate comfortably in the presence of the mother, so the counselor requests that the father and the daughter discuss some topic of interest. If the mother interrupts their discussion, this is potentially important family information. (This diagnostic approach is directly tied to the communicating perspective; namely, action and change, in which every intervention has potential therapeutic benefit.) Finally, the goal-setting stage is reached, and the family is asked to specify the desired changes—not unlike the therapeutic contract in a behavioral context.

Intervention

In the systems outlook, the focus of interventions is on changing the family structure and interaction patterns rather than on changing a person's perception, feelings, or behavior. Strategic counselors are behaviorally oriented, selecting methods that work, focusing on symptoms, and giving less attention to family dynamics, awareness, and insight. Because problem sequences exist in the present and are maintained by the current behavior in the family system, changing requires intervention in the ongoing family process rather than interpretation of past events.

Hypnotic techniques and reframing

From the clinical work of Milton Erickson, Haley adopted hypnotic techniques as ways of managing resistance. Some of these techniques reduce resistance by providing an illusion of choice. For instance, a counselor might ask a resistant family member "Would you like to bring your mother next Thursday or the following Thursday?" The question of whether or not the mother is to be brought at all is bypassed. Another strategy is to provide two choices, one of which is so difficult that the client produces a solution or adopts the less bad and therapeutically beneficial choice.

Reframing, which also emerges from the Ericksonian tradition, is a method by which the counselor restates the situation so that it is perceived in a new way. Reframing is also related to the levels conception of communication—that all communication occurs at two levels, with the message at the second level qualifying what takes place at the content level. Thus the meaning of any event can change with the context. By reframing, a counselor changes the context, enabling participants to remove themselves from self-defeating sequences. For example, a wife constantly nagged and criticized her husband about household chores, reinforcing his reluctance to help, which reinforced her nagging, and so on. The strategic counselor reframed the context by persuading the wife to ask her husband for help because she couldn't do the task. This communication made the husband feel needed and competent and increased his participation in housework.

Paradox, directives, and tasks

Paradoxical intervention is a prototype of the double-bind situation. In the spontaneous paradox, one demands spontaneity. But the demand by its very nature cannot be fulfilled, since demand behavior is not spontaneous by definition. Thus a client can be trapped in a situation where compliance (demand to be spontaneous) involves rule violation (failure to be spontaneous), representing conflicting levels of communication. Strategic counselors use paradox therapeutically by directing the family in effect to disobey the counselor; for example, the family that is told not to change or to slow its efforts disobeys the counselor, resulting in improvement and resistance to relapse.

Tasks do not always involve paradox. Counselors can simply direct family members to interact differently. For example, a strategic counselor may be faced with a father who always supports his young son against his second wife, the new mother in the household. The counselor may see the mother and child together, directing the child to irritate the father and directing the mother to defend the child against the father. This task, combined with a suitable rationale ("let's see how Dad handles problems so your new mom might learn") can lead to a closer relationship between mother and son.

Structural disruption

Conceptually, many of the foregoing techniques can be seen not only as process interventions but as structural interventions, whose aim is to disrupt abnormal family coalitions. As a result of his experience with Minuchin, Haley thinks of the structural aspects of therapy as a developmental change process, in which families go from one abnormal coalition to another before establishing one in which symptoms are no longer necessary. In the example about the new mother in the household, the counselor attempted to disrupt the intense father/child dyad by encouraging the less involved parent, the new mother, to become involved and develop a relationship with the son. In this way, the coalitions could be shifted, enabling the new parent to be more engaged in the family process.

An illustration

An example, condensed from several interviews, may provide a clearer understanding of family-oriented conceptualization and strategic intervention.

Excerpt	*Commentary*
1. **Mother:** John, my son, is failing school and messing up his life.	The information in excerpt 1 tells the counselor that the mother believes that John has the problem and that no one else has anything to do with it.
2. **Counselor:** Dad . . . do you have any ideas here?	In response (excerpt 2), the counselor gathers more information by listening to the father.
3. **Father:** I don't agree. . . . She worries too much. He will be all right. He needs to be his own man. She takes care of him too much!	Excerpts 3, 4, and 5 clearly show disagreement between the mother and the father.
4. **Mother:** Well . . . you should get concerned. You never spend any time with him. . . . You don't have a job now. . . . Why should I do all the work?	

	Excerpt	*Commentary*
5.	*Father:* I don't understand you. I am trying to find work. You always got to harp on my not working.	
6.	*Son:* *[Interrupts and is visibly upset]* Doctor, you want my side of things?	In excerpts 6, 8, and 9, it becomes clear that the son and his problem keep the parents from arguing and exploring the bad feelings between them.
7.	*Counselor:* OK.	
8.	*Son:* Well . . . I just think I got a problem in learning. I can't concentrate. Math is real hard for me.	
9.	*Mother:* We have tried tutors. I don't know. Both of us are very concerned. Can you help John?	
10.	*Counselor:* *[Some time later in the interview]* It seems to me that all of you need a break. You seem to be all working so hard to make this family work. Mom, you have been working hard with John. Dad, you have been looking for work. I wonder if father and mother could go out one night next week, rewarding each other for their efforts. And John can have an evening by himself to watch television without hassles. Can we try this?	The counselor begins to intervene (excerpt 10). He first gives a positive connotation to everyone's efforts. Next, he suggests a task that is intended to disrupt the symptomatic cycle. That is, if the child is taken out of sequence, at least for one night, the couple may have to deal directly with each other, resulting in a rediscovery of the problems and possibilities of their own relationship.

In the above example, the counselor used family information in formulating a treatment strategy. It was apparent that the child's school failure might not be the problem, but the parental relationship itself. Thus carefully developed interventions were needed to remove the child from the sequence, enabling the parents to work on their problems.

Evaluation

Most counseling-process research has focused on the individual, be it the counselor or client. That is, it has studied the counselor's effect on the client and, less frequently, the client's effect on the counselor. In contrast, family researchers using systems-based ideology and interactional-communication theory have explained the counseling process through the interaction between the participants. From an interactional perspective, effects are reciprocal; that is, the behavior of each person affects and is affected by the behavior of every other person.

Haley (1964) developed new procedures to fit the interactional requirement. He studied **family-interaction patterns** of 80 families, developing a noninferential measure of family interactions—a record of the frequency of family members' speech sequences. Conversations were recorded between mother (M), father (F), and children (one child $= C_1$) and the order in which the family members spoke (FC_1, MFC_1, MC_1, MF, and so on). In comparing such frequency counts with the probability of randomness, Haley demonstrated that families follow patterns. Disturbed families used fewer patterns and engaged in them more often than normal families. The process measure also could indicate the effectiveness of family therapy. For instance, a disturbed family might move from only FC and FM patterns to other possible patterns—FC, FM, MF, MC, CM, CF.

Other codings schemas have been developed (Ericson & Rogers, 1973). In addition to designating speech order, as Haley's measure does, these more complex coding procedures provide information about how message content is communicated (for example, by assertion or question) and the relationship of the message to the previous message (for example, supportive or disconfirming).

Recently, counseling researchers have applied transactional-communication **coding systems** to relationship patterns in counseling (Lichtenberg & Barke, 1981) and supervision (Holloway & Wampold, 1983). Lichtenberg and Barke, using the work of Ericson and Rogers, translated messages into those that control (questions demanding answers), those that suggest being controlled (questions seeking supportive responses), and those that neutralize control (noncommittal responses to questions). These coded messages then are used to describe counselor/client interview exchanges.

Statistical analysis has also been affected by the interactional approach. **Sequential analysis** (for example, Markov's chain analysis;

Raush, 1972) enables investigators to identify therapeutic operations (chains of interventions) and the relationship between a therapeutic act and the interaction context. Sequential analysis is used in counseling (Hill, Carter, & O'Farrell, 1983; Lichtenberg & Hummel, 1976) and supervision (Holloway, 1982).

Professional development

The communicating perspective differs from traditional psychotherapy by focusing on the family system, not the symptomatic person, on present family transactions, not past descriptions, and on changing family structure, not on gaining insight. Trainees, however, have difficulty in ing from an individual to a family orientation and tend to treat individuals in a family context and to perceive individuals' psychopathology and interactions with family members as the primary focus.

In preparing family therapists to adopt the interactional model, Haley (1976) suggests **learning by doing.** Of secondary importance is reading verbatim accounts of family-therapy sessions, viewing instructional videotapes, and reading about, discussing, or hearing lectures on family therapy. In addition, an understanding of theory grows out of action and experience; thus theory is presented when trainees can fit what they do into a theoretical frame.

The trainees' first-hand experience with families is a supervised experience. Supervision can be through case-report reviews, case discussions, and observations (audiotape, videotape), but live supervision is preferred (Montalvo, 1973). The supervisor might watch from behind a one-way mirror and call the trainee by phone with suggestions ("Get the family members talking with each other!"). (The supervisor can speak through a "bug" in the trainee's ear or walk into the session, but these techniques are more disruptive.) The assumption of live supervision is that "uninvolved" supervisors can help trainees correct missteps and avoid family-dynamic entanglements that reduce trainees' potency as change agents. To avoid confusion, supervisors and trainees agree beforehand on some basic rules: the trainee is in charge, the supervisor only suggests, the supervisor interrupts only when it is essential, and so on. Thus live supervision protects the families from incompetence and allows inexperienced therapists to learn to do therapy by doing therapy.

The intent of supervision is to directly help trainees solve specific problems in the therapeutic situation, not to help them indirectly by solving their personal troubles. A trainee who has problems with authority figures and who must work with a family of police officers, for example, is taught specific ways to cope with police officers. Therapy outcome is emphasized, not the process.

Commentary

Haley, through his original work on the communication process and his criticisms of traditional psychotherapy, pioneered a new therapeutic practice, which required a new paradigm: interactional communication. This relational orientation resulted in nonlinear thinking, contextual assessment, family-system interventions, and transactional-communication research. Haley, a brilliant synthesizer, encompassed both the form and process of family therapy. He described the way symptoms control others, the power struggles and triangulations, the organizational sequences of a problematic family, and he developed strategic interventions to alleviate symptomatic behavior in families.

Critics, however, suggest that Haley has not integrated the form and process of family therapy but has oscillated back and forth (Hoffman, 1981). To these critics, Haley has shifted from studies of schizophrenic communication to a fascination with small groups and family coalitions, from the development of a strategic model of therapy to an interest in structure, and from a publication (1973) representing the process concern of Erickson to a publication (1976) representing the structural influence of Minuchin.

Many of the same objections made about psychotherapy are also directed at family therapy: lack of a widely accepted theory, little recognition of cultural influences, lack of public service beyond personal health service in private practice and outpatient clinics, and the inadequacy of the research. These criticisms seem warranted. Family therapy is also criticized for the same reason behavioral therapy is criticized—the ethics of the approach. Is reframing a trick to make real problems disappear by simply changing definitions? Does the use of paradox and authoritative directives follow informed consent and responsible decision making? To what degree is human dignity diminished by the use of covert techniques, albeit for seemingly appropriate goals? Of course, these critical questions might arise because Haley couches his treatment approach in a political context, in which he argues vehemently against psychotherapy. Such political rhetoric, often dogmatic, polarizes the therapeutic community.

As in most perspectives, the espoused theory seems different from the theory as practiced. For instance, how does one reconcile Haley's systems orientation (change anywhere within a system will affect the whole system) with his dogmatic propositions (change the family situation to change behavior)? Why not change behavior to change the family situation? Also, is not insight a useful means of behavior change for less resistant families with sufficient capabilities? While the answers to these questions are being developed, the biggest question is whether this new orientation can become a major perspective in a profession dominated by a focus on the individual.

Summary

Counseling function	*Characteristic*
Establishment	Relationship and social-influence variables enhance counselor control.
Conceptualization	Problems are system problems, reflecting faulty family organization.
Intervention	The focus is on family structure and interpersonal relationships.
Evaluation	The interaction is the unit of analysis, requiring new methods of investigation.
Professional development	Learning by doing is emphasized.

Organizing

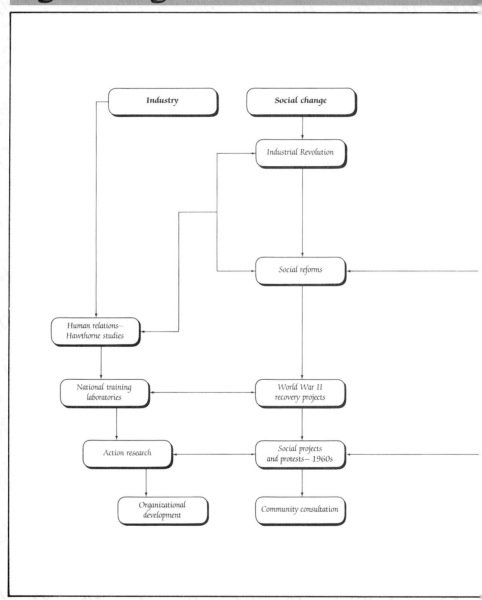

Industry

Social change

Industrial Revolution

Social reforms

Human relations–
Hawthorne studies

National training
laboratories

World War II
recovery projects

Action research

Social projects
and protests– 1960s

Organizational
development

Community consultation

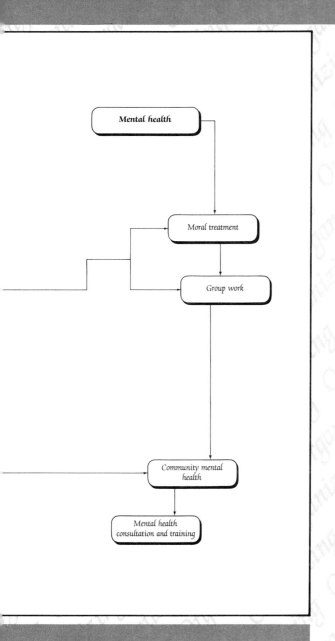

10

Organizing can be likened metaphorically to biology—the making of an organ—the process by which the parts form a body that maintains itself and acts. Although organizing has other connotations—ordering, structuring, efficiency—they have lost their reference to a biological organ, with its intricate functioning of related parts. It is the metaphor of organic biology that defines organizing in this chapter.

Those adopting an organic metaphor make important distinctions between traditional perspectives and an organizing perspective. Traditionally, individualism and autonomy are the frameworks for the counseling process. The emphasis is on helping individual clients examine their actions, take responsibility, and change that which can be changed. But modern corporate society requires a different helping ideology. The organic outlook, although it concerns itself with the functional autonomy of parts, sees these parts only in relation to the whole body, as meaningful only in relation to the environment. This conception broadens the helping possibilities. The external world is not an unmovable reality to which personal adjustment must be made but can be changed. Counselors can help people by changing families, groups, and communities.

Historical background

Historically, mental-health practitioners have shown concern about the environment. During the first half of the 19th century, moral treatment was dominant, along with an optimism about improving mental health by reforming social institutions. This reform logic went something like this: since mental illness is caused by brain malfunction rather than by demonic possession, and since the brain is easily influenced by the environment, therefore the development of therapeutic environments for the cure of mental illness seems prudent. These reform movements helped establish facilities where humane treatment and close relationships between doctors and patients were important. These movements go back to Pinel's work (1806/1977) in Paris; in America, Rush, Beers, and Dix epitomize the movement.

Another social-reform period occurred during the early part of the twentieth century. The United States had moved from an agrarian to an industrial economy, with sharp increases in immigration, urban living, and job specialization. Given these changes in social climate and technology, the demand for services overwhelmed the earlier doctor/patient model. Helping services began to structure their aid in terms of groups—YMCA work, vocational education in the schools, and group work with hospital patients.

A more recent period of social change occurred in the 1960s. The mental-health professions again manifested considerable concern regarding the role of the environment in behavioral problems. This concern was expressed through the establishment of the Joint Commission on Mental Illness and Health and the commission's subsequent recommendations for the development of community mental-health centers (Joint Commission on Mental Illness and Health, 1961). The community mental-health movement challenged psychologists (1) to play a fuller role in the mental-health movements; (2) to assume community roles in addition to their clinical work; (3) to deal not only with the sick but with the healthy; and (4) to address public issues and intervene in social systems. These challenges stimulated the establishment of the Division of Community Psychology within the American Psychological Association and the creation of several university training programs in community psychology.

Environmental concerns and organizing activities have also been part of the history of counseling. As Rockwell and Rothney (1961) point out, the guidance movement was part of the social-reform movement. Environmental ideology also affected the way counseling authors talked about the profession. Williamson (1939b), Wrenn (1962), and Shoben (1962) asked counselors who shape educational systems to be more responsive to students' needs. Counseling journals of the 1960s and 1970s explored social and cultural issues. Stewart and Warnath (1965) described the counselor as a social engineer; Blocher (1966/1974) pointed to an ecology of human development. Recent textbooks have been concerned with community counseling (Blocher & Biggs, 1983; Lewis & Lewis, 1977/1983). Obviously something is going on here; namely, counseling does not have to be restricted to intrapsychic theories or individual modes of practice.

Approach

Most of the earlier chapters discuss counseling in terms of theoretical models within the context of an individual-psychotherapy modality, even though many transcend that mode. This chapter discusses broader systems-based modalities: group work, consultation, organizational development, and community action.

Establishment

Relationship building is common to all counseling-practice modalities. The quality of the relationship is critical, and trust is important. The question of trust is magnified in services to social systems. Social systems, whether families, community groups, or other organizations, tend to become central to an individual's identity and security. When service providers enter the social system, its members interpret their entrance as a weakness in their system and feel threatened. Service providers' first task, therefore, is to establish rapport with the members of the social system. Collaboration is emphasized, and change is not imposed from without but is the responsibility of members of the social system.

But collaboration depends on trust, and gaining trust is especially difficult in organizing activities. In **group work,** group members may fear exposing their difficulties and become passive, sitting silently and asking for lectures, which leads to a focus on the group leader as expert and diminishes the cooperative nature of the group experience. Group leaders can respond to the group's passivity by taking a lower profile and by communicating their own difficulties in new situations ("It will probably take some time and experience for us to get used to each other and feel comfortable with each other. I know it's hard for me to get started in a new group").

In **consultation,** the first stage in the development of the relationship is often a testing of the consultants' competency and integrity. In responding to these challenges, consultants emphasize the peer nature of the relationship, listen to the clients, and remain nonjudgmental. Consultants can reinforce the interdependent nature of the relationship by mentioning their own difficulties in understanding the task and explaining that they depend on the clients for information about the nature of the problem. Without the information from clients, consultants cannot explore relevant alternative actions.

These same issues arise in **organization development** and **community action** (social planning). Traditionally, social planning was done by a small group of experts—government officials or social scientists—although information was sometimes gathered from community workers. Recently, citizen action has developed community-based planning, which enables community members and officials to become collaborators in planning and decision making.

Conceptualization

The primary task for a newly formed group is to determine the **problem** it was formed to solve and the **process** it will use to do it. Without an understanding of the process, members may use the group for reasons other than its purpose (for social approval, for example) and data gathering, problem identification, intervention, and evaluation will suffer. Organizational specialists approach assessment with distinctive concepts and methods, reflecting their social-systems orientation. Thus the presenting problem is always viewed in the **context** of its social system.

The following example illustrates the application of a systems framework to the diagnostic process. The chief of an intensive-care unit (ICU) in a large midwestern hospital asked a psychologist with extensive experience in organizational consultation to help him improve the service of the unit and reduce job turnover. The ICU chief diagnosed the immediate problem as deficiencies in the staff's knowledge and skills and suggested the consultant develop an appropriate educational program.

Preliminary data gathering

The consultant, however, suggested that more information needed to be gathered and, working collaboratively with the chief and staff representatives, used diverse methods to obtain this information—not only about the staff but about the ICU and its environment. The consultant obtained permission to explore hospital staff files and records for data about job turnover, staff illness, patient care, organizational structure (for example, staff/patient ratio, patient-care protocols) and staff demographics (age, educational experience, and ICU experience).

Interviews with administrators and selected nursing staff from the various work shifts elicited perceptions and attitudes about the ICU. Group interviews enabled the consultant and the administrators to explain the project and answer questions about confidentiality and so on. The interviews also enabled the consultant to develop rapport with the staff. Unstructured observations of staff meetings and the ICU yielded information about (1) interpersonal relations within the nursing staff and among nurses, administrators, physicians, patients, and patients' families; (2) physician/nurse communications; (3) nursing care in the ICU; and (4) physical surroundings.

These data-collection methods made it evident that the problem was not a simple education issue but concerned job stress and involved the staff and the work environment. More structured data collection was needed.

Structured data gathering

To focus the diagnostic efforts, surveys were used to explore facets of the problem identified in the prior-assessment phase. These facets fell into three categories: staff-coping resources, job stress, and organizational climate. Information about two of these facets was obtained through standardized instruments that include questions about job stress (Maslach Burnout Inventory; Maslach & Jackson, 1981), work environment (Work Environment Scale; Moos, Insel, & Humphrey, 1974), and life stress (Life Experience Survey; Sarason, Johnson, & Siegel, 1978). Measurement of the staff's coping resources required a specially constructed instrument (Coping Methods Survey; Stone, Jebson, Walk, & Belsham, 1984). The coping methods instrument uses 15 narratives, which incorporate patient-care stressors, and 20 coping methods. It yielded information about the staff's stress perceptions and coping methods.

Periodically, staff meetings were held to discuss preliminary results and to provide an opportunity for the staff to identify problems and discuss them.

Problem identification

Once sufficient data had been gathered, it was possible to formulate a diagnosis. The work environment was identified as the major contributor to job stress. A new intensive-care unit was designed with a staff lounge outside of the unit, nursing stations with all patients in view, and a centralized administration office.

Summary

The example above demonstrates the importance of establishing a process: choosing the assessment team, gathering data. The assessment included the problems' context: social climate, physical design, organizational structure. Although the example suggests that assessment occurs once, it is never finished. In addition, an assessment method can be a successful intervention, such as the group interviews, which had a beneficial effect on the staff.

The task assigned to a consultant is often vague ("help us do a better job"). Other times, the client has defined the problem without regard to its context. Thus a broad data-collection approach, which includes information about the environment, is important. Consultants may also use group dynamics, skills, or power structures, depending on the nature of the organization.

Intervention

Group work

Generally, modern group work can be traced to social-work groups, psychotherapy groups, and to the study of group dynamics. Social-work groups, exemplified by Jane Addams's Hull House, brought together people having common social, economic, and personal problems. Using social reform as a guiding force, these groups organized to improve housing, recreation, education, and working conditions. A major emphasis was the participants' membership in a group with a common goal.

Slowly, groups emerged that were concerned with the personal needs of their members as well as with social causes. In 1905 Joseph Pratt brought together poor tubercular patients for support and medical treatment. Gradually, psychotherapy groups were conceptualized within psychoanalysis (Wolf & Schwartz, 1962), existentialism (Hora, 1959), and behaviorism (Rose, 1976) and used formats such as psychodrama (Moreno, 1946/1959) and gestalt-therapy workshops (Perls, Hefferline, & Goodman, 1951). The psychological experience of each person was an important aspect of these later group therapies.

Advocates of group dynamics believe that group treatment that focuses on the individual person is limited in dealing with group processes. According to the group dynamicists, an appreciation of social psychology (for example, Lewin's field theory) is needed in order to recognize the group as a discrete entity. In this sense, group therapists (for example, Whitaker & Lieberman, 1964) and human-relations counselors (Rogers, 1970) concern themselves with intensive group experiences.

A recent group-work model called the **theme-centered interactional method** (Cohen, 1969, 1972) incorporates many of these preceding influences. The method is appropriate for counselors specializing in helping groups in the community, the work setting, and the school deal with such topics as drug abuse, race relations, police/community relationships, nuclear disarmament, and equity issues.

From her supervision of psychotherapists and leaders in theme-centered workshops, Cohen discovered that the theme and the group's interaction often intermeshed and illuminated personal problems. In one instance, a presenting therapist's insecurity in dealing with a successful although schizoid patient was paralleled by his difficulty in relating to his more experienced coparticipants in the group. Both in therapy and in the group, the insecure therapist was dependent, complacent, and overcautious. During group discussions, other participants also admitted being fearful and dependent in the presence of the group leader, who appeared superior, remote, and all-knowing. The insecure therapist and the other participants were led to recognize that insecurity and dependency can lead to rationalizations for avoiding activity and responsibility ("All one can do when one is with a successful person or in a group of experts is to listen with humility").

Applications of the theme model were broadened by Cohen and introduced into industry (management relations), education (living learning versus dead learning), and personal development (freeing creativity). Principles and procedures evolved, and a model was articulated. Cohen wove many of the historical influences of group work into her model. In her I-we-it triangle, she described the central aspects of social interaction. The *I* (psychological experience of the individual) and the *we* (group interrelationships) represent the group process, the emotional-experiential interactions of group psychotherapy and group dynamics. The *it* (group task) along with the globe concept (group context) are content oriented, focusing on the awareness and cognitive learning of the social-work group of the early reformers.

Methodologically, Cohen and her colleagues found that the thematic approach provides exceptional versatility. Although the workshops are almost always time limited, the time has ranged from a single afternoon to an entire semester. Procedures were codified and guidelines established: (1) assessment of problem precedes theme selection, (2) positive words are used, (3) forms of the pronoun *I* and the present participle of verbs are used ("being myself at work" versus the impersonal "world of jobs").

To start the workshops, group leaders usually open with a formal statement of the theme, which is followed by a few minutes of silence, during which participants think about the theme, feel how it is to be in the group, and connect the theme to their life situations. Group leaders are mindful of balancing themes and interaction: autonomy and interdependence, cognition and feeling, content and interpersonal process, the here-and-now of the group and the there-and-then of the outside world. These balances are necessary so that a focus on one aspect, say interpersonal interactions, is not detrimental to the other aspect, individual psychological experience. To achieve this balance, leaders can stop the interpersonally focused action and ask each member in turn to express their inner thoughts at that moment.

Other group rules and procedures provide a framework to help members relate one to another autonomously. The five rules that follow are examples:

1. *Be your own chairman* (be responsible for your behavior).
2. *Speak as "I"* (state your own experience as clearly as possible).
3. *Give the statement behind your question* (state the unstated words underlying your questions).
4. *Disturbances take precedence* (address emotional interference).
5. *Speak one at a time* (don't talk while others are talking).

In sum, the theme model combines the valid personal experience found in psychotherapy and the organizational obligations of group processes. It keeps the theme focus by using specific procedures to bring participants who become enmeshed in personalized discussions or in group dynamics back to the theme.

More recent group-work methods emphasize one component or the other—career counseling (Knefelkamp & Slepitza, 1976/1978), life skills (Knefelkamp, Widick, & Stroad, 1976)—through which group members address such developmental tasks as midlife changes, retirement, sexual identity, and bereavement. Developmental groups reflect the task orientation of early social work, although the tasks here are personal, while efforts to link individuals to self-help and social-support networks (see Gottlieb, 1981) reflect the experiential dimension of group psychotherapy.

Consultation

Consultation represents a multitude of practices and in fact can be used as a generic term for all the organizing interventions discussed in this chapter. It has been defined in many ways, often leading to confusion and tortured efforts at defining, categorizing, and labeling (see Dustin & Blocher, 1984). The term is neither new nor the unique property of professional psychologists. In a general sense, consultation has roots in the early helping traditions (see Gallessich, 1982).

With advances in civilization, the helping traditions of folk society, which relied on primary relationships, could no longer provide adequate support for industrialized society. In response to technological and social needs, professionalization and institutionalization of human services began to grow. It is in this context that consultation is to be understood; namely, institutions frequently turn to outside professionals for help in the performance of their services. In this sense, it is appropriate to speak of consulting physicians, consulting engineers, consulting educators, and so forth, and this is the sense in which consultation is used here. Consultation refers to a situation in which a professional (the consultant) assists an individual or institution (the penultimate client) in enhancing the quality of services offered to a third party, the ultimate client (see Tharp & Wetzel, 1969). Of course, the nature of the assistance varies (education, behavior modification), and over time, these forms of assistance have developed models, with their associated practices.

Educational consultation evolved from the advisers of the ancient past who equipped others for societal survival and advancement through the transmission of knowledge and skills, such as food preparation and tool construction. In the recent past, educators G. Stanley Hall, William James, Lightner Witmer, and E. Thorndike lectured teachers on the findings from the new field of psychology (Cremin, 1964). Educational consultants take on the roles of adviser, educator, or trainer, transmitting their knowledge and skills to their clients, who in turn apply the learning to human-service needs. An example from mental-health services may clarify.

A consultant was invited to initiate a clinical-supervision system in a large, community mental-health organization. The organization included community agencies and hospitals. The staff had varying educational backgrounds and professional identifications (social workers, counselors, psychologists, and psychiatrists). The consultant used the educational approach, conducting a series of supervision workshops to help the staff develop a common understanding of clinical supervision and its various applications. This example helps to differentiate educational consultation from clinical consultation. In medicine, the physician/consultant examines the client's patients (the ultimate client) in order to make a diagnosis and recommend treatment for the client to carry out. In the educational example above, the focus was on the clients, whom the consultant taught to solve their own problem (supervision).

The teacher/consultee approach was created by mental-health professionals in response to the inadequacy of healer-based consultation (see Caplan, 1970), because the health-care needs of industrial society outstrip the consultation services available in the 19th century clinical model. The goal was to increase available services by improving the skills of an organization's staff in preventing and treating psychological disorders. Central to educational consultation is the spread-of-effect concept. That is, consultants, at the apex of a pyramid, consult with and educate their clients in the middle of the pyramid, who use their newly acquired knowledge and skill to help their clients, the broad base of the pyramid.

Education and training have relied on the development of articulated psychological approaches, such as social-skills training (Curran & Monti, 1982; Goldstein, Sprafkin, & Gershaw, 1976), developmental education (Parker, 1978; Mosher & Sprinthall, 1970; Whiteley, 1977), and human relations (Carkhuff, 1969; Egan, 1975/1982; Ivey & Authier, 1978). A common methodology connects these approaches: based on social learning (Bandura, 1969), training objectives are identified, sequenced, and integrated into a framework through an educational rationale, specific instructions, and appropriate demonstrations or models. After cognitive learning, trainees are given opportunities through behavioral rehearsal, guided practice, feedback, and reinforcement. Further practice of generalized learning strategies and self-management skills, in new settings or in booster sessions, enhances transfer and maintenance of the new learning.

In **behavioral consultation,** the emphasis is on the application of behavioral technology. Target behaviors are defined specifically and objectively and environmental events preceding or following the target behaviors are manipulated to bring about the desired behavior change.

Recently, behavioral technology has been used for such environmental problems as litter prevention, water conservation, and residential-energy conservation (see Geller, Winett, & Everett, 1982). For example, some researcher–consultants (Seligman & Darley, 1977) used consequent strategies to reduce energy use in the home, giving feedback to consumers about energy use along with comparative data (weather conditions, prior use, and control group's use) and a sketched face either smiling or frowning, to indicate levels of reductions or increases. Feedback slips were attached to the residence at frequent intervals and were associated with reductions in energy consumption.

The above example suggests that an established framework and a set of strategies for modifying behavior can be applied to environmental problems and that psychologists can contribute to their solution. The solution of environmental problems may not rely solely on physical/technical breakthroughs.

Organizational development

Organizational-development interventions are aimed at large, complex social systems rather than at individuals (Kelman & Wolff, 1976), although this distinction is not easily maintained in human-service settings. Organizational consultants focus on a number of domains, including work procedures and equipment, administrative structure, managerial and human relations, and the external environment. Their practices have technical, structural, relational, and environmental origins and methods, although the consolidation of organizational consulting in the 1950s (see Beckhard, 1969) resulted in a unified-system approach directed at multiple domains.

A major organizational-development intervention is **process consultation** (see Schein, 1969), reflecting the influence of the early human-relations approach to organizational life (for example, the Hawthorne studies: Roethlisberger & Dickson, 1939; McGregor, 1960) and laboratory training (National Training Laboratories, T-groups: Bradford, Gibb, & Benne, 1964). In the early days, organizational development was characterized by the assumption that through building a climate of trust, people's natural goodness will dominate, thereby solving many problems. This assumption was modified by practitioners and members of training groups (T-groups), who found that conflict is inevitable and group dynamics are important. Therefore, an outside professional may be necessary to facilitate the interaction of a work group or system. For instance, in the example of the intensive-care unit, the consultant met with the ICU's nursing staff at the invitation of the nursing director. The client's system preexisted, and the relationship was viewed as temporary and not voluntary.

Process consultation differs markedly from group work in that no therapeutic relationship exists between the consultant and each member. As in group work, there is a common goal, but stress is put on enabling the group to perform its common work, rather than on improving each member's psychological functioning. That is, the focus is on process events, such as communication patterns, intergroup relations, decision making, and conflict management.

The goal of process consultants is to increase the group's awareness of processes that affect outcomes. With increased sensitivity, it is assumed that members can alter nonproductive patterns and increase their effectiveness. For example, in the first meetings of the ICU consultation, only the younger members participated. The consultant pointed out this pattern—lively participation by new staff members and subdued activity by senior staff—and asked the group to help him understand it. Major issues quickly emerged; one was the appointment of an insider as a nursing supervisor without consultation with senior staff. The underlying issue was the senior staff's negative perceptions of their professional value in the ICU. Eventually, the group as well as the administration became aware of these legitimacy needs and responded appropriately.

Another organizational-development intervention is **action research** (Lewin's recommendation; Marrow, 1980). In conducting research, consultants help clients to become actively involved in the social processes under study. One procedure is the survey-feedback method (Mann, 1957), through which consultants survey employee opinions on such topics as morale, job satisfaction, and organizational climate, and report their findings back to the participants. In the nursing study, a survey was conducted with the ICU staff to identify coping resources. To construct the survey (see Stone et al., 1984), staff members identified stressful situations and coping responses. The data from the survey was given back to the staff, who examined them and, with their superiors, started problem solving and considering changes in the architecture of the new ICU.

Two major premises operate in action research. One concerns group dynamics, in which the client becomes an active participant/observer (Sullivan, 1953/1968), leading to close interaction between consultant and client. The other premise is related to cybernetics (Wiener, 1948/1961) and avers that continuous and accurate feedback is essential to keep systems functioning appropriately.

Community action

The community-action perspective assumes that problems are a function of oppressive social conditions, rather than individual psychopathology, behavioral deficits, or faulty work practices. Community action originated in post–World War II self-help projects in developing countries and in the confrontation politics of the 1960s. Its strategies are aimed at stimulating social change through political action.

Up to this point, discussion has focused on the mental-health tradition or a closely related one. Most mental-health practitioners are uncomfortable in the political arena, believing their goal is to facilitate psychological well-being, not political action. Even consultants believe (or hope) their activities are politically neutral. But from a community-action point of view, one either helps oppressed, disenfranchised groups by altering oppressive social conditions or tacitly supports their oppression by unwittingly perpetuating injustice. Therapists, according to this view, mask oppression by creating false consciousness (that individual change resolves social inequities) and by advocating personal adjustment to society, while consultants are the hired hands of management, helping malignant social institutions to survive.

There are two major forms of community-action consultation: community development and social action. A community-development consultant serves primarily as a technical adviser, while a social-action consultant is a professional organizer. However, both forms of community-action consultation rely on the involvement and sanction of community members.

In the **community-development** model, people are believed to be basically good but are perverted by social circumstances. The goal of the community-development consultant is to begin a process in which community members can experience personal competence through participation, leadership, self-help projects, and local initiative. The consultant brings together segments of a community with a common problem. To foster participatory democracy, the consultant then withdraws to the background, serving only as a technical adviser, while local initiative and indigenous leadership emerge. A recent example of community development as consensus building was the meetings organized to watch and discuss the television film *The Day After,* which depicted the tragedy of nuclear war. Community facilitators gathered diverse community members to watch the film, to discuss nuclear arms issues, and to plan collective actions (for example, lobbying local congressional members and educating the community). In this example, community-development consultants responded to the despair and powerlessness that many citizens experience in contemporary industrial society. Their efforts are aimed at activity, involvement, participation, and self-determination. Community development not only assumes a positive view of the participants, an optimism about their growth and reasonableness, but also assumes that government, bureaucracy, and community officials will be responsive to well-conceived community-development programs.

Social-action consultation makes no such assumptions (see Alinsky, 1972). The principal goal of social action is a shift in power relationships to insure a more humane and equitable distribution of goods. The principal strategy is conflict, which increases the participation of the demoralized and disenfranchised citizenry and establishes the professional organizers' identification with the community. Typically, the establishment (the haves) is lured into attacking the organizer as a dangerous enemy (a communist), thereby gaining credibility with the have-nots. To establish rapport with the indigenous group, the organizer identifies an issue that they are angry about and that can probably be negotiated successfully. For example, an organizer in a nuclear-arms protest group at a government defense site is arrested and receives media exposure. Through the exposure and denunciation by officials, the organizer begins to develop a small nucleus of followers, who identify an issue—the distribution of information at schools concerning the nuclear-arms race. After sufficient agitation (walkouts, class disruption, parental involvement) by students and parents, the school board agrees to meet with the antinuclear group.

In the social-action view, conflict is essential—one cannot negotiate from weakness (Alinsky, 1972). People are selfish and will cooperate only when it is in their self-interest; disenfranchised groups will make gains only with a fight. The haves believe in conflict-free morality, with its consensus building and adjustment promotion, but they will not give up power. The have-nots must seize power and convince the haves, through strength, that it is in the haves' interest to negotiate.

Evaluation

The evaluative research in the organizing perspective usually occurs in relevant settings through field studies, action research, and program evaluation, but it is characterized by weak design and instrumentation. This lack of experimental rigor raises questions about the value of organizing interventions (see Dustin & Blocher, 1984).

A consultation-research study illuminates these attributes of the organizing perspective. Jaffee, Thompson, and Paquin (1978) have described a family-consultation program within an urban police department. The program employed mental-health workers, who worked closely with the police in family crises. These workers were backed up by a management committee, which provided oversight; a professional advisory board, which provided referral; and a research coordinator, who provided evaluation.

The immediate goal of the consultation program was to assist the police in dealing with families in crisis situations. Additional goals reflect the characteristics of the organizing approach: prevention (early detection, referral, and intervention), community awareness (demonstration of the social role of the police; cooperation between mental-health and law-enforcement professionals), and spread of effect (field training for police officers in crisis intervention).

Data were collected with respect to five questions: (1) whether the program duplicated existing community services, (2) whether there were advantages in early intervention, (3) whether the program was preventive, (4) whether the program served the police and social agencies, and (5) whether cooperation between mental-health and law-enforcement professionals was enhanced. The evidence supported the program with respect to these issues. For instance, it was found that a majority of family disturbances occurred when other social agencies were closed. A majority of families contacted by social agencies within 24 hours after the crisis intervention accepted appointments, whereas after 24 hours had elapsed, 30% of them did not accept appointments. Repeat calls for police intervention declined with the introduction of the consultant service, and surveys indicated that police and social agencies supported the service.

The emphasis in this study was on real conditions and followed comprehensive data-collection and program-evaluation procedures. Although the immediate goal of the program was remediation, the thrust was prevention, education, and dissemination. But lack of experimental rigor raises questions about the validity of the family-consultation service. Experimental controls are absent, making causal statements difficult. Some of the evidence is indirect and problematic. That is, data should have been collected directly from the problem families, the ultimate clients. Evidence from these clients about the effects of the organizing interventions should have been systematically gathered. To rely solely on evaluative data from the penultimate clients (police and social agencies) begs the question.

Professional development

Unfortunately, formal training lags behind practices in a new field. Usually, organizing practitioners obtain their training in three ways: on-the-job experiences, formal subspecialty training within an established profession, and training in nontraditional organizations (for example, National Training Laboratories). The focus of this discussion is on selected educational experiences, based loosely on the proposals put forth by Gallessich (1982).

Consultation is viewed as a subspecialty within scientific and professional psychology. Preparation therefore consists of education in psychology, with course work in consultation theory, field work, a minor in an appropriate field like business-management theory and organizational theory, and a comprehensive examination in consultation. After completing academic and practical work in scientific and professional psychology and the minor area, trainees should undertake a year-long course on consultation theory and process, with didactic and supervised laboratory and field experiences.

During the first half of the course, trainees should study the conceptual, historical, and ideological foundations of systems thinking (see Gallessich, 1982). They need to explore models of organizational change, like education and training, clinical consultation, behavioral consultation, organizational development, and community organization. The staffs of various organizations could offer guest lectures, providing case studies of group processes, agency culture, ethical dilemmas, and planned change. After sufficient cognitive learning, trainees need skill-oriented laboratory experiences to develop expertise in building relationships, and in data collection, diagnosis, intervention, evaluation, and ethics. A case-study approach can be used, much like that of the Harvard Business School: case material is provided to small groups, which would use their targeted skills in resolving the problem. Guest lecturers can be used in the simulations; for example, playing the role of business executive in the contracting phase of consultation. Role playing can furnish trainees with high-fidelity practice and real-world feedback.

The second half of the course should be a practicum. The trainee is placed in an organization and develops a consultation project, then either formally evaluates it or proposes a plan to evaluate it. The trainee would be supervised by a seminar of other trainees and a professor. A trainee might, for example, serve a consultation practicum in a boys' training school, developing an incentive program and planning for its evaluation. In developing the program, the student gains experiential knowledge about organizational interventions.

Work in the minor area and preparation for the comprehensive examination should provide trainees the opportunity to develop some substantive depth in a domain of knowledge outside the discipline of psychology but relevant to organizational interventions, such as political science, business, and law.

Commentary

The organizing perspective certainly offers alternative modes of service delivery and in so doing challenges traditional, individual-based helping ideologies. Organizing modalities raise questions about oppressive social conditions, environmental problems, and the interpersonal and organizational context of self-development.

Organizational practitioners challenge traditional helping agents to become aware of the environment, to realize that the promotion of psychological well-being in a dehumanizing social system requires organizational efforts, and to remember that a behavioral technology exists capable of affecting complex environmental issues. These challenges are helpful to a profession otherwise preoccupied with the individual.

Another positive feature of the organizational approach is its emphasis on action research. Too often, applied researchers become enamored with psychological theories, testing propositions in contrived situations, with little formal correspondence to the actual helping process. Organizational researchers challenge these others to tie their investigations to the real conditions or processes of the helping situation.

On the debit side, much of the literature on organizing interventions lacks conceptual clarity and empirical support. In the area of consultation, a great amount of energy has been expended in addressing definitional issues, resulting in elaborate differentiation among goals and activities. Consultation models have been developed without sufficient linkage to psychological theory or empirical evidence. With the exception of behavioral consultation, organizational interventions are diffuse and confusing and are described in terms of service-delivery technology rather than in the language and concepts of psychology or other scientific disciplines.

Beyond these generic weaknesses is the naivete of community-development specialists. They often do not recognize the constraints that prevent cooperation, consensus, and positive change—inadequate time, money, energy, ability, and human resources, which prevent people from participating. Community developers, in trying to keep everything nice, cooperative, and logical, can fall victim to powerful minorities, who receive official attention through pressure tactics and angry confrontation.

Social action has unintended side effects if the action occurs for action's sake without proper planning, recognition of allies within the system, and programmatic development. Prolonged conflict can lead to disdain for those working in the system, even those working for change. Their attitudes may harden, they may become repressive, or they may leave, reducing the resources in the community. Without programmatic development, the problems remain after the battle has been won. The only change is membership in the elite, which is again ripe for overthrow.

The real issue for the organizational perspective is whether helping professionals and society are prepared and willing to maximize opportunities for delivery-system modalities that challenge the historical ideal of individualism.

Summary

Counseling function	Characteristic
Establishment	Trust and collaboration are facilitated by relationship variables and social-influence variables.
Conceptualization	Problems are defined in terms of a systems context.
Intervention	Systems-based modalities are used, including group work, consultation, organizational development, and community action.
Evaluation	Action research in the field-evaluation and program-evaluation methodologies are highlighted.
Professional development	Formal course work and field experiences in consultation are suggested.

Perspective on Perspectives

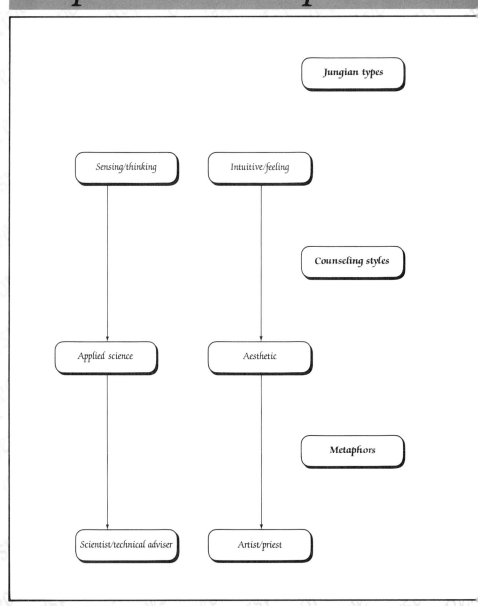

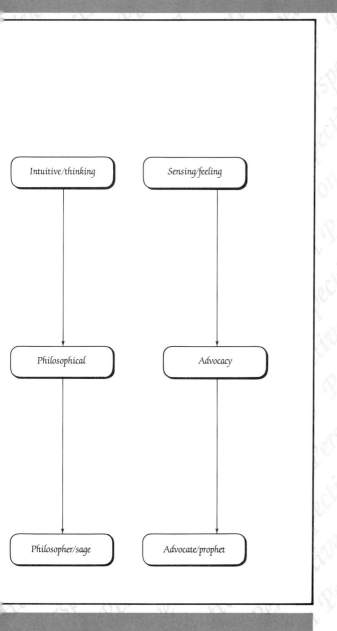

11

Tasks and assumptions

In this chapter the helping perspectives discussed earlier are placed in broad categories to illustrate the prospects and difficulties of an integrated approach to counseling psychology. Much of this chapter is based on similar integrative efforts in the social sciences, especially the work in social-science methodology of Mitroff and Kilmann (1978).

The first task is to classify the psychological dimensions describing the major counseling perspectives. Attempts have been made to differentiate approaches into the dimensions of rational/affective (Patterson, 1966/1973/1980), insight/action (London, 1964), and analytic/experiential (Sundland & Barker, 1962). From personality psychologists, additional dimensions are put forward for consideration: Lockean/Kantian (Rychalk, 1973/1981), pawn/origin (de Charms, 1968), and the nomothetic/idiographic (Allport, 1962). Mitroff and Kilmann used Jung's psychological system to examine differing attitudes toward science. Jungian typology integrates many of the traditional dichotomies and offers a framework for the classification of counseling perspectives.

Four assumptions need to be made before discussing the Jungian typology and the resulting classification system. The first assumption is that a good classification system helps to organize the patterns of counseling practice but does not reduce counselors to a type. Real counselors do not fit into any one type, because of their diverse, sometimes contradictory, behavior. The discussion of perspectives in earlier chapters indicates that counseling is marked by inconsistencies (for example, an emphasis on either individual goals or social goals) and consistencies (for example, an emphasis on relationship conditions).

The second assumption is that characteristics of any particular counseling type are not immutable. Each counseling type is a cluster of potential attributes that vary, depending on historical and situational conditions.

The third assumption is that classification systems are limited. The four major counseling styles that follow may not describe all forms of counseling. These four counseling styles are contrasted in terms of deliberately exaggerated features. Most counselors combine attributes of opposite counseling styles and thereby are not easily defined in terms of any one style.

The final assumption is that no one style is more valid or desirable than the others; every style of counseling has both strengths and weaknesses, and any style can become offensive if pushed to the extreme.

The Jungian system

Jung's psychological system is the foundation of the following classification scheme. Two dimensions of Jung's system, although discussed here in terms of cognitive processing rather than dynamic psychology, are of central importance. One dimension (informational) has to do with the kinds of input data preferred, while the other dimension (decision making) refers to the reasoning process characteristically brought to bear upon the preferred kind of input data.

Jung proposed that information is processed by sensation or intuition. In the **sensation** category are individuals who process information by transmitting physical stimuli directly to awareness. The senses—seeing, hearing, touching—register environmental stimuli, much in the way a photograph represents physical reality. Sensation types are realists, preferring the facts and details of a situation. They take a hard, analytical, practical, present-oriented, and objective stand with regard to reality.

In contrast, individuals referred to as **intuitive** process the incoming stimuli to a greater degree than individuals in the sensing mode, enriching and elaborating the perceived stimuli through semantic or cognitive analysis (see levels-of-processing approach; Craik & Lockhart, 1972). As William James indicated in 1890, "Whilst part of what we perceive comes through our senses from the object before us, another part always comes . . . out of our head" (p. 103). Intuitives are idealists. They are not oriented to the objective parts or the immediate present of a situation but prefer instead to use their cognition in elaborating and construing the hypothetical possibilities of any situation. Unlike sensing types, who analyze a situation into its constituent parts and gather objective data with respect to these parts, intuition types construct conceptualizations of the whole—the gestalt—of any situation.

A similar basic difference occurs in the area of judgment. One way is to use **thinking,** which is a reasoning process and relies on the rules of logic (beginning with a premise and following it to a conclusion) to assess the nature, meaning, and usefulness of things. Its opposite, **feeling,** bases this assessment on human purposes, needs, and concerns. Instead of asking how a person's actions or experiences are understood scientifically, the feeling-oriented observer asks how they follow from the person's needs or goals. Feeling, in contrast to thinking, relies on personalistic value judgments rather than logical abstractions. By feeling, Jung does not mean emotion but a style of reasoning that relates decision making to personal values.

In the Jungian system, each of these two psychological dimensions has two opposite psychological processes, with individuals developing noticeable preferences for and competencies in one mode or the other. Because of the independence of these dimensions (one can take in data either by sensation or intuition and come to some conclusion about the data either by logical or personalistic analysis), they can be combined in four ways to get four personality types: (1) sensing/thinking; (2) sensing/feeling; (3) intuiting/feeling; and (4) intuiting/thinking. Based upon the general characteristics of each Jungian type, and taking into consideration the attributes in each of the discussed counseling perspectives, the following counseling styles are identified: applied science (sensing/thinking), aesthetic (intuiting/feeling), philosophical (intuiting/ thinking), and advocacy (sensing/feeling). The classification system comprises these four styles.

Figure 11-1 shows the various counseling perspectives plotted on Jungian dimensions and placed in counseling-style quadrants. The figure suggests where the perspectives are in relation to others and their approximate locations within one of the four counseling styles. The approach selected to represent a perspective influenced the placement of the perspective. Many perspectives do not easily fit into any one counseling-style quadrant. For example, if Freudian psychoanalysis represented the healing perspective, arguments could be made that it would be placed in the applied-science or philosophical quadrants, due to Freud's commitment to the scientism and rationalism of the 19th century. Therefore, the figure should not be read in terms of absolute differences (for example, that guiding counselors lie at least six units above modifying counselors) nor as indicating permanent and nonoverlapping locations (for example, communicating specialists in family therapy are always placed in the advocacy quadrant).

The four styles

The applied-science and aesthetic styles are discussed first, followed by the philosophical and advocacy styles. The ordering, largely arbitrary, conveys some sense of the changes in style that have occurred during the history and development of counseling. The characteristics of each style are manifestations of an inner psychological attitude. No attempt is made to describe the many aspects of each style or the many forms that each style assumes in counseling.

Applied science

This outlook is that of the technical advisor, who conceptualizes problems in external terms and solves them by the application of scientific principles. The basic approach of the applied-science (AS) counselor is to reduce uncertainty through experimental science. In the AS system, counseling and science are linked, since science alone is capable of making clear progress. In the words of Claude Bernard, a 19th century physiologist,

> With the help of experiment, we analyze, we disassociate these phenomena, in order to reduce them to more and more simple relations and conditions. In two ways we try to lay hold on scientific truth, that is, find the law that

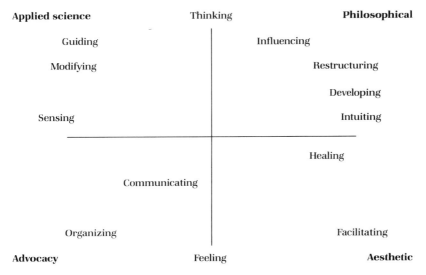

Applied science   Thinking   **Philosophical**

    Guiding   Influencing

    Modifying   Restructuring

                                               Developing

Sensing   Intuiting

                                               Healing

        Communicating

    Organizing   Facilitating

Advocacy   Feeling   **Aesthetic**

Figure 11–1   Four counseling styles as a typology of counseling perspectives

shall give us the key to all variations of the phenomenon. Thus, experimental analysis is our only means of going in search of truth in the natural sciences, and the absolute determinism of phenomena, of which we are conscious *a priori*, is the only criterion or principle which directs and supports us (Bernard, 1865/1957, p. 54).

Perhaps the AS concern for accuracy, precision, control, reliability, reproductivity, and so on, is best represented in the systematic-counseling approach (see Stewart, Winborn, Johnson, Burks, & Engelkes, 1978). In this approach, based on systems theory and technology, the counseling process is broken down into discrete entities, which, along with their postulated interrelationships, are organized and sequenced into a framework in order "to relieve students and beginning counselors of the burden of deciding 'what to do' during the different stages of counseling" (p. vi).

The scientific outlook of AS counselors characterizes their practices, some of which are displayed in table 11-1. The aspect that best captures the counseling-as-science view is the belief that science is value free. The belief arose because science appears to rely on consensual agreement, while value-laden decisions fail to command such agreement. This belief is deeply rooted in the impersonal structure of science, in which scientists discover impersonal facts, erect objective theories, and then test these theories. Knowledge is separate from values. In the counseling context, a similar separation occurs. That is, the domain of decision making for AS counselors is restricted to empirical issues relating to the selection of specific procedures for achieving stated goals, while decisions requiring value judgments (goal selection) are clients' responsibilities. This collaboration enables AS counselors to maintain their

Table 11–1   Characteristics of the applied-science style

Counseling function	Characteristic
Establishment	Relationship and social-influence variables are important, but they serve as a medium through which scientific techniques are used to assist clients.
Conceptualization	Precise, objective, and unambiguous goals are established through accurate, valid, and reliable assessment of external determinants.
Intervention	Treatment selection is based on observational and experimental evaluation.
Evaluation	The preferred mode of inquiry is the controlled experiment.
Professional development	Scientific education, skill training, and detailed procedural specifications for practice provide the major emphases.

value-free approach, even though being completely value free is an unlikely possibility.

Aesthetic

Like the AS counselor, the aesthetic (AE) counselor is characterized by a diverse set of characteristics (see table 11-2). In many ways, the role of AE counselors is similar to that of priests, to whom personal salvation, redemption, humanization, healing, and making whole are central. The overriding counseling concern of the AE counselor is not how science and experimentation can reduce ambiguity, generate knowledge, and thereby assist clients, but how the counselor or experimentation directly affect human welfare. Whereas AS counselors muster technology to serve knowledge, AE counselors muster conceptual skills to serve people. The AS counselor assumes that knowing in the scientific sense automatically results in effective care, while the AE counselor does not identify knowing and caring as the same phenomenon.

Aesthetics play a central role. In Freudian analysis and Rogerian therapy the focal problem is an aesthetic problem—expression. What clients have to express need only be freed from repression. The aesthetic solution is to use methods that will release inward drives—the inward artistry (dream) for public communication in psychoanalysis or the inward drive for personal growth in Rogerian counseling.

Table 11–2   Characteristics of the aesthetic style

Counseling function	Characteristic
Establishment	To a large extent, the interpersonal relationship is therapy.
Conceptualization	Humanistic models are used in which internal conflicts and personal needs are salient. Goals are framed in broad humanistic terms, like personal betterment or personal growth.
Intervention	Psychotherapy interventions are chosen with sensitivity and artistry.
Evaluation	Stories told by clients are taken seriously and used as evidence of desires, wishes, hopes, and fears.
Professional development	Personal learning through therapy, therapy-based supervision, and experiential activities are emphasized.

These humanistic and aesthetic considerations affect counseling functions. The therapeutic relationship becomes of greatest importance (Strupp, 1973). Conceptualization and intervention become opportunities for conflict, which AE counselors see as a beginning of counseling and inquiry. In fact, most AE-counseling theories set up personal dialectics—an explicit confrontation between what one has pretended to be and what one thinks one would like to be—in order to understand psychopathology.

Counseling as art focuses on the internal drama of a personal life as told within a therapeutic relationship. Storytelling is a human science, providing authentic insights into the human condition.

Philosophical

Table 11-3 lists the characteristics of the philosophical (PH) style. In contrast to the technical-advisor tradition (actions and deeds) of the AS style, the PH style relies on the tradition of the sage (beliefs and convictions). Its conceptual/theoretical approach is similar to the poetic approach of AE counselors, but its thinking-based approach is similar to the approach of AS counselors.

The emphasis on conceptualization (intuiting/thinking) is linked to PH counselors' desire to generate multiple explanations for any phenomenon. Whereas AS counselors think of reality as a single, precise,

Table 11–3   Characteristics of the philosophical style

Counseling function	Characteristic
Establishment	Relationship and social-influence variables serve cognitive functions.
Conceptualization	Clients are viewed as active interpreters of their experience. Cognitive-task performances are used to reveal distortions, deficits, and levels of development.
Intervention	Performance-based interventions are used to alter cognitive structures.
Evaluation	Inquiry focuses on conceptual-theory building, based on cognitive/mediational assumptions and using introspective data.
Professional development	A mediational approach is espoused, in which special attention is given to the cognitive development of the counselor.

scientific definition, PH counselors treat reality conceptually, thereby creating multiple realities, which stimulate creative and therapeutic work. The underlying notion is that there is a conceptual conflict (not a motivational conflict as in the AE approach) between competing realities. The PH style accepts such multiplicity and views the creation of therapeutic knowledge as a policy dispute among various assumptions, values, and beliefs. For the PH advocate, the uncovering and the rational analysis of these underlying assumptions are key.

The conceptual and dialectical aspects of the PH style are evident in the interpretation of counseling in terms of cognitive-information processing (Stone, 1980; Wexler, 1974); the connection between relationship-enhancement skills and specific cognitive functions (see Stone, 1980); and the development of cognitive-assessment methods (Cacioppo & Petty, 1981) and intervention strategies (Beck, 1974/1976; Meichenbaum, 1977).

The work of Albert Ellis (1962) reveals these attributes most clearly. His continual persuasive challenges and rational disputations, followed by his clients' articulations of formerly implicit assumptions (irrational statements) demonstrate the PH style. Regardless of one's admiration or horror at the Ellisonian approach, his perpetual challenging of one set of assumptions by another provides the flexibility and creativity for counselors and clients to boldly address problems in living.

Advocacy

Of all the styles, the advocacy (AD) style is the greatest challenge to conventional counseling practices and is the most difficult to characterize in terms of the Jungian system. The difficulty is related to the historical conflict between those who attribute behavior to intrapsychic causes (internalism) and those who attribute behavior to environmental causes (externalism). According to Jung, this conflict has existed throughout history. It has been represented by Nietzsche's Apollonian and Dionysian personalities and James's tenderminded and toughminded types. For Jung, the opposition was defined in terms of introversion and extroversion. Similar differences have been noted in the social sciences (inner directed versus outer directed; Riesman, Denney, & Glazer, 1950/1960) and mental health (intrapsychic versus environmental explanations; Levine & Levine, 1970). This conflict represents a basic orientation about life. The main interest of internals, like the AE and PH counselors, is the inner life of individuals, through which human nature is illuminated, while the externals, like the AS and AD counselors, explain human nature through the individuals' environments.

It is easy to see how the AD style with its external orientation differs from the introverted styles (AE and PH). It is not so clear how the AD style challenges the AS style, since both share extroverted interests. A review of table 11-4 provides some information. These characteristics derive from a prophetic tradition that affirms the objective reality of social facts and a commitment to social action. The commitments are

Table 11–4   Characteristics of the advocacy style

Counseling function	Characteristic
Establishment	The development of a personalistic community is instrumental in carrying out social-action programs.
Conceptualization	Problems are system problems enmeshed in social and political reality.
Intervention	Social-action programs are advocated.
Evaluation	Action research is recommended as a strategy of evaluation, intervention, and professional development.
Professional development	Active participation in the change process is preferred.

reflected in family-therapy assumptions: one cannot separate the client from the family system; all problems are family-system problems; action must be directed at changing the family system; and so on.

The commitments and assumptions of the prophet remind artists (AE) and philosophers (PH) that they cannot sever their art and philosophy from the social situation, but they also challenge the scientific beliefs of AS counselors, suggesting that such beliefs result in an ahistorical and apolitical world view. The AD style uses a personal-knowledge approach (see Polanyi, 1964), in which a person's needs are met by participation with others in addressing the social determinants of behavior.

An example of the AD style is the social-action approach of Saul Alinsky (1972). Alinsky assumes that improvements in mental health result from increases in political power and that therapy channels legitimate grievances into internal attributions—blaming the victim—and perpetuating the power elite.

Afterthoughts

In the original conception of this book, many of the current debates about identity, practice, and scientific inquiry in counseling psychology were thought to relate to differences associated with broad views (perspectives) about the counseling process. In examining a number of counseling perspectives from a common framework (counseling functions based on problem solving), it was discovered that these perspectives illustrate basic psychological differences and interdependencies. The more I reviewed these perspectives, the more apparent it became that a typology of perspectives could illuminate the psychological processes underlying how counselors think about and practice counseling.

But there is a danger in emphasizing a typology, of assuming a fixed or single style of counseling. Counseling must be dynamic, not static. It is not uncommon for a counselor to use one style in one kind of situation and an entirely different style in another. Pure styles probably do not exist, but an opportunity exists (regardless of the particular style in use) to use opposite styles because they are underdeveloped. Thus counselors are capable of developing other styles and of recognizing the blind spots of these styles.

Counseling theories are also dynamic, reflecting different historical periods (the Zeitgeist). Levine and Levine (1970) postulate that an external orientation is emphasized during periods of social reform, while theories emphasizing an internal orientation are prominent during periods of social conservatism. The development of community psychology and community counseling in the 1960s and the growth of private practice of psychotherapy and cognitive therapies in the 1980s bear this out.

The dynamics of personality and history give some understanding of how counseling styles change and suggest a flexible approach to counseling issues and debates. Rigid adherence to a popular style or theory neglects the possibilities of the dialectical opposite (underdeveloped style) and may lead adherents to mistakenly claim validity for popularity.

The typology of perspectives presented here perhaps will serve to sensitize counselors to legitimate differences, to help them respect divergent viewpoints, and to encourage them to try various methodologies. It is time to replace battles about style with the recognition that styles are interrelated. I hope this book is a start.

References

Adler, A. (1939). *Social interest: A challenge to mankind.* New York: Putnam.

Alexander, F., & French, T. M. (1946). *Psychoanalytic therapy.* New York: Ronald Press.

Alinsky, S. D. (1972). *Rules for radicals.* New York: Vintage Books, Random House.

Allport, G. W. (1962). The general and the unique in psychological science. *Journal of Personality, 30,* 405–422.

Bandura, A. (1961). Psychotherapy as a learning process. *Psychological Bulletin, 58,* 143–159.

Bandura, A. (1969). *Principles of behavior modification.* New York: Holt, Rineha. ι & Winston.

Bandura, A. (1971). Psychotherapy based upon modeling principles. In A. E. Bergin & S. L. Garfield (Eds.), *Handbook of psychotherapy and behavior change* (pp. 653–708). New York: Wiley.

Bandura, A., & Adams, N. E. (1977). Analysis of self-efficacy theory of behavioral change. *Cognitive Therapy and Research, 1,* 287–310.

Bandura, A., Adams, N., & Beyer, J. (1977). Cognitive processes in mediating behavioral change. *Journal of Personality and Social Psychology, 35,* 125–139.

Bandura, A., Grusec, J. E., & Menlove, F. L. (1967). Vicarious extinction of avoidance behavior. *Journal of Personality and Social Psychology, 5,* 449–455.

Bandura, A., Jeffrey, R. W., & Gajdos, E. (1975). Generalizing change through participant modeling with self-directed mastery. *Behavior Research and Therapy, 13,* 141–152.

Bandura, A., & Walters, R. H. (1963). *Social learning and personality development.* New York: Holt, Rinehart & Winston.

Bandura, A., & Whalen, C. K. (1966). The influence of antecedent reinforcement and divergent modeling cues on patterns of self-reward. *Journal of Personality and Social Psychology, 3,* 373–382.

Barrett-Lennard, G. T. (1962). Dimensions of therapist response as causal factor in therapeutic change. *Psychological Monographs, 76* (43, Whole No. 562).

Bateson, G., Jackson, D., Haley, J., & Weakland, J. (1956). Towards a theory of schizophrenia. *Behavioral Science, 1,* 251–264.

Beck, A. T. (1967). *Depression: Causes and treatment.* Philadelphia: University of Pennsylvania Press.

Beck, A. T. (1974/1976). *Cognitive therapy and emotional disorders.* New York: International Universities Press.

Beck, A. T., Rush, A. J., & Kovacs, M. (1975). *Individual treatment manual for cognitive/behavioral psychotherapy of depression.* Philadelphia: University of Pennsylvania Press.

Beck, C. E. (1963). *Philosophical foundations of guidance.* Englewood Cliffs, NJ: Prentice-Hall.

Beckhard, R. (1969). *Strategies for organizational development.* Reading, MA: Addison-Wesley.

Bellack, A. S., & Hersen, M. (1979). *Research and practice in social skills training.* New York: Plenum.

Bem, D. (1967). Self-perception: An alternative interpretation of cognitive dissonance phenomenon. *Psychological Review, 74,* 183–200.

Berdie, R. F., & Hood, A. B. (1968). How effectively do we predict plans for college attendance. *Personnel and Guidance Journal, 45,* 487–493.

Berg, K. D., & Stone, G. L. (1980). Effects of conceptual level and supervision structure on counselor skill development. *Journal of Counseling Psychology, 27,* 500–509.

Bergin, A. E. (1962). The effect of dissonant persuasive communications upon changes in a self-referring attitude. *Journal of Personality, 30,* 423–428.

Bernard, C. (1865/1957). *An introduction to the study of experimental medicine.* New York: Dover.

Bertalanffy, L. von. (1968). *General systems theory.* New York: Braziller.

Blocher, D. H. (1966/1974). *Developmental counseling* (2nd ed.). New York: Ronald Press.

Blocher, D. H., & Biggs, D. A. (1983). *Counseling psychology in community settings.* New York: Springer.

Blocher, D. H., & Siegal, R. (1981). Toward a cognitive developmental theory of leisure and work. *The Counseling Psychologist, 9,* 33–44.

Blocksma, D. D., & Porter, E. H., Jr. (1947). A short-term training program in client-centered counseling. *Journal of Counseling Psychology, 11,* 55–60.

Bodin, A. M. (1981). The interactional view: Family therapy approaches of the Mental Research Institute. In A. S. Gurman and P. Kniskern (Eds.), *Handbook of family therapy* (pp. 267–309). New York: Brunner/Mazel.

Bordin, E. S. (1968). *Psychological counseling* (2nd ed.). New York: Appleton-Century-Crofts.

Borgen, F. H. (1984). Counseling psychology. *Annual Review of Psychology, 35,* 579–604.

Box, G. E. P., & Jenkins, G. M. (1976). *Time series analysis: Forecasting and control.* San Francisco: Holden-Day.

Bradford, L. P., Gibb, J. R., & Benne, K. D. (1964). *T-group therapy and laboratory method: Innovation in re-education.* New York: Wiley.

Brewer, J. M. (1932). *Education as guidance.* New York: Macmillan.

Brewer, J. M. (1942). *History of vocational guidance.* New York: Harper.

Budman, S. H. (1981). *Forms of brief therapy.* New York: Guilford Press.

Buehler, C. (1933). *Der menschliche lebenslauf als psychologisches problem* [The human life course as a psychological subject]. Leipzig: Hirzel.

Buss, D. M., & Craik, K. H. (1980). The frequency concept of disposition: Dominance and prototypically dominant acts. *Journal of Personality, 48,* 379–392.

Cacioppo, J. T., & Petty, R. E. (1981). Social psychological procedures for cognitive response assessment. The thought-listing technique. In T. V. Merluzzi, C. R. Glass, & M. Genest (Eds.), *Cognitive assessment* (pp. 309–342). New York: Guilford Press.

Campbell, D. T. (1978). Evolutionary epistemology. In P. A. Schlipp (Ed.), *The philosophy of Karl Popper.* LaSalle, IL: Open Court.

Caplan, G. (1970). *The theory and practice of mental health consultation.* New York: Basic Books.

Carkhuff, R. R. (1969). *Helping and human relations: A primer for lay and professional helpers* (2 vols.). New York: Holt, Rinehart & Winston.

Chickering, A. (1969). *Education and identity.* San Francisco: Jossey-Bass.

Claiborn, C. D. (1982). Interpretation and change in counseling. *Journal of Counseling Psychology, 29,* 439–453.

Claiborn, C. D., Crawford, J. B., & Hackman, H. W. (1983). Effects of intervention discrepancy in counseling for negative emotions. *Journal of Counseling Psychology, 30*, 164–171.

Claiborn, C. D., Ward, S. R., & Strong, S. R. (1981). Effects of congruence between counselor interpretations and client beliefs. *Journal of Counseling Psychology, 28*, 101–109.

Cohen, R. C. (1969). From couch to circle to community: Beginnings of the theme-centered interactional method. In H. M. Ruitenbeek (Ed.), *Group therapy today: Styles, methods and techniques* (pp. 256–267). New York: Atherton Press.

Cohen, R. C. (1972). Style and spirit of the theme-centered interactional method. In C. J. Sager and H. Kaplan (Eds.), *Progress in group and family therapy* (pp. 852–878). New York: Brunner/Mazel.

Combs, A. W., & Snygg, D. (1959). *Individual behavior: A new frame of reference for psychology.* New York: Harper (reprinted from Snygg and Combs, 1949).

Corrigan, J. D., Dell, D. M., Lewis, K. N., & Schmidt, L. D. (1980). Counseling as a social influence process: A review. *Journal of Counseling Psychology, 27*, 395–441.

Craik, F. I. M., & Lockhart, R. S. (1972). Levels of processing: A framework for memory research. *Journal of Verbal Learning and Verbal Behavior, 11*, 671–684.

Cremin, L. A. (1964). *The transformation of the school.* New York: Vintage Books. (Reprinted from Knopf, 1961.)

Crites, J. O. (1969). *Vocational psychology.* New York: McGraw-Hill.

Crites, J. O. (1981). *Career counseling: Models, methods, and materials.* New York: McGraw-Hill.

Cronbach, L. (1975). Beyond the two disciplines of scientific psychology. *American Psychologist, 30*, 116–127.

Cross, K. P. (1971). *Beyond the open door: New students to higher education.* San Francisco: Jossey-Bass.

Curran, J. P., & Monti, J. P. (1982). *Social skills training: A practical handbook for assessment and treatment.* New York: Guilford Press.

Day, H. I., Berlyne, D. E., & Hunt, D. E. (Eds.). (1971). *Intrinsic motivation: A new direction in education.* Toronto: Holt, Rinehart & Winston.

de Charms, R. (1968). *Personal causation: The internal affective determinants of behavior.* New York: Academic Press.

Dell, D. M. (1973). Counselor power base, influence attempt, and behavior change in counseling. *Journal of Counseling Psychology, 20*, 399–405.

Dewey, J. (1916). *Democracy and education.* New York: Macmillan.

Dewey, J. (1933/1960). *How we think: A restatement of the relation of reflective thinking to the educative process.* Lexington, MA: Heath.

Dollard, J., & Miller, N. E. (1950). *Personality and psychotherapy: An analysis in terms of learning, thinking, and culture.* New York: McGraw-Hill.

Dustin, D., & Blocher, D. H. (1984). Theories and models of consultation. In S. D. Brown and R. W. Lent (Eds.), *Handbook of counseling psychology* (pp. 751–784). New York: Wiley.

D'Zurilla, T. J., & Goldfried, M. R. (1971). Problem solving and behavior modification. *Journal of Abnormal Psychology, 78*, 107–126.

Egan, G. (1975/1982). *The skilled helper.* Monterey, CA: Brooks/Cole.

Ekstein, R., & Wallerstein, R. (1958/1972). *The teaching and learning of psychotherapy.* New York: Basic Books.

Ellenberger, H. F. (1970). *The discovery of the unconscious: The history and evaluation of dynamic psychiatry.* New York: Basic Books.

Ellis, A. (1962). *Reason and emotion in psychotherapy.* New York: Stuart.

Ellis, A., & Harper, R. A. (1975). *A new guide to rational living.* Hollywood, CA: Wilshire.

Epting, F. R. (1984). *Personal construct counseling and psychotherapy.* New York: Wiley.

Ericson, P., & Rogers, L. E. (1973). New procedures for analyzing rational communication. *Family Process, 12,* 245–267.

Erikson, E. H. (1950/1963). *Childhood and society.* New York: Norton.

Erikson, E. H. (1968). *Identity: Youth and crisis.* New York: Norton.

Eysenck, H. J. (1952). The effects of psychotherapy: An evaluation. *Journal of Consulting Psychology, 16,* 319–324.

Eysenck, H. J., & Rachman, S. (1965). *The causes and cures of neurosis: An introduction to modern behaviour therapy based on learning theory and the principles of conditioning.* London: Routledge & Kegan Paul.

Ferenczi, S. (1920). *Further contributions to the theory and technique of psychoanalysis.* (J. Suttie, Trans.). London: Hogarth, 1950.

Festinger, L. (1957). *A theory of cognitive dissonance.* Stanford, CA: Stanford University Press.

Ford, J. (1979). Research on training counselors and clinicians. *Review of Educational Research, 49,* 87–130.

Fox, L. (1962). Effecting the use of efficient study habits. *Journal of Mathematics, 1,* 75–86.

Frank, J. D. (1961/1973). *Persuasion and healing.* Baltimore: Johns Hopkins University Press.

Frankl, V. E. (1960). Paradoxical intention: A logotherapeutic technique. *American Journal of Psychotherapy, 14,* 520–535.

Franks, C. M. (Ed.). (1969). *Behavior therapy: Appraisal and status.* New York: McGraw-Hill.

Gallessich, J. (1982). *The profession and practices of consultation.* San Francisco: Jossey-Bass.

Geller, E. S., Winett, R. A., & Everett, P. B. (1982). *Preserving the environment: New strategies for behavior change.* New York: Pergamon Press.

Gelso, C. J., & Johnson, D. H. (1983). *Explorations in time-limited counseling and psychotherapy.* New York: Teachers College Press.

Goldfried, M. R. (1971). Systematic desensitization as training in self-control. *Journal of Consulting and Clinical Psychology, 37,* 228–234.

Goldfried, M. R., & Davidson, G. C. (1976). *Clinical behavior therapy.* New York: Holt, Rinehart & Winston.

Goldfried, M. R., & Merbaum, M. (Eds.). (1973). *Behavior change through self-control.* New York: Holt, Rinehart & Winston.

Goldfried, M. R., & D'Zurilla, T. J. (1969). A behavioral-analytic model for assessing competence. In C. D. Spielberger (Ed.), *Current topics in clinical and community psychology* (Vol. 1, pp. 151–196). New York: Academic Press.

Goldstein, A. P. (1971). *Psychotherapeutic attraction.* New York: Pergamon Press.

Goldstein, A. P., Heller, K., & Sechrest, L. B. (1966). *Psychotherapy and the psychology of behavior change.* New York: Wiley.

Goldstein, A. P., Sprafkin, R. P., & Gershaw, N. J. (1976). *Skill training for community living.* New York: Pergamon Press.

Goodman, D. S., & Maultsby, M. C., Jr. (1974). *Emotional well-being through rational behavior training.* Springfield, IL: Charles C Thomas.

Goor, A., & Sommerfeld, R. A. (1975). A comparison of problem-solving processes of creative students and non-creative students. *Journal of Educational Psychology, 67,* 495–505.

Gordon, C., & Gergen, K. (1968). *Self and social integration.* New York: Wiley.

Gottlieb, B. (1981). *Social networks and social support.* Beverly Hills, CA: Russell Sage Foundation.

Gottman, J. R., & Glass, G. V. (1979). Time-series analysis of interrupted time-series experiments. In T. Kratoschwill (Ed.), *Single subject research: Strategies to evaluate change* (pp. 197–226). New York: Academic Press.

Gottman, J., Markman, H., & Notarius, C. (1977). The topography of marital conflict: A sequential analysis of verbal and nonverbal behavior. *Journal of Marriage and the Family, 39,* 461–478.

Greenspoon, J. (1962). Verbal conditioning and clinical psychology. In A. J. Bachrach (Ed.), *Experimental foundations of clinical psychology* (pp. 510–553). New York: Basic Books.

Greenwald, A. G. (1981). Self and memory. In G. H. Bower (Ed.), *Psychology of learning and motivation* (Vol. 15, pp. 202–236). New York: Academic Press.

Gurman, A. S., & Kniskern, D. P. (1981). Family therapy outcome research: Knowns and unknowns. In A. S. Gurman and D. P. Kniskern (Eds.), *Handbook of family therapy* (pp. 742–775). New York: Brunner/Mazel.

Haley, J. (1964). Research on family patterns: An instrument. *Family Process, 3,* 41–55.

Haley, J. (1973). *Uncommon therapy: The psychiatric techniques of Milton Erickson, M.D.* New York: Norton.

Haley, J. (1976). *Problem-solving therapy.* San Francisco: Jossey-Bass.

Haley, J. (1977). Toward a theory of pathological systems. In P. Watzlowick & J. H. Weakland (Eds.), *The interactional view: Studies at the Mental Research Institute, Palo Alto, 1965–1974* (pp. 31–48). New York: Norton.

Hartmann, H. (1939/1958/1964). *Ego psychology and the problem of adoption.* New York: International Universities Press.

Harvey, O. J. (1967). Conceptual systems and attitude change. In C. W. Sherif and M. Sherif (Eds.), *Attitude, ego involvement, and change.* New York: Wiley.

Harvey, O. J., Hunt, D. E., & Schroder, H. M. (1961). *Conceptual systems and personality organization.* New York: Wiley.

Heider, F. (1958). *The psychology of interpersonal relations.* New York: Wiley.

Heppner, P. P., & Dixon, D. N. (1978). Effects of client perceived need and counselor role on client's behaviors. *Journal of Counseling Psychology, 25,* 514–519.

Heppner, P. P., & Dixon, D. N. (1981). A review of the interpersonal influence process in counseling. *Personnel and Guidance Journal, 59,* 542–550.

Heppner, P. P., & Handley, P. G. (1981). A study of the interpersonal influence process in supervision. *Journal of Counseling Psychology, 28,* 437–444.

Heppner, P. P., & Heesacker, M. (1982). Interpersonal influence process in real-life counseling: Investigating client perceptions, counselor experience level, and counselor power over time. *Journal of Counseling Psychology, 29,* 215–223.

Heppner, P. P., & Heesacker, M. (1983). Perceived counselor characteristics, client expectations, and client satisfaction with counseling. *Journal of Counseling Psychology, 30,* 31–39.

Heppner, P. P., & Petersen, C. H. (1982). The development and implications of a personal problem-solving inventory. *Journal of Counseling Psychology, 29,* 66–75.

Hill, C. E., Carter, J. A., & O'Farrell, M. K. (1983). A case study of the process and outcome of time-limited counseling. *Journal of Counseling Psychology, 30,* 3–18.

Hirsch, P., & Stone, G. L. (1982). Attitudes and behavior in counseling skill development. *Journal of Counseling Psychology, 29*, 516–522.

Hoffman, L. (1981). *Foundations of family therapy.* New York: Basic Books.

Hoffman, M. A., & Spencer, G. P. (1977). Effect of interviewer self-disclosure and interviewer-subject sex pairing on perceived and actual behavior. *Journal of Counseling Psychology, 24*, 383–390.

Hogan, R. A. (1964). Issues and approaches in supervision. *Psychotherapy: Theory, Research, and Practice, 7*, 139–141.

Holloway, E. L. (1982). Interactional structure of the supervision interview. *Journal of Counseling Psychology, 29*, 309–317.

Holloway, E. L., & Wampold, B. E. (1983). Patterns of verbal behavior and judgments of satisfaction in the supervision interview. *Journal of Counseling Psychology, 30*, 227–234.

Hora, T. (1959). Existential group psychotherapy. *American Journal of Psychotherapy, 13*, 83–92.

Hosford, R. E. (1969). Behavioral counseling: A contemporary overview. *The Counseling Psychologist, 1*(4), 1–33.

Hovland, C. I., Janis, I. L., & Kelley, H. H. (1953). *Communication and persuasion: Psychological studies of opinion change.* New Haven, CT: Yale University Press.

Hunt, D. E. (1971). *Matching models in education.* Toronto: Ontario Institute for Studies in Education.

Hunt, D. E., Greenwood, J., Noy, J. E., & Watson, N. (1973). *Assessment of conceptual level: Paragraph completion method.* Toronto: Ontario Institute for Studies in Education.

Hunt, D. E., & Sullivan, E. H. (1974). *Between psychology and education.* Hinsdale, IL: Dryden Press.

Hurst, J. C. (1978). Chickering's vectors of development and student affairs programming. In C. A. Parker (Ed.), *Encouraging development in college students.* Minneapolis: University of Minnesota Press.

Ivey, A. E., & Authier, J. (1978). *Microcounseling: Innovations in interviewing, counseling, psychotherapy, and psychoeducation* (2nd ed.). Springfield, IL: Charles C Thomas.

Ivey, A. E., & Simek-Downing, L. (1980). *Counseling and psychotherapy: Skills, theories, and practice.* Englewood Cliffs, NJ: Prentice-Hall.

Jackson, D. D. (1957). The question of family homeostasis. *Psychiatric Quarterly, 31*, 79–90.

Jaffe, P. G., Thompson, J. K., & Paquin, M. J. (1978). Immediate family crisis intervention as preventative mental health: The family consultation service. *Professional Psychology, 9*, 551–560.

James, W. (1950). *The principles of psychology.* New York: Dover. (Reprinted from Holt, New York, 1890.)

Jepsen, D. A. (1979). Assessing career decision processes as developmental change. Paper presented at the meeting of the American Personnel and Guidance Association, Las Vegas, April.

Johnson, D. H., & Gelso, C. J. (1980). The effectiveness of time limits in counseling and psychotherapy. *The Counseling Psychologist, 9*, 70–83.

Joint Commission on Mental Illness and Health. (1961). *Action for mental health.* New York: Basic Books.

Jones, M. C. (1924). The elimination of children's fears. *Journal of Experimental Psychology, 7*, 382–390.

Kagan, H., Krathwohl, D., Goldberg, A., Campbell, R. J., Schauble, P. G., Greenberg, B. S., Danish, S. J., Resnikoff, A., Dowes, J., & Bandy, S. B. (1967). *Studies in human interaction: Interpersonal recall stimulated by videotape.* East Lansing, MI: Michigan State University.

Kagan, N., & Schauble, P. G. (1969). Affect simulation in interpersonal process recall. *Journal of Counseling Psychology, 16,* 309–313.

Kanfer, F. H., & Phillips, J. S. (1970). *Learning foundations of behavior therapy.* New York: Wiley, 1970.

Kasdorf, J., & Gustafson, K. (1978). Research related to microcounseling. In A. E. Ivey and J. Authier (Eds.), *Microcounseling: Innovations in interviewing, counseling, psychotherapy and psychoeducation* (2nd ed.) (pp. 323–376). Springfield, IL: Charles C Thomas.

Kazdin, A. E. (1978). *History of behavior modification.* Baltimore: University Park Press.

Kazdin, A. E. (1984). Statistical analyses for single-case experimental designs. In M. Hersen & D. H. Barlow (Eds.), *Single case experimental designs* (pp. 285–324). New York: Pergamon Press.

Kazdin, A. E., & Wilcoxon, L. (1976). Systematic desensitization and nonspecific treatment effects: A methodological evaluation. *Psychological Bulletin, 83,* 729–758.

Kell, B. L., & Burow, J. M. (1970). *Developmental counseling and therapy.* Boston: Houghton Mifflin.

Kell, B. L., & Mueller, W. J. (1966). *Impact and change: A study of counseling relationships.* Englewood Cliffs, NJ: Prentice-Hall.

Keller, K. E., Biggs, D. A., & Gysbers, N. C. (1982). Career counseling from a cognitive perspective. *Personnel and Guidance Journal, 60,* 367–370.

Kelley, H. H. (1967). Attribution theory in social psychology. In D. Levine (Ed.), *Nebraska symposium on motivation* (pp. 192–240). Lincoln, NE: University of Nebraska Press.

Kelly, G. A. (1955). *The psychology of personal constructs.* New York: Norton.

Kelman, E., & Wolff, G. (1976). Data feedback and group problem-solving: An approach to organizational development in schools. *Psychology in the Schools, 13,* 421–426.

Knefelkamp, L. L., & Slepitza, R. A. (1978). A cognitive-developmental model of career development: An adaption of the Perry Scheme. In C. A. Parker (Ed.), *Encouraging development in college students.* Minneapolis: University of Minnesota Press. (Reprinted from *The Counseling Psychologist,* 1976, *6,* 53–58.)

Knefelkamp, L. L., Widick, C. C., & Stroad, B. (1976). Cognitive-developmental theory: A guide to counseling women. *The Counseling Psychologist, 6,* 15–19.

Kohlberg, L. (1969). *Stages in development of moral thought and action.* New York: Holt.

Kohlberg, L., & Kramer, R. (1969). Continuities and discontinuities in childhood and adult moral development. *Human Development, 12,* 93–120.

Kohut, H. (1971). *The analysis of self.* New York: International Universities Press.

Kopel, S., & Arkowitz, H. (1975). The role of attribution and self-perception in behavior change. *Genetic Psychology Monographs, 92,* 175–212.

Kovacs, M., Rush, A. J., Beck, A. T., & Hollon, S. D. (1981). Depressed outpatients treated with cognitive therapy or pharmacotherapy: A one-year follow-up. *Archives of General Psychiatry, 38,* 33–39.

Krumboltz, J. D. (1964). Parable of a good counselor. *Personnel and Guidance Journal, 43,* 110–126.

Krumboltz, J. D. (1965). Behavioral counseling: Rationale and research. *Personnel and Guidance Journal, 44,* 383–387.

Krumboltz, J. D. (1966a). Behavioral goals for counseling. *Journal of Counseling Psychology, 13,* 153–159.

Krumboltz, J. D. (Ed.) (1966b). *Revolution in counseling. Implications of behavioral science.* Boston: Houghton Mifflin.

Krumboltz, J. D., & Schroeder, W. W. (1965). Promoting career planning through reinforcement. *Personnel and Guidance Journal, 44,* 19–26.

Krumboltz, J. D., & Thoresen, C. E. (1964). The effect of behavioral counseling in group and individual settings on information seeking behavior. *Journal of Counseling Psychology, 11,* 324–335.

Krumboltz, J. D., & Thoresen, C. E. (Eds.). (1969). *Behavioral counseling: Cases and techniques.* New York: Holt, Rinehart & Winston.

Krumboltz, J. D., & Thoresen, C. E. (Eds.). (1976). *Counseling methods.* New York: Holt, Rinehart & Winston.

Krumboltz, J. D., Varenhorst, B., & Thoresen, C. E. (1967). Nonverbal factors in the effectiveness of models in counseling. *Journal of Counseling Psychology, 14,* 412–418.

Lamaze, F. (1958). *Painless childbirth: Psychoprophylactic method.* London: Burke.

Lang, P. J., Melamed, B. G., & Hart, J. H. (1975). Automating the desensitization procedure: A psychophysiological analysis of fear modification. In M. L. Kietzman, S. Sutton, & J. Zubin (Eds.), *Experimental approaches to psychopathology* (pp. 289–324). New York: Academic Press.

Lazarus, A. A. (1958). New methods in psychotherapy: A case study. *South African Medical Journal, 32,* 660–664.

Leary, T. (1957). *Interpersonal diagnosis of personality.* New York: Ronald Press.

Leitenberg, H. (Ed.). (1976). *Handbook of behavior modification and behavior therapy.* Englewood Cliffs, NJ: Prentice-Hall.

Levine, M., & Levine, A. (1970). *A social history of helping services: Clinic, court, school and community.* New York: Appleton-Century-Crofts.

Levy, L. H. (1963). *Psychological interpretation.* New York: Holt, Rinehart & Winston.

Lewin, K. (1936). *Principles of topological and vectoral psychology.* New York: McGraw-Hill.

Lewis, M. D., & Lewis, J. A. (1977/1983). *Community counseling: A human services approach.* New York: Wiley.

Lichtenberg, J. W., & Barke, K. H. (1981). Investigation of transactional communication relationship patterns in counseling. *Journal of Counseling Psychology, 28,* 471–480.

Lichtenberg, J. W., & Hummel, T. J. (1976). Counseling as a stochastic process: Fitting a Markov chain model to initial counseling interviews. *Journal of Counseling Psychology, 23,* 310–315.

Lindsley, O. R. (1960). Characteristics of the behavior of chronic psychotics as revealed by free-operant conditioning methods. *Diseases of the Nervous System, Monograph, 21,* 66–78.

Littrell, J. M., Lee-Borden, N., & Lorenz, J. (1979). Developmental framework for counseling supervision. *Counselor Education and Supervision, 18,* 129–136.

Loevinger, J. (1976). *Ego development: Conceptions and theories.* San Francisco: Jossey-Bass.

Loevinger, J., Wessler, R., & Redmore, C. (1970). *Measuring ego development* (Vols. 1, 2). San Francisco: Jossey-Bass.

Loganbill, C., Hardy, E., & Delworth, U. (1982). Supervision: A conceptual model. *The Counseling Psychologist, 10,* 3–42.

London, P. (1964). *The modes and morals of psychotherapy*. New York: Holt, Rinehart & Winston.

Lopez, F. G., & Wambach, A. (1982). Effects of paradoxical and self-control directives in counseling. *Journal of Counseling Psychology, 29*, 115–124.

Lorr, M., & McNair, D. M. (1963). An interpersonal behavior circle. *Journal of Abnormal Social Psychology, 67*, 68–75.

Mager, R. F. (1962). *Preparing instructional objectives*. Belmont, CA: Fearon.

Mahoney, M. J. (1974). *Cognition and behavior modification*. Cambridge, MA: Ballinger, 1974.

Malan, D. H. (1963). *A study of brief psychotherapy*. London: Tavistock Publications.

Malan, D. H. (1976). *Toward the validation of dynamic psychotherapy: A replication*. New York: Plenum.

Mann, B., & Murphy, K. C. (1975). Timing of self-disclosure, reciprocity of self-disclosure, and reactions to an initial interview. *Journal of Counseling Psychology, 22*, 304–308.

Mann, F. C. (1957). Studying and creating change: A means to understanding social organization. *Research in Industrial Human Relations*. Industrial Relations Association, No. 17, 146–167.

Mann, J. (1973). *Time-limited psychotherapy*. Cambridge, MA: Harvard University Press.

Marquis, J. M., & Morgan, W. K. (1969). *A guidebook for systematic desensitization*. Palo Alto, CA: Veterans Administration Hospital.

Marrow, A. J. (1980). *The practical theorist: The life and work of Kurt Lewin*. New York: Basic Books.

Maslach, C., & Jackson, S. (1981). The measurement of experienced burnout. *Journal of Occupational Behavior, 2*, 1–15.

Masserman, J. H. (1943). *Behavior and neurosis: An experimental psycho-analytic approach to psychobiologic principles*. Chicago: University of Chicago Press.

McCain, L. J., & McCleary, R. (1979). The statistical analysis of the simple interrupted time-series quasi-experiment. In T. D. Cook & D. T. Campbell (Eds.), *Quasi-experimentation: Design and analysis issues for field settings* (pp. 233–294). Chicago: Rand McNally.

McGregor, D. (1960). *The human side of enterprise*. New York: McGraw-Hill.

McGuire, W. J. (1969). The nature of attitudes and attitude change. In G. Lindzey & E. Aronson (Eds.), *The handbook of social psychology* (Vol. 3, 2nd ed., pp. 136–314). Reading, MA: Addison-Wesley.

McNeill, J. T. (1951). *A history of the cure of souls*. New York: Harper & Brothers.

Meichenbaum, D. (1973). *Therapist manual for cognitive behavior modification*. Waterloo, Canada: University of Waterloo.

Meichenbaum, D. (1977). *Cognitive behavior modification: An integrated approach*. New York: Plenum.

Meichenbaum, D., & Butler, L. (1978). Cognitive etiology: Assessing the streams of cognition and emotion. In K. Blakstein, P. Pilner, & J. Palivy (Eds.), *Advances in the study of communication and affect: Assessment and modification of emotional behavior* (Vol. 6, pp. 139–163). New York: Plenum.

Meichenbaum, D., & Jaremko, M. (1983). *Stress prevention and reduction*. New York: Plenum.

Mendonca, J. D., & Siess, T. F. (1976). Counseling for indecisiveness: Problem-solving and anxiety-management training. *Journal of Counseling Psychology, 23*, 339–347.

Merluzzi, T. V., Glass, C. R., & Genest, M. (1981). *Cognitive assessment*. New York: Guilford Press.

Mesmer, F. A. (1949). *Mesmerism: A translation of the original medical and scientific writings of F. A. Mesmer, M.D.* London: McDonald.

Michael, J., & Meyerson, L. A. (1962). A behavioral approach to counseling and guidance. *Harvard Educational Review, 32,* 382–402.

Miller, G. A. (1956). The magical number seven, plus or minus two: Some limits on our capacity for processing information. *Psychological Review, 63,* 81–97.

Miller, N. E., & Dollard, J. (1941). *Social learning and imitation.* New Haven, CT: Yale University Press.

Millon, T. (1981). *Disorders of personality. DSM-III, Axis II.* New York: Wiley-Interscience.

Mischel, W. (1973). Toward a cognitive social learning reconceptualization of personality. *Psychological Review, 80,* 252–283.

Mitroff, I. I., & Kilmann, R. H. (1978). *Methodological approaches in the social sciences.* San Francisco: Jossey-Bass.

Montalvo, B. (1973). Aspects of live supervision. *Family Process, 12,* 343–359.

Moos, R. H., Insel, P., & Humphrey, B. (1974). *Combined preliminary manual for the Family Environment Scale, Work Environment Scale, and the Group Environment Scale.* Palo Alto, CA: Consulting Psychologists Press.

Moreno, J. L. (1946/1959). *Psychodrama* (2 vols.). Beacon, NY: Beacon House.

Mosher, R. L., & Sprinthall, N. A. (1970). Psychological education in secondary schools: A program to promote individual and human development. *American Psychologist, 25,* 911–924.

Mowrer, O. H., & Mowrer, W. M. (1938). Enuresis—a method for its study and treatment. *American Journal of Orthopsychiatry, 8,* 436–459.

Mueller, W. J., & Kell, B. L. (1972). *Coping with conflict: Supervising counselors and psychotherapists.* New York: Meredith.

Munroe, R. (1955). *Schools of psychoanalytic thought: An exposition, critique, and attempt at integration.* New York: Holt, Rinehart & Winston.

Munsterberg, H. (1899). *Psychology and life.* Boston: Houghton Mifflin.

Murphy, K. C., & Strong, S. R. (1972). Some effects of similarity self-disclosure. *Journal of Counseling Psychology, 19,* 121–124.

Neimeyer, G. J., & Neimeyer, R. A. (1981). Personal construct perspectives on cognitive assessment. In T. V. Merluzzi, C. R. Class, & M. Genest (Eds.), *Cognitive assessment* (pp. 188–232). New York: Guilford Press.

Neisser, U. (1967). *Cognitive psychology.* New York: Appleton-Century-Crofts.

Neufeld, R. W. J. (1977). *Clinical quantitative methods.* New York: Grune & Stratton.

Nisbett, R. E., Wilson, T. D. (1977). Telling more than we know: Verbal reports on mental processes. *Psychological Review, 84,* 231–259.

O'Leary, K. D., Turkewitz, H., & Taffel, S. J. (1973). Parent and therapist evaluation of behavior therapy in a child psychological clinic. *Journal of Consulting and Clinical Psychology, 41,* 279–283.

Parker, C. A. (Ed.). (1978). *Encouraging development in college students.* Minneapolis: University of Minnesota Press.

Parsons, F. (1909). *Choosing a vocation.* Boston: Houghton Mifflin.

Patterson, C. H. (1966/1973/1980). *Theories of counseling and psychotherapy* (3rd ed.). New York: Harper & Row.

Paul, G. L. (1966). *Insight versus desensitization in psychotherapy: An experiment in anxiety reduction.* Stanford: Stanford University Press.

Perkins, M. J., Kiesler, D. J., Anchin, J. C., Chirico, B. M., Kyle, E. M., & Federman, E. J. (1979). The Impact Message Inventory: A new measure of relationship in counseling/psychotherapy and other dyads. *Journal of Counseling Psychology, 26,* 363–367.

Perls, F. S., Hefferline, R. E., & Goodman, P. (1951). *Gestalt therapy*. New York: Dell.

Perry, W. G., Jr. (1970). *Forms of intellectual and ethical development in the college years*. New York: Holt, Rinehart & Winston.

Petty, R. E., & Cacioppo, J. T. (1981). *Attitudes and persuasion: Classic and contemporary approaches*. Dubuque, IA: Brown.

Piaget, J. (1970). Piaget's theory. In P. H. Mussen (Ed.), *Carmichael's manual of child psychology* (Vol. 2, 3rd ed., pp. 707–732). New York: Wiley.

Pinel, P. (1977). *Treatise on insanity*. In D. N. Robinson (Ed.), *Significant contributions to the history of psychology 1750–1920* (pp. xi–288). Washington, D.C.: University Publications of America. (Reprinted from the translation of D. D. Davis, which was published in Sheffield in 1806 by W. Todd.)

Polanyi, M. (1964). *Personal knowledge*. New York: Harper & Row.

Posner, M. I. (1978). *Chronometric explorations of the mind*. Hillsdale, NJ: Erlbaum.

Raimy, V. C. (1943). *The self-concept as a factor in counseling and personality organization*. Unpublished doctoral dissertation, Ohio State University.

Rank, O. (1929/1945). *Will therapy and truth and reality*. New York: Knopf.

Raush, H. L. (1972). Process and change: A Markov model for interaction. *Family Process, 13*, 275–298.

Rice, L. N., & Greenberg, L. S. (1984). *Patterns of change: Intensive analysis of psychotherapy process*. New York: Guilford Press.

Rice, L. N., & Wagstaff, A. K. (1967). Client voice quality and expressive styles as indexes of productive psychotherapy. *Journal of Consulting Psychology, 31*, 557–563.

Richards, C. S. (1975). Behavior modification of studying through study skills advice and self-control procedures. *Journal of Counseling Psychology, 22*, 431–436.

Richardson, B., & Stone, G. L. (1981). Effects of a cognitive adjunct procedure within a microtraining situation. *Journal of Counseling Psychology, 28*, 168–175.

Riesman, D., Denney, R., & Glazer, N. (1950/1960). *The lonely crowd: A study of the changing American character*. New Haven, CT: Yale University Press.

Riskin, J., & Faunce, E. F. (1970). Family interaction scales. *Archives of General Psychiatry, 22*, 504–537.

Rockwell, P. J., & Rothney, J. W. M. (1961). Some social ideas of pioneers in the guidance movement. *Personnel and Guidance Journal, 40*, 349–354.

Roethlisberger, F. J., & Dickson, W. J. (1939). *Management and the worker*. Cambridge, MA: Harvard University Press.

Rogers, C. R. (1939). *The clinical treatment of the problem child*. Boston: Houghton Mifflin.

Rogers, C. R. (1942). *Counseling and psychotherapy*. Boston: Houghton Mifflin.

Rogers, C. R. (1951/1965). *Client-centered therapy*. Cambridge, MA: Houghton Mifflin.

Rogers, C. R. (1957). Necessary and sufficient conditions for therapeutic personality change. *Journal of Consulting Psychology, 21*, 95–103.

Rogers, C. R. (1958). A process conception of psychotherapy. *American Psychologist, 13*, 142–149.

Rogers, C. R. (1959a). A tentative scale for the measurement of process in psychotherapy. In E. A. Rubinstein & M. B. Parloff (Eds.), *Research in psychotherapy* (pp. 96–107). Washington, D.C.: American Psychological Association.

Rogers, C. R. (1959b). A theory of therapy, personality, and interpersonal relationships, as developed in the client-centered framework. In S. Koch (Ed.),

Psychology: A study of science. Vol. III. Formulations of the person and the social context (pp. 184–256). New York: McGraw-Hill.

Rogers, C. R. (1961). *On becoming a person: A therapist's view of psychotherapy.* Boston: Houghton Mifflin.

Rogers, C. R. (1969/1982). *Freedom to learn: A view of what education might become.* Columbus, OH: Merrill.

Rogers, C. R. (1970). *Carl Rogers on encounter groups.* New York: Harper & Row.

Rogers, C. R. (1977). *Carl Rogers on personal power.* New York: Delacorte.

Rogers, C. R., & Dymond, R. (Eds.). (1954). *Psychotherapy and personality change.* Chicago: University of Chicago Press.

Rogers, C. R., Gendlin, E. T., Kiesler, D. J., & Truax, C. B. (Eds.). (1967). *The therapeutic relationship and its impact.* Madison: University of Wisconsin Press.

Rogers, T. B., Kuiper, N. A., & Kirker, W. S. (1977). Self-reference and the encoding of personal information. *Journal of Personality and Social Psychology, 35,* 677–688.

Rose, S. (1976). *Group therapy: A behavioral approach.* Englewood Cliffs, NJ: Prentice-Hall.

Rotter, J. B. (1954/1973/1980). *Social learning and clinical psychology.* New York: Johnson.

Rush, A. J., Beck, A. T., Kovacs, M., & Hollon, S. (1977). Comparative efficacy of cognitive therapy and pharmacotherapy in the treatment of depressed outpatients. *Cognitive Therapy and Research, 1,* 17–37.

Russell, R. K., & Sipich, J. F. (1973). Cue-controlled relaxation in the treatment of test anxiety. *Journal of Behavior Therapy and Experimental Psychiatry, 4,* 47–49.

Ryan, T. A., & Krumboltz, J. D. (1964). Effect of planned reinforcement counseling on client decision-making behavior. *Journal of Counseling Psychology, 11,* 315–323.

Rychlak, J. F. (1973/1981). *Personality and psychotherapy* (2nd ed.). Boston: Houghton Mifflin.

Sarason, I. G., Johnson, J. H., & Siegel, J. M. (1978). Assessing the impact of life changes: Development of the Life Experiences Survey. *Journal of Consulting and Clinical Psychology, 46,* 932–946.

Scheid, A. B. (1976). Client's perception of the counselor: The influence of counselor introduction and behavior. *Journal of Counseling Psychology, 23,* 503–508.

Schein, E. H. (1969). *Process consultation.* Reading, MA: Addison-Wesley.

Schmidt, L. D., & Strong, S. R. (1970). "Expert" "inexpert" counselors. *Journal of Counseling Psychology, 17,* 115–118.

Schroder, H. M., Driver, M. J., & Streufert, S. (1967). *Human information processing.* New York: Holt, Rinehart & Winston.

Schultz, J. H., & Luthe, W. (1959). *Autogenic training: A psychophysiologic approach in psychotherapy.* New York: Grune & Stratton.

Seligman, C., & Darley, J. M. (1977). Feedback as a means of decreasing residential energy consumption. *Journal of Applied Psychology, 62,* 363–368.

Selman, R. L. (1980). *The growth of interpersonal understanding: Developmental and clinical analyses.* New York: Academic Press.

Shannon, C., & Weaver, W. (1949). The mathematical theory of communication. *Bell System Technical Journal, 27,* 379–423, 623–656.

Shantz, C. V. (1975). The development of social cognition. In E. M. Hetherington (Ed.), *Review of child development research* (Vol. 5). Chicago: University of Chicago Press.

Shapiro, D. (1965). *Neurotic styles.* New York: Basic Books.

Shapiro, D. (1980). *Meditation: Self-regulation strategy and altered states of consciousness.* New York: Aldine.

Shapiro, D., & Schwartz, G. E. (1972). Biofeedback and visceral learning: Clinical applications. *Seminars in Psychiatry, 4,* 171–184.

Shapiro, M. B. (1966). The single case clinical-psychological research. *Journal of General Psychology, 74,* 3–23.

Sheehy, G. (1981). *Pathfinders.* New York: Morrow.

Shoben, E. J. (1949). Psychotherapy as a problem in learning. *Psychological Bulletin, 46,* 366–393.

Shoben, E. J. (1962). Guidance: Remedial function or social reconstruction? *Harvard Educational Review, 32,* 430–443.

Singer, J. (1974). *Imagery and daydream methods in psychotherapy.* New York: Academic Press.

Skinner, B. F. (1953). *Science and human behavior.* New York: Macmillan.

Sloane, R. B., Staples, F. R., Cristol, A. H., Yorkston, N. J., & Whipple, K. (1975). *Psychotherapy versus behavior therapy.* Cambridge, MA: Harvard University Press.

Stein, M. L., & Stone, G. L. (1978). Effects of conceptual level and structure on initial interview behavior. *Journal of Counseling Psychology, 25,* 96–102.

Stephens, W. R. (1970). *Social reform and the origins of guidance.* Washington, D.C.: National Vocational Guidance Association.

Stephenson, W. (1953). *The study of behavior: Q-technique and its methodology.* Chicago: University of Chicago Press.

Stewart, L. H., & Warnath, C. F. (1965). *The counselor and society: A cultural approach.* Boston: Houghton Mifflin.

Stewart, N. R., Winborn, B. B., Johnson, R. G., Burks, H. M., Jr., & Engelkes, J. R. (1978). *Systematic counseling.* Englewood Cliffs, NJ: Prentice-Hall.

Stoltenberg, C. (1981). Approaching supervision from a developmental perspective: The counselor complexity model. *Journal of Counseling Psychology, 28,* 59–65.

Stone, G. L. (1980). *A cognitive-behavioral approach to counseling psychology.* New York: Praeger.

Stone, G. L. (1984). Counseling. In R. Corsini (Ed.), *Encyclopedia of Psychology* (Vol. I). New York: Wiley.

Stone, G. L., Jebson, P., Walk, P., & Belsham, R. (1984). Identification of stress and coping skills within a critical care setting. *Western Journal of Nursing Research, 6,* 201–211.

Stone, G. L., & Kelly, K. (1983). Effects of helping skills on attitudes toward psychological counseling. *Counselor Education and Supervision, 22,* 207–214.

Stone, G. L., & Noce, A. (1980). Cognitive training for young children: Expanding the counselor's role. *Personnel and Guidance Journal, 58,* 416–420.

Storms, M. D., & Nisbett, R. E. (1970). Insomnia and the attribution process. *Journal of Personality and Social Psychology, 16,* 319–325.

Strohmer, D. C., Haase, R. F., Biggs, D. A., & Keller, K. E. (1982). Process models of counselor judgment. *Journal of Counseling Psychology, 29,* 597–606.

Strong, S. R. (1968). Counseling: An interpersonal influence process. *Journal of Counseling Psychology, 15,* 215–224.

Strong, S. R. (1971). Experimental laboratory research in counseling. *Journal of Counseling Psychology, 18,* 106–110.

Strong, S. R. (1978). Social psychological approach to psychotherapy research. In S. L. Garfield & A. E. Bergin (Eds.), *Handbook of psychotherapy and behavior change* (2nd ed.) (pp. 101–135). New York: Wiley.

Strong, S. R., & Claiborn, C. D. (1982). *Change through interaction*. New York: Pergamon Press.

Strong, S. R., & Dixon, D. N. (1971). Expertness, attractiveness, and influence in counseling. *Journal of Counseling Psychology, 18*, 562–570.

Strong, S. R., & Matross, R. P. (1973). Change process in counseling and psychotherapy. *Journal of Counseling Psychology, 20*, 25–37.

Strong, S. R., & Schmidt, L. D. (1970). Expertness and influence in counseling. *Journal of Counseling Psychology, 17*, 81–87.

Strong, S. R., Wambach, C. A., Lopez, F. G., & Cooper, R. K. (1979). Motivational and equipping functions of interpretation in counseling. *Journal of Counseling Psychology, 26*, 98–107.

Strupp, H. H. (1973). The interpersonal relationship as a vehicle for therapeutic learning. *Journal of Consulting and Clinical Psychology, 41*, 13–15.

Strupp, H. H. (1976). Clinical psychology, irrationalism, and the erosion of excellence. *American Psychologist, 31*, 561–571.

Suinn, R. M., & Richardson, F. (1971). Anxiety management training: A nonspecific behavior therapy program for anxiety control. *Behavior Therapy, 2*, 498–510.

Sullivan, H. S. (1953/1968). *The interpersonal theory of psychiatry*. New York: Norton.

Sulloway, F. G. (1979). *Freud, biologist of the mind: Beyond the psychoanalytic legend*. New York: Basic Books.

Sundland, D. M., & Barker, E. N. (1962). The orientation of psychotherapists. *Journal of Consulting Psychology, 26*, 201–212.

Super, D. E. (1964). A developmental approach to vocational guidance. *Vocational Guidance Quarterly, 13*, 1–10.

Super, D. E. (1980). A life span, life space approach to career development. *Journal of Vocational Behavior, 16*, 282–298.

Tharp, R. G., & Wetzel, R. J. (1969). *Behavior modification in the natural environment*. New York: Academic Press.

Thoresen, C. E., & Coates, T. J. (1980). What does it mean to be a behavior therapist? *The Counseling Psychologist, 7*, 3–21.

Touchton, J. G., Wertheimer, L. C., Cornfeld, J. L., & Harrison, K. H. (1978). Career planning and decision making: A developmental approach to the classroom. In C. A. Parker (Ed.), *Encouraging development in college students*. Minneapolis: University of Minnesota.

Truax, C. B. (1961). A scale for the measurement of accurate empathy. *Psychiatric Institute Bulletin, 1*, 12.

Truax, C. B. (1962a). A tentative scale for the measurement of therapist genuineness of self-congruence. *Discussion Papers*, Wisconsin Psychiatric Institute, University of Wisconsin, 35(b).

Truax, C. B. (1962b). A tentative scale for the measurement of unconditional positive regard. *Psychiatric Institute Bulletin*, Wisconsin Psychiatric Institute, University of Wisconsin, 2, 1(a).

Truax, C. B. (1966). Reinforcement and nonreinforcement in Rogerian psychotherapy. *Journal of Abnormal Psychology, 7*, 1–19.

Truax, C. B., & Carkhuff, R. R. (1967). *Toward effective counseling and psychotherapy*. Chicago: Aldine.

Ullman, L. P., & Krasner, L. (Eds.). (1965). *Case studies in behavior modification*. New York: Holt, Rinehart & Winston.

Ullman, L. P., & Krasner, L. A. (1969/1975). *A psychological approach to abnormal behavior*. Englewood Cliffs, NJ: Prentice-Hall.

Vance, F. L. (1968). The psychological interview as discovery machine. In C. A. Parker (Ed.), *Counseling theories and counselor education.* New York: Houghton Mifflin.

Van Dusen, R. A., & Sheldon, E. B. (1976). The changing status of American women: A life cycle perspective. *American Psychologist, 31,* 106–116.

Wark, D. M. (1976). Teaching study skills to adults. In J. D. Krumboltz &. C. E. Thoresen (Eds.), *Counseling methods* (pp. 265–268). New York: Holt, Rinehart & Winston.

Watson, J. B., & Rayner, R. (1920). Conditioned emotional reactions. *Journal of Experimental Psychology, 3,* 1–14.

Watzlawick, P., Beavin, J. H., & Jackson, D. D. (1967). *Pragmatics of human communication.* New York: Norton.

Weber, M. (1958). *The protestant ethic and the spirit of capitalism.* New York: Scribner's.

Werner, H. (1957). *Comparative psychology of mental development* (rev. ed.). New York: International Universities Press.

Wexler, D. A. (1974). A cognitive theory of experiencing, self-actualization, and therapeutic process. In D. A. Wexler &. L. Rice (Eds.), *Innovations in client-centered therapy* (pp. 49–116). New York: Wiley.

Wexler, D. A., & Butler, J. M. (1976). Therapist modification of client expressiveness in client-centered therapy. *Journal of Consulting and Clinical Psychology, 44,* 261–267.

Wexler, D. A., & Rice, L. (Eds.). (1974). *Innovations in client-centered therapy.* New York: Wiley.

Whitaker, D. S., & Lieberman, M. A. (1964). *Psychotherapy through the group process.* New York: Atherton.

Whitehead, A. N., & Russell, B. (1910). *Principia mathematica.* Cambridge, England: Cambridge University Press.

Whiteley, J. C. (1977). Developmental counseling psychology. *The Counseling Psychologist, 6,* 2–69.

Wicklund, R. A. (1975). Objective self-awareness. In L. Berkowitz (Ed.), *Advances in experimental social psychology* (Vol. 8, pp. 233–275). New York: Academic Press.

Widick, C., & Simpson, D. (1978). Developmental concepts in college instruction. In C. A. Parker (Ed.), *Encouraging development in college students.* Minneapolis: University of Minnesota Press.

Wiener, N. (1948). *Cybernetics; Or control and communication in the animal and the machine.* New York: Wiley.

Wiener, N. (1961). *Cybernetics: Or control and communication in the animal and the machine.* 2nd ed. Cambridge, MA: MIT Press.

Williamson, E. G. (1939a). The clinical method of guidance. *Review of Educational Research, 9,* 214–217.

Williamson, E. G. (1939b). *How to counsel students.* New York: McGraw-Hill.

Williamson, E. G. (1950). *Counseling adolescents.* New York: McGraw-Hill.

Williamson, E. G. (1965). *Vocational counseling.* New York: McGraw-Hill.

Williamson, E. G., & Biggs, D. A. (1975). *Student personnel work: A program of developmental relationships.* New York: Wiley.

Williamson, E. G., & Biggs, D. A. (1979). Trait-factor theory and individual differences. In H. M. Burks, Jr., & B. Stefflre (Eds.), *Theories of counseling* (pp. 91–131). New York: McGraw-Hill.

Wilson, E. O. (1975). *Sociobiology: The new synthesis.* Cambridge, MA: Harvard University Press.

Wolf, A., & Schwartz, E. K. (1962). *Psychoanalysis in groups.* New York: Grune & Stratton.

Wolpe, J. (1958). *Psychotherapy by reciprocal inhibition.* Stanford, CA: Stanford University Press.

Wolpe, J. (1978). Cognition and causation in human behavior and its therapy. *American Psychologist, 33,* 437–446.

Wolpe, J., & Lazarus, A. A. (1966). *Behavior therapy techniques.* New York: Pergamon Press.

Wrenn, C. G. (1962). *The counselor in a changing world.* Washington, D.C.: American Personnel and Guidance Association.

Yankelovich, D. (1974). *The new morality: A profile of American youth in the seventies.* New York: McGraw-Hill.

Yates, A. J. (1970). *Behavior therapy.* New York: Wiley.

Zajonc, R. B. (1980). Feeling and thinking: Preferences need no inferences. *American Psychologist, 35,* 151–175.

Zytowski, D. G., & Rosen, D. (1982). The grand tour: 30 years of counseling psychology in the *Annual Review of Psychology. The Counseling Psychologist, 10,* 69–81.

Author index

212

Subject index

217